ROUTLEDGE LIBRA⌐
IMMIGRATION AND

CW00687945

Volume 19

# POINT OF ARRIVAL

# POINT OF ARRIVAL

## A Study of London's East End

CHAIM BERMANT

Routledge
Taylor & Francis Group

LONDON AND NEW YORK

First published in 1975 by Eyre Methuen Ltd

This edition first published in 2023
by Routledge
4 Park Square, Milton Park, Abingdon, Oxon OX14 4RN

and by Routledge
605 Third Avenue, New York, NY 10158

*Routledge is an imprint of the Taylor & Francis Group, an informa business*

*British Library Cataloguing in Publication Data*
A catalogue record for this book is available from the British Library

ISBN: 978-1-032-31713-7 (Set)
ISBN: 978-1-032-36920-4 (Volume 19) (hbk)
ISBN: 978-1-032-36923-5 (Volume 19) (pbk)
ISBN: 978-1-003-33447-7 (Volume 19) (ebk)

DOI: 10.4324/9781003334477

**Publisher's Note**
The publisher has gone to great lengths to ensure the quality of this reprint but points out that some imperfections in the original copies may be apparent.

**Disclaimer**
The publisher has made every effort to trace copyright holders and would welcome correspondence from those they have been unable to trace.

'Aliens' arriving at Irongate Stairs,
a contemporary impression by W. Rainey

# Point of Arrival

## A STUDY OF
## LONDON'S EAST END

Chaim Bermant

EYRE METHUEN
LONDON

First published 1975
© 1975 Chaim Bermant

Printed in Great Britain for
Eyre Methuen Ltd
11 New Fetter Lane, London EC4P 4EE
by Willmer Brothers Limited, Birkenhead

ISBN 0 413 28060 8

# Contents

# Illustrations

MAP

The East End *endpaper*

*drawn by Edgar Holloway*

Acknowledgements and thanks for permission to reproduce the plates are due to the Tower Hamlets Local History Library for the frontispiece and plates 1a, 2 and 4; to the Radio Times Hulton Picture Library for plates 1b, 3, 5a, 6a, 6b, 7a, 7b, 7c, 9 and 10; to the Greater London Council for plate 5b; to the Port of London Authority for plate 8; to the Mary Evans Picture Library for plate 11a; to the Illustrated London News and Sketch Ltd for plate 11b and to Ron McCormick for plates 12a and 12b.

# Acknowledgements

There are so many intriguing sides to the East End that this book often threatened to run away with itself. I am grateful to Mrs Chloe Green for helping to keep it within bounds. I should also like to thank Mr A. Hellicar, formerly Local History Librarian of the Tower Hamlets Reference Library, Mile End and Avrom Stencl for permission to quote his poem on Whitechapel. I am indebted also to Dr William Fishman of Queen Mary College, London, Dr Patrick Snoddy of the Irish National Museum and Dr Charles Marmoy, Hon. Secretary of the Huguenot Society for reading different parts of this book and saving me from some errors of judgement and fact, and to Mrs Beatty Pearlman who deciphered my typescript and reduced it to readable form.

*Jerusalem*                                            CHAIM BERMANT
*March 1974*

# Foreword

Much of the old East End is gone, but here and there one still finds a crumbling terrace stained with life, and in spite of all the new building there is hardly an area of London where the past may be more perceptibly felt.

I was concerned in these pages to recall something of this past and to compare the experiences of the various immigrant groups – the Huguenots, Irish, Jews and Pakistanis – who have made their home there, for the East End was, and to an extent still is, the point of arrival. Here was their first and sometimes their last taste of England. Here, in many cases, was the only England they were to know.

None of the groups was particularly welcomed and their arrival occasioned considerable acrimony, and none more than the Jews. If the Huguenots spoke a different language, they were of the same faith. If the Irish were of a different faith, they spoke (approximately) the same language. The Jews were different in every possible respect, as, indeed, are the Pakistanis, but the latter at least stem from what was a province of the Empire, and, like the Irish, have a moral claim on the goodwill of England. The Jews had none and most of them came when, as a result of setbacks suffered by British arms in South Africa, there was intense anti-alien feeling in this country. There was also severe unemployment and a serious housing shortage in the East End. Their arrival could thus not have been less timely, and it aroused a large body of polemic literature.

Moreover, the Jews, like the Irish, are people of the word, but whereas the Irish love of words is mainly verbal, the Jews are more inclined to express themselves in writing and one sometimes had the impression that the Jewish immigrant hardly drew breath before he launched his own paper. Few of the journals survived their first year, and fewer still survived their founders, but they left a wealth of material for the social historian. There is, as a result, a certain imbalance between the space accorded to the Jews and that given to the other immigrant groups, but quite apart from the controversy they excited, the Jews formed the largest single immigrant group; they remained a distinct group for the longest period, and made the most lasting impact on their neighbourhood, and one may therefore perhaps be forgiven the fuller attention accorded to their sojourn.

*Jerusalem*                                          CHAIM BERMANT
*March 1974*

# Point of Arrival

# ONE

# Pagan Place

In 1897 the Reverend A. S. Barnett, Vicar of St Judes', White-chapel, wrote to *The Times* to lament that 'after six years of work, after everything has been done which money can provide or thought can suggest, I have to confess that in the past year the church has been as little used as ever'.[1]

Other letters followed which differed in detail but agreed on one substantial point, that the East End was a sadly pagan place. The Church of England, which had been receiving like reports from about the time of the Reformation, stirred itself into action and a few months later appointed the Reverend Canon Walsham How as Suffragan Bishop of East London. The appointment was welcomed on all sides as a timely and necessary step and *John Bull*, a weekly journal then mainly concerned with church affairs, commented:

> We understand that a definite district in the East of London, bounded westwards by the City, Islington and Highbury, and eastward to the river Lea, will be assigned to the Bishop. This district is about six miles in length from north to south, and scarcely four miles in breadth, the size of many a rural parish, but it has a vast population – more than four times as great as the whole Diocese of St. Asaph, which only contains about a quarter of a million. Poplar, Limehouse, the Isle of Dogs, Stepney, Spitalfields, Bethnal Green, Hoxton, Bow, and other places, all of which would rank as towns out of the metropolis are included in the proposed sub-diocese.

The commentator drew breath, then went on to describe the inhabitants:

The district is teeming with people who are almost as removed from Christian influences as savages in the wilds of Africa, and the administration of the new sub-diocese will require not only hard work, but a diligent study of character and tact. Bishop How, we may be sure, will approach the uncivilised inhabitants of his new diocese ready to take any advantage of any inclination for better things, even when what he esteems the best of all cannot be pushed prominently to the front.[2]

The journal was not singular in its view. Different papers sent special correspondents into the area, as if it was a dark and distant continent and they all came back with harrowing tales: 'Whence all those dwarfs and hunchbacks, those creatures bent double, those crooked and bandy and rickety babes?' asked one writer, those 'sickly mothers nursing sickly babes; sickly girls toying in a sickly manner with sickly weaver boys; listless, emaciated middle-aged women; dreadful old women as ugly as sin, who looked as though they supported nature on a diet of lucifer matches and gin.'[3]

George R. Sims, a popular author who toured the area for the *Daily News*, found a child of four, 'neglected, ragged, grimed, and bare-legged', alone in a bare attic in charge of her baby sister:

The little sentinel's papa – this we unearthed of the deputy of the house later on – was a militiaman and away; her mamma was gone out on 'a arrand', which, if it was anything like her usual 'arrands', would bring her home about dark, very much the worse for it. Think of that little child keeping guard on that dirty sack for six or eight hours at a stretch ... sitting there till night and darkness came on, hungry, thirsty, and tired herself, but faithful to her trust to the last minute of her drunken mother's absence. 'Bless yer! I've known that young un sit there eight 'our at a stretch. I've seen her there of a mornin' when I've come up to see if I could get the rint, and I've seen her there when I've come again at night', says the deputy. 'Lord, that ain't nothing – that ain't.'[4]

The East End, however, was not merely sunk in paganism and poverty, but, to judge from the daily press, it was steeped in vice,

the home of every type of delinquent: thieves, brigands, cut-
throats, coiners, forgers, bigamists, profligate priests, unfrocked
priests, absconding priests, pederasts in holy orders and towards
the end of the century, as regular as the successive editions of a
penny dreadful, came the grisly details of the Jack the Ripper
murders. There were descriptions of sinister, sweaty-locked,
hook-nosed Hebrews in Whitechapel, nefarious Lascars in Shadwell, opium-smoking Chinamen in the dens of Limehouse, of
drunken, ruffianly, wife-beating Irishmen everywhere, and even,
to the stupefaction of the public, reports of a 'dragball' in
Whitechapel:

> It appeared from the evidence that, in consequence of informa-
> tion which reached the police, a ball of very extraordinary, if
> not immoral, character was about to take place in a hall in
> Mansell Street. . . . It appeared to be a fancy ball, and a number
> of the dancers were magnificently attired, and although quite
> half of the dancers wore female attire, the officers soon dis-
> covered that there were not half a dozen women in the place,
> the supposed females being merely men in women's clothes.
> These, however, danced together, kissed each other, and
> behaved in anything but an orderly manner.. . .[5]

The sort of scene one might have expected in some effete
corner of Vienna or Berlin, and was altogether out of keeping
with the traditional, homespun, villainy of East London. Readers
must have drawn some comfort from the fact that the defendant,
Adolf Voizanger, was German.

Well might the East End's own paper, the *East London Observer*
(founded in 1857 and now sadly defunct) protest that the reporters
from Fleet Street were ignorant, snobbish and mischievous, and
that their reports were a libel on, if not a fair, at least not an
unattractive, and hard-working area of the metropolis, that they
came looking for misery, degradation and squalor and found
them, though such scenes could equally be found behind the
proud façades of West London.

This was true. There were many East Ends and the casual
reader of the *East London Observer* could come away thinking
that it was a place given over to temperance meetings, sermons,
hymn-singing and prayer, relieved by the occasional bout of
mayhem. Its advertisements, too spoke of gentility:

Mrs. and the Misses Straugham beg to inform the public that
the duties of their establishment will be resumed on January
13th, 1859, when they will have vacancies for four young
ladies to board and educate on moderate terms. [6]

Sheridan Literary Club, Cannon Street Road, announce a
Soirée and Ball. A full and efficient band and recherché supper.
Every means will be taken to render this the Ball of the Season.
Tickets 5/-, including supper, 7/6. [7]

A Grand Night for Masqueraders, Monday March 25th. Y.
Zaplin's Grand Ball Masque will be held at the elegant and
spacious Assembly Rooms, King's Arms Tavern, Beaumont
Street, Mile End. The Musical arrangements will be of a
nature which no previous celebration has approached. [8]

And more modestly:

A Soirée Musicale will be held at the Salem Church, Wapping. [9]

But whatever the truth of the situation – and we shall examine
it in due course – the public had a fixed idea on the scene, which
conjured up instant visions of squalor and which was confirmed
by a series of dramatic events in the final decades of the century.
The impression, though mistaken, helped the East End in
many ways. The rich remembered it in their wills as if it was a
sanctuary for old horses. Public schools and universities vied
with each other to establish settlements in the area. It was studded
with philanthropic institutions of every sort, ragged schools,
shoe-blacks' brigades, soup kitchens, boot and clothing guilds,
orphanages, asylums, dispensaries, night refuges, industrial
schools, shelters for falling women and sanctuaries for fallen
ones.
The impression also hindered in that, with a few exceptions
(and they mostly Jewish), people with money – or, as they were
referred to in the papers, 'persons of quality' – did not come to
the area, and those without left it as soon as they made some.
Bishop How himself was given a stately house in Clapton, within
his diocese, but without the East End of lore. [10] The East End
was poor, but it was not entirely dishonest. It was the service
area of the metropolis, the servants' quarters of the stately home
that was London. Here, with its vast warehouses flanking the

river like a prison wall, were the great docks which fed London, and stored the merchandise which supplied its wealth. Here were the stevedores, and ballast heavers, and coal-whippers, and ships' chandlers and rope-makers, and, till the end of the century, ship-builders. Here were the bakeries and sugar refineries, and Mann's brewery, and Charrington's brewery and Truman, Hanbury and Buxton, and Bryant and May's match-works. Here were the hand-loom weavers of Spitalfields and Bethnal Green, crouch-backed but nimble fingered, still trying to compete with the machines, and often starving in the attempt. Here were the shoemakers who shod it, and here, pressed shoulder to shoulder, in grimy attics, were the Jewish garment makers who clothed it. The East End lived on London, but London lived on the East End and given a major strike in the area, as the dock strike of 1889, all commerce threatened to come to a halt.

But, to use an Americanism, the East End was also the skid row of the metropolis, a resort of the helpless, the feckless and the unfortunate, the place where one finally settled as one declined in life. But it is also – and this is what has always given the East End its vibrant, hopeful, bustling character – the point of arrival, where English and Irish, Flemings and Huguenot, Jews and Pakistanis, settled to start a new life.

# TWO

# The Garden Suburb

To the north, the wooded glades of Hackney; to the south, the Thames; to the east, the Lea; and to the west, lofty and massive, the walls of London.

A twelfth-century writer regarded that part of Essex which was to become East London as a tranquil paradise:

> On all sides without the houses of the suburb are the citizens' gardens and orchards, planted with trees both large and sightly and adjoining together. On the north side are the pastures and plain meadows, with brooks running through them, turning water-mills with a pleasant noise. Not far is a great forest, a well-wooded chace, having good covert for harts, bucks, does, boars and wild bulls. The corn-fields are not of a hungry, sandy mould, but as the fruitful fields of Asia, yielding plentyful increase, and filling the barns with corn.[1]

Much of the area formed the Manor of Stepney, a fief of the Bishop of London and inhabited at the time by about a thousand souls, mostly peasants. There was a church dedicated to St Dunstan, a former Bishop of London, and a number of monastic houses, including Holy Trinity Priory, St Katharine's Hospital, and the Benedictine convent of St Leonard, where Chaucer's prioress learned her French:[2]

> And French she spak ful faire and fetysly
> Aftur the schole of Stratford atte Bowe
> For Frensch of Parys was to her unknowe.

The building which dominated and to an extent still dominates the area was the Tower of London, built by William the Conqueror between the city walls and the Thames, not so much for the defence of London, as to overawe it.

Stepney then, as now, helped to feed London. It provided the corn, the flour and bread, and 'the great forest' described above was its favourite hunting-ground. When a Bishop of London sought to enclose it for his own amusement in 1292, he encountered fierce opposition. Londoners, he was told, 'had from time immemorial used to hunt within the aforesaid woods and without, hares, foxes, conies and other beasts where and when they would', and although the Bishop invoked the help of Edward I, the citizens' claim was upheld.[3]

The growth of London attracted many foreigners to Stepney, and a foreigner in those days was someone who came from the next county or town. The worst encumbrances of the feudal system were beginning to be eased, but even in the fourteenth century the small peasant cultivator was almost a chattel of the estate. London, however, was a city of free men. Its freedom was contagious and the peasants and labourers of Stepney were amongst the first to be freed from feudal duties. But there was an important sense in which Stepney was freer even than the City. Within the walls every trade and craft was controlled by guilds which laid down conditions of entry and which, on the whole, tended to be hostile to newcomers. There were no such restraints beyond the walls. Whoever had a trade could come and ply it, and the hitherto agricultural population of Stepney was augmented by a sizeable group of artisans, craftsmen and small merchants.

In 1349 Stepney was struck by the Black Death. It raged through the hamlets of Ratcliff, Shadwell and Limehouse, which had sprung up along the north shore of the Thames. It coursed northwards to Bethnal Green and eastwards to Mile End and Stratford. London, as Piers Plowman noted, was cut off from its main source of bread:[4]

> It is nought long y-passed
> There was a careful commune
> When no cart com to towne
> With bread fro' Stratforde.

About a third of Stepney perished in the plague.[5] A more dreadful visitation lay ahead but Stepney proved resilient, especially as the labour shortage resulting from the plague pushed up wages and brought a new influx of labourers from the country to the towns. By the end of the fourteenth century Stepney had a population of about two thousand. New churches were built, including a large Cistercian abbey near the Tower at East Smithfield, on the site of a burial pit of the 1349 plague. With the exception of St Katharine's Hospital, which was saved by the pleading of Anne Boleyn, all the religious houses were swept away with the dissolution of the monasteries in 1539. The Cistercian Abbey over the burial pit is now the site of the Royal Mint.

The passing of the monasteries, which had given the area a dignity it lacked in later years, was noted with regret even by many Protestants, and Stow, whose *Survey of London*, published in 1598 is a major source book of the period, recalled them with many a nostalgic sigh, especially a row of small cottages, kept by priors for the bed-ridden poor:

> In my youth, I remember, devout people, men as well as women of the city, were accustomed often times, especially on Fridays, weekly to walk that way purposely there to bestow their charitable alms; every poor man or woman lying in their bed within their window, which was towards the street, open so low that every man might see them, a clean linen cloth lying within their window, and a pair of beads to show that there lay a bed-rid body, unable but to pray only ...[6]

The site of these cottages became a gun-foundry. In 1570 a bell foundry was established by Robert Mot on what is now the north side of Whitechapel High Street, on the site at present occupied by Woolworths. In 1738 the foundry moved to more commodious premises across the way, where it still remains behind its eighteenth-century façade, as busy and active as ever, with visitors stumbling among its forges and casting rooms. Hence came some of the most celebrated bells of the world, including those of St Mary le Bow (the 'Bow Bells'), Great Tom of St Paul's, Big Ben of Westminster, the bells of Canterbury, Durham, Lichfield and Winchester Cathedrals, and the Liberty Bell of Philadelphia. It is currently producing hundreds of small replicas of this bell for the bicentenary of the American Declaration of Independence in 1776.

The overseas adventures of Henry VIII and Elizabeth I led to a rapid expansion of the navy. The earliest Thames-side shipyards were within the city limits, but the noise of the shipwrights, caulkers and carpenters grew insufferable and the yards moved down river to Rotherhithe and Deptford on the south bank and Ratcliff and Blackwall on the north. This was part of a trend noticed already in the fourteenth century when the City, finding its air 'corrupted and infected' by the local abattoirs, ordered that 'all oxen, sheep, swine or other large animals for the sustenance of our City aforesaid to be slaughtered, should be taken to the village of Streteford on the one side and the village of Knytebrigge on the other side of the said City and there be slaughtered'.[7] Knightsbridge was later to become part of fashionable London. Stratford, as part of the East End, continued to be a depository for nuisances.

The growth of London under the Tudors made the docking facilities at the City wharves inadequate. Ships too were growing in size and the larger ones, finding it difficult to pass the cumbersome piers of London Bridge, stopped downriver at Ratcliff. The sacking of Antwerp – Europe's premier port – by the Spaniards in 1576 gave a further boost to London and its suburbs and the riverside hamlets of Ratcliff, Wapping, Shadwell, Limehouse and Poplar grew till they formed an almost continuous line. Beyond Limehouse there was a large area caught in a bend of the river known as Stepney Marsh. It was drained in the sixteenth century by Vanderdelf, a Dutchman, and the reclaimed area became known as the Isle of Dogs. The inhabitants of this area were, to use a contemporary expression, mainly of 'the meaner sort', shipwrights, seamen, watermen, though here and there could be found the grander homes of men of substance. Sir Walter Raleigh had a house in Poplar, Sir Humphrey Gilbert in Limehouse, Frobisher in Ratcliff.[8]

The population of Stepney as a whole increased thirteenfold during the course of the fifteenth and sixteenth centuries and by 1580 it was estimated to be 14,000. The growth of new industries in the area affected the City Guilds and they protested against what they regarded as unfair competition:

They made counterfeit indigo, musk, saffron, cochineal, nut-megs, wax, steel and other commodities, but they were but bunglers at their business. They took excess of apprentices and kept them not for full time according to law. They prac-tised deceits having none appointed to oversee them and their works. For they belonged to none of the companies of London and so were under no control or restraint.[9]

There was much truth in these complaints, for Stepney, being unable to compete with the City for quality, competed for cheap-ness and there was no doubt that some of the new artificers, not having the prolonged training demanded by the Guilds, were indeed 'bunglers at their business'.

The north bank of the Thames was a built-up area from the Tower to the mouth of the Lea. Mile End grew eastwards to Bow, Bow westwards to Mile End. The open spaces were being swallowed up. Stow watches these developments with dismay. He recalled an area of 'fair hedgerows, of elm trees, with bridges and easy stiles to pass over into pleasant fields, very commodious for the citizens to therein walk, shoot, and otherwise to recreate and refresh their dull spirits in the sweet and wholesome air.' And now? There was 'continuous building throughout of garden houses and small cottages ... tenter yards, bowling alleys and such like ...'. The whole eastern approach to the City, he com-plained, was 'so encroached upon that it scarce remaineth a sufficient highway for the meeting of carriages and droves of cattle; much less is there any fair, pleasant or wholesome way for people to walk on foot; which is no small blemish to so famous a City to have so unseemly and unsavoury a passage thereunto'.[10]

The effect of all this was more than unsavoury, it constituted an immediate danger to health. Street crowded upon street, house upon house, with gables thrusting forward till they almost met, and little light or air between. A petition to Elizabeth I drew attention to the resulting squalor:

> ... a great part are very poor, and such as must live of begging and worse means. And they heaped up together and in a sort smothered with many families of children and servants in one house. And the Plague, or popular sickness, when that might happen in the City would, by the contiguity of the buildings,

spread and invade the whole City and confines and so endanger the Queen's own life . . .[11]

In 1580 Elizabeth made a proclamation limiting building on the outskirts of London, and like proclamations were made in the reign of James I, but in so far as they were followed their effect was to increase congestion, for the population continued to rise and, in the absence of new buildings, people overcrowded the old ones. Large houses were cut up into small and small into smaller ones still, on a pattern which was to become familiar in later years, until whole families were confined to one room. And if the homes were not always sanitary, the streets were little better.

The slaughterhouses of Stratford polluted the air. Dung, offal, carcasses and entrails were cast into roadside ditches or rivers – rivers which provided drinking-water for the population.

Worse still were the factories. In the reign of Charles I a chemical works was established at Wapping for the extraction of alum from urine and the local inhabitants petitioned the King that they 'cause so noisome a savour and evil air to all parts thereabouts, and to all passengers on the way to the river Thames, that they were . . . continually choked up with the daily and continuous stink and most noisome and infectious smell'. They further complained that the refuse discharged into the river poisoned large quantities of fish. When that had no effect, they added that the infected water was used by the local breweries, and that some of it could find its way into the King's beer.[12]

A commission of inquiry headed by the President of the Royal College of Physicians was immediately appointed. It found the nuisance every bit as pernicious as described and an order was made prohibiting the discharge of excrement into the Thames 'whereof beer is made for His Majesty's Service'.[13]

The crowded houses, the narrow streets, the unsanitary employments, the foul habits made the area particularly vulnerable to any passing pestilence. The Black Death which swept the country in 1349 returned for longer or shorter visitations almost every year. There was a serious outbreak in Stepney in 1603 which killed six hundred and fifty people; another in 1625 which killed nearly three thousand. Then came the final and

deadliest visitation. There are numerous accounts of it and perhaps the best is to be found in Defoe's *Journal of the Plague Year*,
which, though not an eye-witness report, is accepted as an
accurate reconstruction.

In 1664 two men living in Drury Lane died of a mysterious
disease. They had lately returned from Holland where the plague
had been raging throughout the summer. Two physicians and a
surgeon called to examine them and quickly confirmed the worst.
The Black Death had returned.

At first there was no reason to suspect that it would be an
outbreak of catastrophic proportions. Mortality figures in the
autumn of 1664 and in the early part of 1665 were low, but then
as the temperature rose the incidents multiplied.

In the seventeenth century, as in the fourteenth, there was no
known remedy for bubonic plague; the only defence was flight.
The Court fled to Oxford; the rich scattered in all directions.
At the East End of the town, wrote Defoe, 'the consternation
was very great':

> ... the richer sort of people, especially the nobility and the
> gentry from the west-part of the City thronged out of town
> with their families and servants; and this was more particularly
> seen in Whitechapel, that is to say the Broad Street where I
> lived: indeed nothing was to be seen but waggons and carts,
> with goods, women, servants, children, etc., coaches filled with
> people of the better sort.[14]

People of the not so good sort could only stand and watch them
hurrying by.

There was no parish in or about London, wrote Defoe, where
the plague 'raged with such violence as in the two parishes of
Aldgate and Whitechapel'.[15] Seventy-one people died in the
third week of July, one hundred and forty-five in the fourth,
and two hundred and twenty-eight in the first week in August.
The figures continued to climb. In one day in September one
hundred and fifty-four people died in Stepney alone. Daniel
Lysons, writing a century later, described it 'as a striking instance
of mortality scarcely to be paralleled in any other parish in the
United Kingdom'.[16]

Shops were shut, the streets were all but deserted. Infected
houses were sealed up. The healthy were locked in with the sick,

the dead with the living. The death carts, creaking slowly over the cobbles, could not keep up with the spread of death.

Watchmen were placed outside infected homes to enforce the quarantine and to run errands for the afflicted. London, wrote Defoe, 'might be said to be all in tears':

> ... the voice of mourning was truly heard in the streets; the shrieks of women and children at the windows and doors of their houses, where their dearest relations were dying or perhaps just dead, were so frequent to be heard as we passed the streets, that it was enough to pierce the stoutest hearts in the world to hear them.[17]

Different causes, each more bizarre than the other, were advanced as the cause of the plague. Dogs and cats were for a time suspected as carriers and forty thousand dogs and two hundred thousand cats were slaughtered in a week.[18] Some seeing it as a sign that the world was about to end, abandoned themselves to debauchery. Others, taking it as a sign of divine wrath, went ranting through the streets calling on the world to repent. Many, wrote Defoe, were driven out of their minds and went 'roaring and crying, and wringing their hands along the streets; some would go praying and lifting up their hands to heaven, calling upon God for mercy'.[19]

The plague raged on. Local cemeteries were not large enough and great pits were dug for the dead. Defoe described one: 'about forty feet in length, and about fifteen or sixteen foot broad; and at the time I first looked at it about nine foot deep; but it was said that they dug near twenty foot deeper in one part of it, till they could get no further for the water'.[20] And into this the bodies were heaped by the cartload throughout the hours of darkness. Within a fortnight the pit had taken its fill – one thousand one hundred and fourteen bodies – and had to be sealed up.

Then, with the cooler weather, the plague declined in extent and virulence. London began to breathe again. During September deaths in the city had averaged about seven thousand a week. By November they declined to two thousand. By Christmas the Royal Family felt it safe to return from Oxford. The plague was over. The official mortality rolls put the deaths in the capital at about seventy thousand. Defoe suggests that the true figure was nearer a hundred thousand.

Over fifteen thousand people died in Stepney and the neighbouring parishes. Grass grew among the cobbles of Whitechapel.
The area had lost its bustling, boisterous character. What had
been a lusty, teeming township was so sapped that, in the words
of an eighteenth-century historian, 'it might be mistaken for a
green field'.[21]

It did not remain so for long. In the next few years East London
was to display its chief quality – resilience. The gaps left by the
dead were filled. The survivors were fruitful and multiplied.
New industries and new people moved in. Within fifteen years
of the Great Plague there were eighty thousand people in the
eastern suburbs, now grown into one continuous conurbation.
The East End was becoming a city in its own right, with all the
problems of a city.

# THREE

# On the Waterfront

There is nothing like a grisly murder to put a place on the map and early in the nineteenth century the East End experienced something like a massacre. It was immortalised later by De Quincey in *Murder As One of the Fine Arts*:

Never throughout the annals of Christendom has there indeed been any act of one solitary individual armed with power so appalling over the hearts of men, as that exterminating murder by which, during the winter of 1812, John Williams, in one hour, smote two houses with emptiness, exterminated all but two entire households, and asserted his supremacy over all the children of Cain.[1]

De Quincey had the date wrong. The murders took place in December 1811, but he did not exaggerate the horrors which it aroused and the panic which ensued so that for weeks on end people hesitated to stir from their homes after the hours of darkness, and within their homes sat anxious and afraid. De Quincey, some three hundred miles from the scene of the crime, recalled,

One lady, whom I personally knew, living at the moment during the absence of her husband, with a few servants in a large solitary house, never rested until she had placed eighteen doors, each secured by ponderous bolts and bars and chains between her own bedroom and any intruder of human build.[2]

The murder took place in Ratcliff Highway, near the river, an area of narrow, winding streets and alleys, badly lit and badly policed, a drab huddle of mean houses and mean shops, sordid taverns and low-class lodging houses inhabited mainly by seamen, many of them foreign, and as De Quincey suggested, the navies of Christendom were a receptacle for ruffians and cut-throats from the four corners of the globe.

It was a Saturday in December and the time round midnight. Christmas was near and the streets were crowded and noisy, and the taverns full. Marr, who kept a small hosiery shop at No. 29, saw his last customer out, ordered his assistant, a lad of thirteen lately up from the country, to close for the night, and asked Mary, a young servant girl, to fetch some oysters for supper. They were a small household and, apart from his two servants, there was his wife, a young, lusty, attractive woman of twenty-two, and their eight-month-old baby.

Marr had left it late to send out his servant, for by midnight things had quietened down even on Ratcliff Highway, and she walked up and down without finding a shop open. She then tried more distant streets with the same result and got lost in the course of her wandering. By the time she was back at No. 29 it was one in the morning and the windows were shuttered and the doors barred.

She rang the bell and rapped the knocker – gently for she was afraid of waking the baby. There was no reply. She knocked again, still no reply. She put her ear to the door: silence. Then, as she was about to knock a third time, she heard footsteps, a heavy tread on the stairs leading downwards from the bedrooms, then on the landing, finally on the creaking floorboards of the passage towards the front door. And there they stopped. Mary panicked. She hammered the door with both her fists, she kicked, she screamed. A neighbour roused from his sleep put his head out of the window and found her convulsed with fear and by now, all but voiceless. Her master and all his family had been murdered, she cried, she was sure of it.

The neighbour, a local pawnbroker, put on a coat, grabbed a poker, climbed over the brick wall separating his house from Marr's and lowered himself into the yard. The back door was ajar and the entrance dimly lit by a light from the landing. He did not get far before he sensed the slithery feel of blood under-foot; a step later he stumbled upon a body. The papers the next day carried the details:

Mr. Marr was found lying near a window, dead, with his skull broken. His wife, who, it would seem, had come to his relief from below on hearing the scuffle, had been met by the villains at the top of the stairs, where she was found, her head too shockingly mangled for description. The shop-boy to all appearances, had made more resistance than the rest; for the counter which extends for the whole length of the shop, lay bespattered with his blood and brains from one length to the other, and his body lay weltering in gore.[3]

And the slaughter did not stop there. The baby was dead in its cradle, its throat cut from ear to ear. An iron mallet was found nearby, with the initials J.P. on the handle. It was generally believed that robbery was the motive, that the thieves had been surprised by the return of Mary before they could get their hands on anything. The Government offered a reward of £500 for information leading to an arrest; the Prince Regent offered a further £50.[4]

A few days later there came news of another massacre, at New Gavel Lane, a few hundred yards from the scene of the first. The victims this time were a Mr Williamson, keeper of the King's Arms tavern, his wife, and their maid Bridget. All three had their throats cut, Bridget, so deeply, that her head was almost severed from her body, and Williamson, who had put up some resistance, was found with his hands lacerated and hacked, his right leg broken and bone protruding through his stocking.[5] The ferocity of the attack showed at once that the Williamsons and the Marrs had been killed by the same man, or men.

Turner, a lodger at the King's Arms, had woken to see a man crouched over the body of Mrs Williamson, but stayed to see no more. He grabbed a sheet, lowered himself out of the window and raised the alarm. Help came immediately but the killer climbed out of a back window and made his way across wasteground and into the mists. A Mr Stroud who had been at the King's Arms shortly before it closed had noticed a tall man in a shabby greatcoat loitering near the door and had mentioned him to Williamson, but such figures appear to have been fairly common in the neighbourhood and Williamson had taken no notice, but the description tallied with the brief glimpse which

Turner had had of the man bent over Mrs Williamson. A number of tall men were taken into custody and questioned but all were able to establish their innocence. [6] At the inquest the Coroner expressed the sense of public disquiet:

> While the exertions of the police, with the ordinary powers of parochial officers, are insufficient to protect men's persons from the hands of violence, and the Coroner has to record the most atrocious crimes without the probability of delivering the perpetrators to justice and punishment; our houses are no longer our castles and we are unsafe in our beds. [7]

A special militia was established to police the area during the hours of darkness and there were constant patrols armed with cutlass and pistol empowered to detain anyone whose appearance or conduct gave grounds for suspicion. As there were a great many such people in Ratcliff the jails were soon overflowing. The Government offered a further reward of £500. A hue and cry was sent out throughout the country and a special watch was kept at ports, but the police were still no nearer their man, and they still had only one reliable clue to work on – the iron mallet found beside Mr Marr, with J.P. on the handle.

On Christmas Eve the police arrested a young German seaman called Richter. He had been seen drinking at the King's Arms shortly before the murder, but denied that he knew Williamson. His lodgings in an upstairs room at the Pear Tree tavern, which had been fitted up as a dormitory, were searched and, under his bed, they found a damp pair of trousers lately cleaned of mud. They had been left to him by a foreign sailor, said Richter. Who? He couldn't remember. Further searches yielded a tool-box with the initials J.P. Two Germans, a couple of Scotsmen and an Irishmen were also living at the Pear Tree. The police questioned them all. They had found some mud-stained stockings near the bed of Williams, the Irishman, and according to a local washerwoman he had sent her a blood-stained shirt for cleaning after the death of Marr. The evidence was not particularly damning, for mud was not uncommon in the Thames-side streets, and neither was bloodshed. Williams said that he had been drinking and playing cards with some Irish coal-heavers and had been involved in a brawl. [8] His explanations did not satisfy the police and he was held for further questioning.

TERRA EPI LVNDONIENSIS

*[Latin text of Domesday Book, in medieval script]*

1a. Latin text of Domesday Book relating to Stibenhede (Manor of Stepney)

1b. The Great Plague from a contemporary broadsheet *The Intelligencer*,
26 June, 1665

2. Huguenot weavers' houses in Spitalfields, photograph c. 1903

In the meantime a new and more hopeful lead appeared from an entirely new quarter. Cahill, an Irishman picked up for desertion at Marlborough, Wiltshire, claimed that it was a case of mistaken identity and that he was employed by a Mr Williamson on Ratcliff Highway. At this two officers raced up by special post-chaise to fetch him and, travelling for fourteen hours without a break, returned to London near midnight on Saturday, 28 December. The late hour notwithstanding the magistrates assembled to examine him there and then. Cahill, faced with a charge of murder, quickly confessed that he was a deserter. He had never heard of Williamson, he said, and had never been to Ratcliff Highway. Why then did he mention both at the Marlborough hearing? Because he wanted to cover up his tracks. But why Williamson and Ratcliff? They happened to come to mind, he said. When the magistrates adjourned the hearing they were confident that they had found the killer.[9]

And they had, but it wasn't Cahill. Williams, the other Irishman arrested a few days before and unaware that the magistrates themselves were far from convinced about his guilt, had concluded that he was doomed and hanged himself from a rafter in his prison cell.

There then followed a bizarre rite. At 9 a.m. on 31 December, with the kerchief with which he had hanged himself still round his neck, his feet bare, his hair blowing in the wind, and dressed in blue pantaloons and a white shirt, Williams was placed face upward in an open cart, the mallet with which he had slaughtered the Marr family like a sceptre by his side, while a procession of local dignitaries assembled round him. The whole of the East End had turned out to see the cavalcade and stood bent against the cold while it took its slow course, pausing first outside 29 Ratcliff Highway, in tribute to the Marr family, and then at the King's Arms, in tribute to the Williamsons, and finally to a point where Canon Street and Ratcliff Highway met. A shallow grave had been prepared and the body of Williams was slowly lowered into it. And then, amid the enthusiastic shouts of the multitude, a stake was driven through his heart, the traditional punishment meted out by the Church to its suicides.[10]

If the Marr and Williamson murders placed the Ratcliff Highway and the surrounding riverside parishes of Shadwell, Wapping and Limehouse in a lurid light, they had never been the last redoubt of innocence. They lived on the river, and the river meant plunder. 'The immense depredations committed on every species of Commercial Property in the River Thames,' wrote the City Magistrate, Patrick Colquhoun, in 1800, 'has long been felt a grievance of the greatest magnitude, exceedingly hurtful to the Commerce and Revenue of the Port of London.'[11]

Over ten thousand ships used the river in an average year and they were all considered fair game, especially the great West Indiamen, laden with sugar, tobacco and rum, which because of their size had to anchor in midstream. At night thieves would swarm over them like soldier ants over a carcass, and some even operated in broad daylight. There were full-time thieves and part-time thieves and Colquhoun was convinced that 'all classes of aquatic labourers'[12] were implicated in the plunder. And those not directly involved could derive a profitable income by divert-their eyes from those who were. Everyone was aware of what was going on, and on some parts of the river labourers were unpaid and in others they even paid to be employed, so rich were the pickings; and until comparatively recent times there appears to have been a tacit assumption that plunder was a fringe benefit of waterside work.

Colquhoun calculated losses from theft in an average year at about £$\frac{1}{2}$ m.[13] There were river pirates who cut away the cordage, spars, oars and sometimes even the anchor and cable. There were what he called 'Heavy Horsemen' who boarded the ships with coats-of-many-pockets and came away laden with sugar, coffee, pimento, cocoa and ginger and staggered ashore like sows in labour. There were 'Light Horsemen' who were allowed to buy the 'sweepings' of goods fallen through broken casks and who saw to it that breakages were abundant. There were the watermen in small craft who buzzed round the big ones and were, according to Colquhoun, 'extremely loose in their morals', and who acted as middlemen between thieves on board and receivers on shore.[14] Small boys digging around in the Thames mud were also employed to smuggle goods ashore at low tide, and thus served an apprenticeship from which they graduated to more profitable forms of theft. One young thief, and he no more than an apprentice, kept a carriage and mistress on his takings.[15]

Every time a cargo was trans-shipped it was at the mercy of

thieves and diminished at every stage of its handling, from ship
to lighter, from lighter to shore, and on the crowded quays
themselves. Journeymen, coppers, excisemen, all were in the
game, coming with sacks and aprons, and even bladders to siphon
off gin and rum. The receivers, usually in business as ships'
chandlers, grocers or junk dealers, remained open at all hours
of the day and night.[16] Everything was vendible, and everyone
was on the lookout for something to vend. It made for a certain
keenness and vivacity, and if there was poverty in the riverside
parishes, it was poverty tampered by loot. This is not to say that
the riverside was amoral. A pickpocket would have been ostracised or handed over to the police, but tampering with cargo –
or 'knocking-off' as it was called later – was merely the East End
exacting its own tribute. It was a means of supplementing the low
wages paid by the shipowners.

The establishment of the Marine Police in 1798 curbed the
traffic somewhat, but as long as ships discharged in mid-river
and there was open access to the quays and wharves the depredations could not be stopped. In 1799, the West India Company,
which had suffered most from the piracy, obtained a charter to
build a dock on the north bank of the Thames by the Isle of
Dogs. It was completed two years later amid loud fanfares from
the press:

> The grand and magnificent work which is now to become the
> receptacle of a great portion of our national wealth, and which
> if we consider the stupendous scale on which it had been
> planned, the celerity with which it had been executed, and the
> accommodation it must afford to our commerce, is an object
> of universal admiration, was yesterday, for the first time,
> opened to the service of the public;[17]

The dock, half a mile in length and twenty-four acres in
extent, was large enough to take over four hundred vessels of
three hundred tons each. It was an immediate success, and further
docks were built along the north side of the river, by the London
Dock Company, the East India Dock Company (whose buildings
were designed by Rennie), the Regent Canal Dock, and finally,
almost in the shadow of the Tower of London, St Katharine's
Dock. St Katharine's, built by Telford, was cut in 1828 and by
the time it was opened London had a surplus of docking facili-

ties,[18] and the docks, in spite of continuing process of re-organisation and amalgamation, were in frequent financial difficulties.

The largest ships afloat could now come into dock and discharge their goods straight into the warehouses, whose walls rose in an almost continuous line high above the river and dwarfed the nearby dwellings. Dockers and other labourers were admitted through a gate in the morning and searched as they left at night. The warehouse walls gave the whole area the aspect of a prison-cum-fortress, and presented either an endless blank façade to the streets or gazed out upon it through small barred windows. The whole character of the waterside parishes was transformed. The river could still be approached via narrow streets and stairs through gaps in the warehouse walls, but the broad vistas, the sight of ships and sails, the hint of far away places and distant shores were obscured.

The process begun by the docks was carried further by the railways, which began to insinuate their way into the East End in 1839, and thrust their way round it and over it and under it in loops and crossings, with a cutting here and a viaduct there, splitting up neighbourhoods and throwing whole streets into permanent gloom. East London was a developer's paradise. Property was cheap, and the population was neither articulate nor influential, nor of the sort which could be easily organised in protest. A local paper complained that the railway companies were carving up London: 'they appear to have been so carried away, as to regard the public as created for the convenience of railway schemes, instead of the old idea that railways were to be created for the convenience of the public'.[19]

The riverside parishes, with their higgledy-piggledy streets and alleys and tall gabled houses round narrow courtyards, were lacerated by the lines. In Wapping many of its inhabitants were made homeless by the demolition of whole streets. There was no attempt to rehouse them and they moved northwards beyond Whitechapel High Street to find rooms among the sordid lodging-houses and teeming slums of Spitalfields.[20]

The Tower alone was safe from the developer's hand. Nearby, within its shadow, stood one of the few buildings in East London to have survived from antiquity, St Katharine's Convent. Founded by Matilda, wife of King Stephen, in 1148, as a memorial to her two children, it was re-established by Eleanor, widow of Henry III. One of the few such institutions to have been untouched by the dissolution of the monasteries, it was by the nineteenth century the oldest ecclesiastical foundation in London. With its cloistered walks, its cobbled quadrangle, its gothic arches and ancient timbers, it looked like a Cambridge College stranded on the edge of the East End. Beyond was the clamour and bustle of Ratcliff Highway, the hoarse cries of street vendors, the clatter of great drays on cobbled stones, within there was peace, an island of tranquillity in a sea of noise. In 1825 it was found to be in the way of Telford's plan for St Katharine's dock, and a building which had withstood even the wrath of Henry VIII was pulled down and transferred to Regent's Park but the Foundation returned to the East End in 1950.

The Annual Register for 1763 described the Ratcliff Highway as a place 'of dissolute sailors, blackmailing watermen, rowdy fishermen, stock-fish hawkers, quarrelsome chairmen, audacious highwaymen, sneak-thieves and professional cheats . . . footpads, deserters, prisoners of war on parole, bravos, bullies and river vultures', and perhaps because it had changed so little and retained both its colour and notoriety, it became the subject of legend and song:

> List ye, jovial sailors gay,
> To the rigs of Ratcliff Highway.

> I fell in with a lady so modest and meek,
> She eats thirteen faggots and nine pigs feet,
> Three pounds of beef, and to finish the meal,
> Ate eight pounds of tripe and an old cow-heel.

> I met with another borne down with fear.
> She guzzled down thirteen pots of beer.
> She threw up her heels and played the deuce,
> And broke her nose at Paddy's Goose.

> You jovial sailors, one and all,
> When you in the port of London call,
> Mind Ratcliff Highway and the damsels loose,
> The William, The Bear and Paddy's Goose.

> You sailors bold my song obtain,
> And learn it on the raging main.

Dickens came down this way in search of colour and found almost excess of it:

> Down by the Docks, the seamen rove in mid-street and mid-day, their pockets inside-out and their heads no better. Down by the Docks the daughters of wave-ruling Britannia also rove, clad in silken attire, with uncovered tresses streaming in the breeze, bandana kerchiefs floating from their shoulders and crinolines not wanting.... Down by the Docks the Children of Israel creep into any gloomy cribs and entries they can hire, and hang slops there, pewter watches, souwester hats, water-proof overalls — 'firth rate articleth Jack'. ... Down by the Docks the apothecary sets up in business on the wretchedest scale – chiefly on lint and plaster for the strapping of wounds – and with no bright bottles and with no little drawers. Down by the Docks, the shabby undertaker's shop will bury you for next to nothing after the Malay or Chinaman has stabbed you for nothing at all ...[21]

Down by the Docks, he could have added, the living-room was the street and the drawing-room the Gin Palace.

In the eighteenth century, beer, traditionally the Englishman's drink, was overtaken by spirits, though both were drunk in vast quantities, especially in East London where work was hard, hours were long and thirsts were great. Workers in the local sugar refineries consumed two gallons of beer a day. Water, where it was available – the local water supply was deficient right up to modern times – was offensive in smell and taste, and not infrequently poisonous, though it soon became evident that gin, taken in copious quantities, if less lethal than the local water, was not entirely healthy either, and in 1825 the Bishop of London complained of 'a most frightful increase of intemperance'.[22]

Dr Gordon, a physician at the London Hospital in Whitechapel Road, which had to cope with many of the effects of excessive drinking, said that the consumption of spirits had introduced a new malady to the local working man – indigestion: 'I attribute it as a physician, to the facility which the poor people possess of procuring, without loss of time, without inconvenience, and without shame, day and night, Sunday and working-day, any quantity of spirits.'[23]

An American visitor was appalled by the scene!

The local classes of the Great Metropolis are as bad as the lower classes of any metropolis can be; they are perhaps more depraved, more dissolute than any other. Drunkenness is a vice practised to an unparalleled extent in the community. A stranger will be struck with astonishment at the number of drunken persons he will meet in the metropolis; nor less so at the superb edifices that are raised by the proceeds of those who indulge in this darling vice, and by their voluntary contributions. These are called Gin Palaces. First because the chief spirit, the favourite liquor of the lower orders is Gin; and secondly, because the edifices in their fitting up resemble palaces in their costliness and grandeur. Had Hogarth lived in the present era he would have improved upon his celebrated picture. The contrast between the magnificent structure and the squalid and ragged misery which support such grandeur by its own ruin, is a picture which was not of his time. The contrast is startling to a degree. The houses are open to a very early hour of the morning, and do more business between four and eight a.m. than in all the rest of the day. . . . Another startling point to an American is the sight of women going in for their quarter as commonly as men.[24]

Dickens noted that the gin palaces were 'invariably numerous and splendid in precise proportion to the dirt and poverty of the surroundings,'[25] but the fact is that they did add a touch of splendour to areas which were otherwise drab. They, the churches, and the local workhouse were about the only buildings of particular distinction in the neighbourhood. In the 1830s, Commercial Road, built to link the City with the docks, cut a broad swathe through the riverside parishes, and it was continued eastwards as far as the river Lea by the East India Dock Road. Both were as straight as a French boulevard, and as wide, though not as elegant, and they were lined mainly with commercial properties, but here and there was a large house with a garden and carriage drive inhabited by some merchant, retired sea-captain, or senior official of the dock companies, but the gentry began to vanish as the noise and congestion increased, and as the railways gave them easy access to the new suburbs sprouting round Epping Forest. And when they went, company clerks, dock foremen, proprietors of the large shops followed. The area bounded by Commercial Road/East India Dock Road and the river became almost solidly working-class, with street upon narrow street of houses of a pocket-Georgian variety, with a continuous parapet line at the top hiding the chimneys and roofs from view, two windows at the top and one at the bottom, with identical door and identical curtains, with a few schools, a few churches, a great many pubs, no parks or playing fields, and a curtain of smoke and grit from the surrounding factories.[26]

There were citizens who managed to lead a cheerful and even respectable life amid such scenes, and bring up their children to respectability, but in areas such as Ratcliff Highway, as a local paper observed, they fought a losing battle:

> ... In this long street of Crimps, Slop-sellers, flaring Gin-palaces, Sailors' Boarding-houses, equi-vocal Coffee shops, and flash Dancing Saloons, there are steady, hard-working, respect-able and *wealthy* tradesmen, with staid matrons and pure-minded daughters, existing and growing up amidst all the filth and depravity that defective police arrangements permit to pollute the local atmosphere. ... How many a respectable woman has been forced into the roadway to avoid a reeking crowd that some easy, swinging gin-palace door belches forth? ... How many a modest woman is forced into the roadway to avoid the half-dozen caricatures of her sex, who, wildly drunk, are walking abreast occupying the whole of the footway, and singing, or rather screeching, snatches of obscene songs at the very top of their voices?[27]

Prostitution was rife in Victorian England in the West End as well as the East End, and Ratcliff Highway was the working man's Regent Street. The prostitutes' trade mark was a red bandana round their shoulders and a small cane in their hand, but in many cases by the time they were on the Highway they were at the end of their careers, spent, drunken wretches, and their attempts at youthful finery made them a pathetic spectacle. Hardly a day passed without a batch of them being brought before the magistrates for drunkenness, assault or theft, and sometimes all three, but the traffic continued, and so did the exodus of the respectable and the well-to-do.[28] But they did not entirely vanish. There were petty-traders with homes above their shop, publicans who had to live with their trade, mechanics who had to be within easy reach of their machines, old people clinging to the old scenes, and, above all, the saving grace of the East End, clergymen of all denominations, though not all of them lived with their work. A Vicar of Shadwell began his inaugural sermon on the text: 'Woe is me that I sojourn in Mesach, that I dwell in the tents of Kedar', and made his home in the Strand.

# FOUR

# Profitable Strangers

The prosperity of Tudor England attracted many foreigners and they formed small colonies in and around London. The Crown viewed them with favour, for they brought new skills and revenues, but the surrounding population envied their prosperity and resented their competition. There were anti-alien riots in 1517 and apprentices and watermen (who were always good for a riot whatever the occasion) ran wild through the streets of Spitalfields sacking the homes of Flemings, Frenchmen and Italians. Dr Beale, Canon of St Mary's, Spitalfields, protested 'that English merchants could have no utterance; for the merchant strangers brought in all silks, cloth of gold, wine, oil and other merchandise'.[1] And that was not the limit of their intrusion. 'I saw on a Sunday this Lent, six hundred strangers shooting at the popinjay,' protested a London merchant.[2]

Henry VIII decreed that 'no strange artificer should keep more than two servant strangers',[3] but the law was applied half-heartedly, and the aliens continued to come in and, according to a survey made by the Lord Mayor of London in 1551, there were some forty thousand of them living in and around London, 'besides women and children, for the most part heretics fled from other countries'.[4] This would have brought the full figure up to about a hundred thousand – a wild exaggeration, but symbolic of the sort of estimates that were to be made in later centuries whenever there was any sizeable influx of newcomers. Though England was an open country right up to our own times, the stranger was never a welcome figure and in English eyes a few could seem like many.

The first substantial body of immigrants to settle in England were the Huguenots who began to arrive in Elizabethan times. The extent of their influx varied with their treatment in France. The peak was reached after the Revocation of the Edict of Nantes in 1685, when over a hundred thousand, most of them destitute, made their homes in England. They proved themselves to be ideal citizens. 'They labour truthfully', wrote a bishop, 'they live sparingly. They are good examples of labour, travail, faith and patience. The towns in which they live are happy; for God doth follow them with His blessing.'[5] They were greeted with a warmth and sympathy which no refugees in England had encountered before or since. A public subscription on their behalf raised over £200,000.[6] Charles II issued a special proclamation according them 'all privileges and immunities for the liberty and free exercise of their trade and craft';[7] privileges which they put to immediate use and within a few years they were prospering as cutlers, watchmakers, instrument makers, jewellers, opticians, locksmiths, hatters, glovers but – above all – in every branch of the silk industry. Within a few years too, their neighbours were complaining of competition.

Elizabeth and James I had made attempts to set up a silk industry in England, but it only began to flourish with the Huguenots. They made Spitalfields, abutting on the City wall, their main base and turned out large quantities of lustrings, velvets, brocades, damasks. Spitalfields silks began to be spoken of in the same breath as Lyons and Tours and England attracted a good part of the trade hitherto monopolised by France.[8] 'Profitable strangers' was the name applied to the bustling newcomers, and they were indeed.[9]

'The English', noted an eighteenth-century writer, 'have now so great an esteem for the workmanship of the French refugees that hardly anything now vends without a Gallic name.'[10]

Spitalfields, at the end of the seventeenth century, was an area of fields and gardens. The influx of refugees led to a rapid spate of building, but it was not rapid enough, and two or three families were crammed into every house. By 1775 the area was bricked over, and Walter Harrison lamented:

These fields now consist of a great number of streets, lanes and alleys, principally inhabited by the descendants of those French refugees who fled thither in 1686 . . .[11]

The more prosperous of the refugees, the merchants, retailers, dyers, built elegant homes in Spital Square, with imposing façades, though the interiors were usually unpretentious, but in the main the area was working class.[12] The weavers' homes were built in long rows, in cramped narrow streets and they caught what light there was through large windows built along the entire length of their attics which housed their looms. They brightened their surroundings with flowers and window boxes, and wherever there was an inch of soil open to the sky they planted a garden. The very names of the streets, Blossom Street, Fleur de Lys Street, Flower and Dean Street, suggest a certain gaiety, but the East End, like other working-class areas, has always had a genius for misnomer, and they may have sought in the street-names the cheer they failed to find in the streets.

The evidence on the appearance of the area is contradictory. On the one hand we have Harrison's lament that the fields were all built over; on the other a description of Spitalfields as an artisan's paradise, 'each man plying his craft in an essentially rural landscape of fields and hedgerows',[13] with flowers by his door, a singing bird by his loom and a song in his heart. Each weaver had his own individual patterns, and 'a lady of fashion could visit a weaver's cottage to select material for a dress'.[14]

'The conditions under which the original Spitalfields weavers pursued their handicraft were as idyllic as their domestic surroundings', wrote a historian of the British silk industry.[15] Each master could employ two or three journeymen weavers, and an apprentice or two, and they all formed part of the households, working together, eating together, praying together.

The day began at 5.45 a.m. when the tenor bell at Christ Church summoned the men to their labour, and closed when the curfew bell rang at a quarter to eight.[16] There were half-hour breaks for lunch and tea, and, from all accounts, the men applied themselves to their work with great zeal.

The Church was central to their existence. There were sixteen Huguenot churches in and around Spitalfields and a seventeenth in Wapping. Jean Durel, minister of the fashionable French Protestant Church in the Savoy, near the Strand, translated the Anglican liturgy into French, but in East London they tended to adhere to the liturgy they used in France. Their churches were austere, inside and out, as was their manner of dress. They sang their old hymns with their old fervour, and there was something timeless about the tone and contents of the weekly sermon. Their clergy were determined to maintain, within eighteenth-century England, a corner of seventeenth-century France. The Huguenots tried as far as possible to speak French at home and, as late as the mid-eighteenth century, many of the working men in the area could speak no English.[17] Their urge for self-improvement started with the local parochial schools maintained by the community and continued throughout their lives. Even while they were at their looms a child of the family would read aloud to raise its elders' minds to higher things.[18] A strong sense of community existed. The prosperous merchants took their duties to their less fortunate brethren sternly. They established soup kitchens and charity schools, and distributed money, but – and here one sees a local influence creeping in – 'many of them spent so much on Spiritous Liquors', wrote a contemporary observer, 'that the Managers rightly judged it better to relieve them with provisions'.[19]

There were several learned societies in the area. One founded by a local publican which enjoyed particular popularity was the Mathematical Society. It had its own clubroom and a library of over three thousand books. The subscription was 4d a week and members could be fined a penny for failing to attend meetings. Sessions began with an hour of private study followed by a lecture on some more or less abstruse philosophical subject.[20] Among the members of the society were John Dollond, a weaver whose son became an optician and founded the famous firm which still bears his name.

The first half of the eighteenth century seems to have been the golden age of the Spitalfields Huguenots. There were about fifteen thousand of them in the neighbourhood, according to figures supplied by local consistories, but, as they were habitually nervous of external authority, they may have concealed their true number. What is certain is that Spitalfields was soon too small for all the newcomers and they set up looms in nearby Bethnal Green. The new area was contiguous to the old, so that they continued to form a compact colony, but they found it difficult to remain distinct from their neighbours, and the particular way of life which they had preserved against every adversity did not long survive freedom.

In 1782, L'Eglise De La Artillery Lane commemorated its jubilee with a special service and what should have been a celebration became a lament. The Minister, M. Bourdillon, declared that the church was dying and berated his congregants for their lack of zeal and for failing to bring up their sons in the ways of their fathers:

> ... churches which their ancestors had reared as a glorious monument of the generous sacrifices which they had made of their country, their employments in the sacred cause of conscience, for the open profession of the truth, whereas now, through the growing aversion of the young for the language of their fathers, from whom they seem almost ashamed to be descended – shall I say more? – because of inconstancy in principles of their faith, which induces so many to a sort of infatuation to forsake the ancient assemblies in order to follow novelties unknown to their fathers, and listen to teachers whose only gifts are rapture and babble, and whose sole inspiration consists of a self-sufficiency and pride. Alas! What savages have been made here and elsewhere during this jubilee of fifty years. [21]

Savages was hardly an exaggeration for, by the end of the century, Spitalfields was one of the most riotous corners of London and Bethnal Green was, if anything, worse.

On 3 October, 1763, wrote a local paper:

> Several thousand journeymen weavers assembled in Spitalfields and in a riotous and violent manner broke open the house of one of their masters, destroyed his looms, and cut a great quantity of rich silk to pieces, after which they placed his effigy in a cart, with a halter about his neck, an executioner on one side and a coffin on the other. They then drove it through several streets, hung it on a gibbet and burnt it to ashes . . . [22]

They rioted again in 1765 and 1766. On the latter occasion the tumult was so great and the damage so extensive that the Guards were called out from the Tower of London. These outbreaks now became an annual event, each one more serious than the other. In 1769 fourteen of the ringleaders were apprehended, and two were hanged outside the Salmon and Ball, a

Bethnal Green tavern, instead of the usual place of execution. But if the desire was to cow the local population it had no effect. Troops were quartered in the local taverns, but what finally brought peace to the neighbourhood was the 1773 Spitalfields Act under which masters and weavers regulated prices and wages by mutual agreement.

It is difficult to reconcile the picture of master and journeyman together as one family, bookish, studious, working in their small cottages, busy in their little gardens, good churchmen and true, with the reports of riot and arson, murder and mayhem one found in the press.

It could perhaps be suggested that, as the Huguenots prospered and moved out, the Irish moved in, and certainly of the fourteen ringleaders arrested after the 1769 riots several had Irish names. Of the two actually hanged, one, Valine, was probably Huguenot and the other, Doyle, was Irish.[23] A more likely answer, however, was that the rioters were indeed Huguenots, but that they were demoralised by destitution. It was one thing to struggle for one's faith against a known enemy and another to cope with the insidious creep of hunger. Wars brought dislocation of trade, peace brought competition from France, and in war and peace there was the smuggling of French silks on a scale large enough to upset the market. In 1763 several thousand journeymen went in procession from Spitalfields to St James's to petition George III on 'the miserable condition themselves and their families were reduced to by the clandestine importation of French silk'. The riots were pleas for protection. Their family experience, their own training, had made them stoic, patient and docile, but once roused they were not easily subdued. Their struggles excited wide sympathy and for a time it was feared that the turbulence in Spitalfields might form the basis for a populist rising in the East End. By fixing wages, the Spitalfields Act put an end to the agitation and brought a stability to the area which was unknown elsewhere in the textile industry.

The Spitalfields weavers formed an aristocracy of labour and, when wages elsewhere in the industry were six to seven shillings a week, the Spitalfields wage was 12/6. The disparity was too large to be overlooked even by the most benign manufacturers and many moved their looms to Lancashire, the Midlands and

Essex which were unaffected by the Act. This at once lowered the number of jobs and the tone of the neighbourhood. A booklet published in 1806 on *The Distress Peculiar to the Poor of Spitalfields* referred to 'the extreme poverty of the neighbourhood' and ascribed the main cause to 'the gradual removal of the more affluent people into other parishes, while their former dwellings here soon became divided and subdivided into small lodgings, which are immediately occupied by an accession of casual poor'.[24] The arrival of newcomers from Wapping dislodged by the building of London docks brought further changes. 'Here', one was told, 'the poor literally support the poor'.[25] The rich had fled to a world of their own.

The rest of the story is one of attrition and heartbreak. The spread of the power loom brought about the repeal of the act in 1824 and although eleven thousand weavers pleaded that it was their 'greatest blessing', the measure took its course and wages fell to starvation level. By 1837 a family would be lucky to earn as much as 25 shillings a week.

The occasional loom could still be heard clattering away even after the end of the century. There were forty-six handloom weavers at work in the East End as late as 1914[26], but they were kept in trade for old times' sake or were producing a special article for a very specialised market. Spitalfields and Bethnal Green had effectively ceased to be of any significance to the silk trade by the middle of the nineteenth century, and with the trade went the final traces of Huguenot life.

The Reverend Isaac Taylor, vicar of St Matthew's, Bethnal Green, wrote towards the end of the century:

> The descendants of the immigrants still continue to inhabit the district. Many of them still cherish the proud traditions of their ancestry; many of them, though now, perhaps clad in rags, bear the old historical names of France. . . . In addition to their surnames and their traditions, the only relic which these exiles retain of their former prosperity and gentle nurture is a traditional love of birds and flowers.[27]

In 1849 a local inhabitant observed: 'I meet with many names, evidently French; but I have never been able to find among those parties anything like a traditional account of their origins. They have a vague tradition that their ancestors did come from

France at one time; but why and wherefore they are not able to say.'[28]

And this, hardly more than a century and a half from the Revocation of the Edict of Nantes. The actual observable traces of Huguenot life had vanished much earlier.

Why, in a society notoriously slow to assimilate strangers, did the Huguenots fade out so fast? First, they were few. One historian wrote that eighty thousand Huguenots settled in Britain, another put the figure at between forty to forty-five thousand. The well-to-do tended to settle round Leicester Square and Soho and Savoy. Artisans made their homes in East London, and it is unlikely that their number was much above fifteen thousand. They came in three main waves, the first, arising mainly from the dragonades in 1681–82; the second, and largest, arrived after the Revocation between 1686–88, and the third, after the renewal of persecution between 1698–1700.[29] Thereafter, the anti-Protestant fury died down, the influx stopped, and those Huguenots whose longing for France outlasted their memories of persecution no doubt went back. Those who remained did attempt to maintain a sort of Zion in exile, but it was difficult. They suffered from the fact that, unlike other immigrant groups, they were, in a sense, too readily acceptable. Their very industriousness may have occasioned resentment, and the Weavers' Company protested against their privileges;[30] but they arrived in England almost under Royal patronage, and such was their popularity that even the Catholic James II authorised collections in the churches towards their upkeep. William III, who included a large body of Huguenot officers in his army, helped generously. And apart from the external political circumstances – as victims of England's particular enemy, the premier Catholic power of Europe – which made them welcome, they had unique qualities to commend them. They were men steeled by torment, high-minded, idealistic, who had proved by their very flight that they were ready to face every hazard and forego every material advantage for the sake of their faith, and the Englishman, though not too religious a being himself, has always had an instinctive admiration for the martyr – except where, as with the Irish – he was himself the cause of their martyrdom. The Huguenot, moreover, was a Protestant in a Protestant land, and there were thus no obstacles to his assimilation except for those he imposed himself. For a while he maintained his own distinct community, with its own language, its own customs and rules, even on the frequency which they had to preach. (A minister who failed to preach – or provide a substitute – was fined a guinea; an elder, who forgot his turn to invite the minister to Sunday dinner, was fined half a crown.)[31] They had their own soup kitchen, alms houses, charity school, their own general hospital – which was the first in the country to admit lunatics as patients. They virtually introduced the Mutual Benefit Society to England. (In the Society of Parisians, for example, they paid an entrance fee of 2/6, and a monthly contribution of 1/-. They met on the last Saturday of the month and paid four pence for the evening's entertainment – and tuppence per absence. Sick benefits were 8/- a week for the first year, 4/- thereafter and £5 on death.)[32] Though loving the French language, the attitude of Huguenots to France and French culture was necessarily ambivalent. There was something unFrench about their very Protestantism, and as they had had to flee from France for their lives they experienced no conflict of loyalties during the many wars between Britain and their country of origin. During the 1745 rising of the Young Pretender the master-weavers of Spitalfields offered George II the services of three thousand men, mostly of Huguenot descent.[33] Some families adopted English names. One elder of the Church, Abraham de la Neuve Maison, became Abraham Newhouse.[34] Pellegrins became Pilgrims and Dubois, Wood.[35] The use of French lapsed in the street, then at home, and finally even in the Huguenot institutions.

The rate of intermarriage between Huguenots and their English neighbours, as the local parish registers indicate, was high.[36] Also as a result of their hard work and enterprise, many a Huguenot artisan rose to be master or merchant, and usually marked his ascent by moving out of Spitalfields altogether. And once removed from Huguenot neighbours and Huguenot institutions, his absorption into English life was immediate. There was every reason for it. In the seventeenth century anyone moving from France to England was moving from a comparatively advanced to a comparatively backward country. By the eighteenth century, possibly because of the flight of Huguenots, the roles had been reversed. Her strength, her prosperity, her political institutions, her triumphs over French arms on land and at sea, had made England the foremost power in Europe. One could glory in the name of Englishman, and many Huguenots did.

By the beginning of the nineteenth century Huguenot hand-loom weavers must have been few and far between, and it was fairly clear that the work force at the bottom of the Spitalfields weaving trade was largely, if not entirely, English or Irish.

Yet, the public still thought of Spitalfields as a Huguenot settlement long after it had ceased to be so, and when in 1816 an appeal was launched to relieve distress in the area, £37,000 was raised – including £5,000 from the Prince Regent.[37] The effect of such appeals and generosity was to make the area a magnet for every mendicant, sob-story vendor, professional beggar, and idler in the kingdom. Many families with a claim to respectability and a modicum of funds felt compelled to get out. Spitalfields became a dank, nefarious slum, one of the most dangerous corners of London, with all the squalor of Ratcliff Highway, but none of its tanginess or colour.

Of the Huguenot settlement there remains nothing but derelict churches. One, L'Eglise Neuve, built in 1743 in Brick Lane, is still standing. First a Huguenot church, then a Methodist Chapel, and finally a synagogue, it may soon become a mosque.

# FIVE

# Troublesome Strangers

Where there were Irish there was trouble. They were many, mobile, rowdy and poor and they seemed to carry their poverty like an epidemic. As early as 1413 there was a statute ordering 'that all Irishmen and Irish clerics and beggars called chamber-dykins be voided out of the realm'.[1]

There were laws restricting the movement of Irish in the sixteenth and seventeenth centuries. In 1629 the City of London protested that 'the realm hath of late been pestered with a great many Irish beggars, who live here idly and dangerously and are an ill-example to the natives of the Kingdom'.[2] There were anti-Irish riots in Spitalfields in 1736, in Wapping in 1768, in Shadwell in 1786. In the first case weavers protested that the Irishmen were undercutting their wages.[3] In the second there was an affray between Irish coal-heavers and English sailors, resulting in many injuries, much destruction of property and some deaths. Several heavers were arrested, but no sailors, and two of the heavers, Murphy and Duggan, were hanged.[4] In Shadwell there was a further affray. This time the police descended in force and seven men, all Irish, were hanged.[5]

An Irish writer, J. Denvir, was later to claim:

We know how, by studied insults to his creed and country, the hot-blooded Irish Celt is often made to appear the aggressor. In any case, he is nearly always the greatest sufferer, for even if he comes off victorious in the fight with his opponents, the law is pretty sure to claim him in the end as the chief victim.[6]

This, needless to say, had not been the opinion of their English neighbours, and in 1810 a resident of East London complained:

The quarrelsome, riotous, and indeed, blood-thirsty disposition of the lower orders of Irishmen, when intoxicated with gin or whisky, has long called for exemplary punishment. Some of the streets of districts most afflicted by them almost weekly exhibit a nocturnal row. The brutal temper is most prevalent among them – strange as it may seem – when out of their native land. One would imagine that men emigrating from their own country in search of better employ in another, would be meek and humble, and make it a primary object to conciliate the good opinion of the people who allot them an asylum. The very reverse, however, is the case. Opinion to a degree of disgust (the common failing of the most ignorant) they arrogate to themselves a superiority over the common ability of whatever country they fly to.[7]

The British armies and navies which fought Napoleon were filled with Irishmen. When they were discharged after Waterloo they roamed the country in ravenous bands looking for bread and work and the London Mendicity Society protested that Irish beggars were overwhelming the country.[8] The Reverend Thomas Malthus warned a Parliamentary Committee on emigration that the Irish influx was 'fatal to the happiness of the labouring classes in England'.[9]

Malthus had made a detailed study of Irish agrarian problems and had found that, though Ireland's population had been doubling every forty-five years since the end of the seventeenth century, her agricultural output had remained static. In England the enclosure movement had led to the creation of large agricultural holdings. In Ireland there was an opposite tendency with small holdings parcelled among many sons into smaller ones until they were insufficient to feed a family and men drifted off to become landless labourers.[10] Moreover, farmers rarely enjoyed security of tenure and were therefore disinclined to spend money on improvement. But even where they might have been ready to spend money, they rarely had money to spend. Irish farming was starved of capital. The great landlords, members of the Protestant ascendancy, derived their revenues from Ireland and spent them in England. The result was misery. The picture Dean Swift painted of rural Ireland at the beginning of the eighteenth century was substantially true a century later:

> . . . a bare face of nature, without houses or plantations – filthy cabins, miserable, tattered, half-starved creatures, scarce in human shape; one insolent, ignorant, oppressive squire to be found in 20 miles riding . . . a bog of 15 miles round; every meadow a slough; every hill a mixture of rock, heath and marsh; and every male and female from the farmer inclusive to the day labourer, infallibly a thief and consequently a beggar, which in this island are terms convertible. There is not an acre of land in Ireland turned to have its advantage, yet it is better improved than the people – and all the evils are effects of English tyranny.[11]

When the harvests were good they were barely sufficient to feed the population. When they were bad there was starvation and a drift towards England.

But there were other factors which brought the Irish to England. A Parliamentary Committee on emigration chanced upon the fully obvious fact that 'two different rates of wages and two different conditions of labour cannot permanently co-exist'.[12] Though England and Ireland were, in law, part of one kingdom, the one was rich and getting richer, the other was poor and getting poorer, and there were therefore natural forces compelling the surplus population of the latter to seek jobs in the former. England, moreover, had a Poor Law which, though it gave little, and that grudgingly, at least kept starvation at bay. There was no such law in Ireland until the middle of the nineteenth century. One could hope for alms from the Catholic Church, but the Church was itself not rich and at a time of hunger there was nothing for it but to head for England. The journey often meant a walk of a hundred miles to the nearest port, and then a crossing which was always unpleasant, frequently hazardous, and sometimes fatal. The principal freight of the shipping lines was cattle, sheep and pigs. There was rarely cabin accommodation and passengers remained on deck washed by the spray. Some winters were so fierce that they were frozen to the boards. One boatload of passengers, travelling from Sligo to Liverpool, was battened down against a storm and, in the ensuing commotion and darkness, seventy-two of them were trampled to death.[13]

Once in port they were often too hungry and exhausted to dis-
embark and had to be carried ashore by police.[14]

A Liverpool charity might feed them for a day, and then
began the long trek south. In summer and autumn there was
always the hope of work on the farms, picking peas, making
hay, stacking corn. In the winter, where they had not earned
enough to return home, they made for the cities.

'... there is nothing equal to the eagerness with which the
Irish labourer will look for work', said an observer in 1827,
'if he hears of work within ten miles to be done in the country,
he immediately applies; there are no people who wish to be
employed more than they do'.[15]

They were a little too eager, which was in itself a cause of
unpopularity. Where the wage was low, the work hard, the
hours long and the conditions noxious, whether in the fetid
heat of a slaughterhouse, the stench of a tannery, the darkness
and constriction of a ship's hold or a tunnel, one found the
Irish, great, shaggy, lumbering giants, like Clydesdale horses.
Their bulk, their build went ill with one's idea of starving
victims of a hungry land. It was as giants that the Irish figured
in popular lore (and *Punch* cartoons), with massive shoulders,
hairy face, gnarled hands, clay pipe in mouth, shovel (or shil-
lelagh) at the ready, prepared for any task where much brawn
and little brain were called for. They seemed a race apart, specially
bred for hardship, and hardy they were. They did not mix too
well with the English, not at all well with the Welsh, and were
explosive when brought within sight of the Scotch[16], and they
had to be kept in their own encampments and secluded gangs
but when bent upon a job they had no equal. They formed the
core of the floating armies of labourers who built the canals,
the docks, the railways and transformed the face of England.
They were needed, but they were not popular.

Ireland was in an almost constant state of insurrection throughout the nineteenth century, so that being Irish was bad enough;
what made it worse was the fact that most of them were Catholic.

Catholics in the United Kingdom were denied civil rights and,
when an attempt to ease their conditions was made at the end
of the eighteenth century, the Protestant mob rose in anger and
went rampaging through the streets of London, burning,
plundering, maiming. The Irish had built a humble chapel in

Spitalfields and another in Wapping. Both were razed. There would have been serious bloodshed, but for the restraint which an Irish priest kept on his outraged flock.[17]

The public recoiled at the violence, but not so far as to evince much sympathy for Catholics, and it was not until 1829 that a Catholic relief act was passed.

The press gave prominence to reports of oppression and mis-government in those parts of Italy which were still under Papal rule and built up a picture of Catholicism as evil tempered by incompetence. The average Catholic was regarded as a person of dubious loyalty, if not an active agent of subversion, a view which seemed to be confirmed by the daily reports coming out of Ireland.

The antipathy worked both ways, for if some disliked the Irish because they were nearly all Catholics, others disliked Catholics because they were nearly all Irish, but their number was not large, they lived in compact neighbourhoods; they presented no great problem. Then came the flood.

The cause, as before, was hunger, but hunger on an un-precedented scale. The potato harvest had failed before, but if one year was bad there was always the hope that the next one would be good, or at least adequate, but in 1846, the potato crop failed disastrously; the following two years were not much better. There was famine throughout the land and demoralisation was complete.[18] 'Those farmers who could manage to prepare the land for tillage', wrote an Irish paper, 'have not the courage to encounter a third or fourth adverse season. Such a climax of social disorganisation is without parallel.'[19] It was as if the very land had turned upon its inhabitants, and they scattered in all directions. Within less than a decade two million people – over a fifth of the population – left Ireland.[20] Most of them settled in America, but about five hundred thousand made their home in England, more than doubling the size of the Irish community.[21] They poured into Shadwell, Wapping, Limehouse and Poplar and made the north bank of the Thames their own. They crowded into Spitalfields and pushed into Bethnal Green.

There was wide sympathy for the starving Irish so long as they remained in their own country, and a relief fund, launched by the Rothschilds, got massive support. But there was little sympathy for those Irish who managed to scramble ashore in

England, and complaints poured in of the distress caused by their invasion. 'We allude to an evil which threatens to over-power all means of remedy, unless it meets with a speedy and efficient check', declared *Chambers' Journal*, 'and this is the over-running of Great Britain by pauper Irish vagrants.' And it went on:

> If we establish a House of Refuge or Nightly Shelter to afford temporary relief to houseless strangers, the charity is swamped by vast migratory hordes of Irish; if we establish a school of industry for the purpose of receiving the half-beggar, half-criminal children who crowd our streets, we find we are only attracting ragged families from Roscommon. . . . Attempts to repress mendacity, crime and disorder, are little better than burlesque, so long as such an inexhaustible fountain of misery is permitted to pour forth its polluting stream over the land.[22]

In order to benefit from the Poor Law proof of domicile had to be shown and the Irish of course had none. They were thus given only temporary help, sheltered and fed for a night, kept under lock and key, like a prisoner awaiting extradition, and then shipped back to Ireland. Those who came in for help, said a Poor Law official, 'know they must be removed, and when once we have possession of them, the officers take care that they do not escape'. But once in Ireland they did not always remain. The Mayor of Wexford, for example, had a private fund for passing paupers back to England, and some made the journey two or three times.[23]

'The hordes of starving vagrant Irish', as A. Redford writes in his study of labour immigration, 'pushed into the interior of the country, carrying with them, famine, fever, dysentery and smallpox. Improvident, drunk, slovenly, lazy and stupid, they were thus, "necessarily given the lowest paid work", and, as a result, "formed a submerged class always tending to drag down their neighbours' standard of living".'[24]

Yet they seemed content and the Hammonds, in their economic history of England, suggested 'that it was the Irish, with their low standards of cleanliness and comfort who best adapted themselves to the conditions of town life. They found dirt and they multiplied it lavishly, but they preserved a contented spirit however degraded their surroundings.'[25]

Local health officers were sometimes aghast at the customs
which the Irish brought with them, especially the extended
funeral wake, with the cadaver assuming the function of a
household prop!

> With the lower orders, in these districts, it is often treated
> with as little ceremony as a carcass in a butcher's shop. Nothing
> can exceed their desire for an imposing funeral; nothing can
> surpass their efforts to obtain it, but the deceased remains
> share none of the reverence which this anxiety for their be-
> coming burial would indicate ... the body is never absent
> from their sight – eating, drinking, sleeping, it is still by their
> side; mixed up with all the ordinary functions of daily life,
> till it becomes as familiar to them as when it lived and moved
> in the family circle. From familiarity it is a short step to
> desecration. The body, stretched out upon two chairs, is
> pulled about by the children, made to serve as a resting place
> for any article that is in the way, and is not seldom the hiding
> place for the beer bottle or gin if any visitor arrives inoppor-
> tunely.[26]

Wages were low, unemployment was high, rents were rising
and, where the Irish newcomer found a roof over his head at
all, it was by crowding in among those who had come a little
before him. In one East London parish with a high intake of
Irish there were 2·7 people to each bed.[27] And no matter how
cramped a family might be there was always room for a visiting
relative or a lodger. A public health official described one house
where:

> There were swarms of men and women, boys and girls in
> scores of each, using jointly one single common privy; grown
> persons of both sexes sleeping in common with their married
> parents; a woman suffering travail in the midst of the males
> and females of three separate families of fellow lodgers in a
> single room; an adult son sharing his mother's bed during
> her confinement . . .[28]

As a result of such overcrowding, life, wherever possible, was
lived in the street or, where funds permitted, in the pub. This
was a problem which every temperance reformer encountered.
The pub was not merely a place where one could drink and get

drunk – though it would be wrong to underestimate its function in that respect – it was the local club room, a place where a man might meet friends, talk, gossip, celebrate a gay event, seek solace through a grave one.

A vivid picture of Irish life in London is shown in a novel *Kate Gearey* by a Miss Mason. Published in 1852, it tells the story of Kate's arrival in London where, hungry and alone, she finds shelter in a teeming Irish slum. Here about a thousand souls are huddled together in the warren of alleys which form the neighbourhood, and they can be roughly divided into three groups – those in regular work, those who work now and then, and those who never work at all. 'The first', we are told, 'are exclusively women, generally blessed with a lazy drunken husband and a large family of small children, all of which they contrive to support out of eight shillings a week.

> ... and for this pittance they must rise at five on a cold winter's morning, be on their milk-walk before six, return at eleven, and after snatching a hasty meal, which they must prepare for themselves and children, go forth again to their toilsome round, labouring under a heavy yoke, again to return in the evening, exhausted and hungry, to find the hearth cold, Pat at the beer-shop, the youngest child fretful, the elder sickening with the measles.[29]

As one continues through the book, one suspects that the author is an early progenitor of Women's Lib, for while the story is concerned mainly to draw attention to the plight of the Irish poor (it closes with a direct appeal on their behalf), the men are, with exceptions, a nefarious pack of sluggards, braggarts, criminals and drunks; and although not all the women are noble, all the truly noble characters are women. Kate and her friends are raised out of the lower depths by a guardian angel, the daughter of a titled Protestant family, a Catholic convert who for the sake of her faith renounces rank, wealth and the hand of a belted Earl, to spend the rest of her days among the Irish poor, whom she regards as the living confirmation of God's presence:

> There can be no more convincing proof of the divine origin of Catholicism than the tenacity with which the lower order of

Irish adhere to the most minute precepts of a creed which they cherish as clearly as their own existence.[30]

The plot is absurd and at times unconsciously funny. The writer clearly loved the Irish and understood them, although she romanticised them and thus tended to exaggerate both their faults and their virtues. Yet there was an essential truth in her picture of the devout Irish woman who, however harassed and hard-pressed, was the one indomitable spirit of the Irish family. Perhaps the very resolve of Irish wives encouraged fecklessness in their men – in the last resort the children were being cared for, why not relax? But the women did not suffer in silence. If anything, they suffered volubly. Many an Irish childhood was marred by the sound of altercation in the night, and many an Irish woman began her working day by nursing a pair of black eyes.

Henry Mayhew, whose work on *London Labour and the London Poor*, first published in 1851, brought him into contact with a great many Irish, remarked on the chastity of the women. As street-sellers, they were exposed to the attention of every passing lecher. English girls in a like position, he found, formed easy connections with the other sex:

> With the Irish girls the case is different; brought up to a street life, used to whine and blarney, they grow up to womanhood in street-selling, and as they rarely form impure connections, and as no one may be induced to offer them marriage, their life is often one of street celibacy.[31]

It was sometimes suggested, wrote a contributor to the *Dublin Review*, that the purity of the Irish Catholic woman was 'the result of a natural coldness of temperament':

> ... nothing can be more preposterous than such an hypothesis ... For in the first place human nature is always substantially the same, and to no sins is it more naturally inclined than the sins of the flesh. And secondly, the Irish are an imaginative, and irascible, and, as is often said, an unstable people; and surely, these are the qualities which, more than any others, predispose to sins against purity. Lastly, the Irish are virtually the same race as the Welsh ... yet the Welsh are known to be the most immoral people in Europe, excepting, perhaps, the Swedes.

No, he concluded, 'it is no difference of race and temperament which has created this remarkable feature in the Irish character. ... It is the Catholic faith which makes them as a body chaste and pure.'[32] And, of course, the social and family restraints which were a part of that faith.

If, as sometimes happened, an Irish woman succumbed to temptation, the sense of betrayal was dreadful. She could be ostracised, maimed and sometimes even murdered by her outraged menfolk. Mayhew relates a hideous story told to him by a young girl:

When I was quite a child, Sir, I went to a funeral. ... it was of a young woman that died after her child had been born a fortnight, and she wasn't married; that was Illen. Her body was brought out of the Lying-in-Hospital ... and was in the Churchyard to be buried; and her brother, that hadn't seen her for a long time, came and wanted to see her in her coffin, and they took the lid off, and then he cursed her in her coffin afore hus; she'd been so wicked.

'Mary, my darling', her mother told her later, 'If you starruve be virtuous. Rimember poor Illen's funeral.'[33] The result of such tireless insistence on virtue was that if an Irish girl – like the Jewish girls who came after her – was seduced, she felt there was nothing for her but the streets. 'When the uneducated Irish woman has fallen into licentious ways', wrote Mayhew, 'she is, as I once heard it expressed, the most "savagely wicked".'[34] Irish men experienced no such pressures to be virtuous, and the Irish prostitutes who thronged Rosemary Lane and Ratcliff Highway, in their bright kerchiefs, were in part a byproduct of Irish chastity.

If the author of *Kate Gearey* went out of her way to do justice to the Irish women, she was perhaps less than fair to the Irish men. Certainly they were not all lazy – at least while on the job. If they were, they would have been less unwelcome to their Cockney neighbours. Nobody employed the Irish out of charity. If they were given a job it was because they did it better than the English, or because no Englishman could be found to do it.

The company secretary of St Katharine's Docks, said in 1835, that he preferred to employ English dockers, for they were more educated and intelligent, but they were 'of limited capacity as regards hard labour':

The Irish employed at the docks are generally powerful men and are certainly capable of giving the company in certain species of labour ... a better return for their pay than the generality of the English. We generally class them in gangs together finding they work to more advantage. When so selected, and we usually take them for the performance of such labour as requires great athletic powers, we have no reason to complain of their conduct whilst within the walls of the docks.[35]

Mayhew visited a lodging house used by Irish newcomers, and found that six men, who had arrived only the day before, were all out looking for work. In another, a shabby hole devoid of all furniture except a few old mattresses, he found a number of men lolling about lazily, and he asked one if they had tried to find work. 'Ah, sure, and that they have', he was told, 'it's the docks they have tried, worrus luck.'[36]

But if the Irish were eager to find work, and eager to work when it was found, they were unsteady in their effort and inclined to ease off after a while. They could survive on less and were content with less, and if five days' work brought in enough to keep body and soul together, they rested on the sixth, and if they caroused too much on the seventh, they rested also on the first. They were naturally of an independent nature and given a shilling in their pocket, excessively so. They liked to come and go as they wished, with the result that wherever the Irish were to be found in any number, one began to see notices: NO IRISH NEED APPLY. An Irish paper, *The Nation*, took this as proof absolute 'that an unmitigable and ferocious hatred of the Irish people, resident in England, is fondly cherished by the great majority of all sects, parties and persuasions of the English people.'[37] *The Tablet*,[38] then, as now, a leading Catholic weekly periodical, thought that there was a great deal of animosity against the Irishman's religion, but not against the Irishman himself.

Indeed we are convinced that there is in England a far greater personal dislike of Scotchmen than of Irishmen; that the close, cautious, crafty Scotch character is far more hated by our countrymen than the open, generous, impulsive Irish character. There has always been a tendency in England to show this

kind of particular hatred against Scotchmen ... But yet
Scotchmen have never found themselves excluded from any
employment for which they were fitted.

Why not? The paper went on to deliver what it thought were
a few necessary home truths:

The fact is that there are two classes of Irish labouring people
who differ about as widely as light and darkness ... There
are many who are industrious, methodical, orderly, thrifty and
generous in the highest degree ... But ask anyone to show
you where '*the* Irish' live. He will take you to a miserable
cul-de-sac, which you are afraid of penetrating, and which,
bad as it is physically, bears a moral character even worse ...
There are times when no policeman who is careful of his life
dare show himself within that sacred enclosure. And though
the respect felt and paid to priestly character protects the
English priest who ventures there at the worst moments of
turbulence, it is, we believe, generally admitted that in them
no one but an Irish priest can operate with any great and
signal success.

The sad conclusion which the writer reached was that if,
indeed, there was some bias amongst the English against the
Irish, it was not wholly unjustified. To which the usual Irish
reply was that the things said against them weren't true, that
their so-called defects were really proof of their joie de vivre,
and that, in any case, it was all the fault of the English. John
Denvir, a publicist constantly involved in defending the Irish
name, did concede that they liked a drink, but added quickly:
'It is not true that they drink more than people of other nationalities, but being naturally demonstrative, they put themselves in
evidence when under the influence of intoxicants, where an
Englishman would go and sleep off their effects.'[39]
Englishmen tended to regard the Irishman as a congenital
scoundrel, dirty, lying, thieving, drunken, parasitical, bellicose,
incorrigible and irredeemable. Mayhew believed that ninety per
cent of London's criminal class was Irish. A prison chaplain,
relating the results of a lifetime spent among criminals, declared:
'... anyone with an eye for form may perceive, at a glance, that
the generality of these unfortunate persons have small, ill-shaped

skulls, with (among the Irish particularly) foreheads villainously low.'[40]

The *Nation* believed that in England the Irish 'are not regarded as human beings; they are looked upon as some noxious animal – some creature poorly imitating the human form – some outlandish, extraordinary and monstrous thing, to be carefully excluded from all social intercourse and all civilised society'.[41]

In essence, as W. L. Arenstein, a student of Victorian life, has pointed out, the belief in the inferiority of the Irish was part of the belief in the superiority of the English:

> Paddy was regarded as a consequence not of environment but of centuries old racial inheritance, as a hard-drinking, hard-fighting, peasant, emotionally unstable, ignorant and indolent ... the Anglo-Saxons bred in the forests of Germany were the true carriers of civilisation.[42]

The Irish, as we shall see in a later chapter, changed, but the old attitudes to them persisted, partly because, where they came to be less drunken and tumultuous, and more responsible, they were generally regarded as English. And tumultuous, drunken Englishmen were sometimes taken as Irish.

3. St. Katharine's Dock, 1840-50

4. High Street, Whitechapel, 1837

# SIX

# The Double Burden

The London Irish suffered from a double handicap. To be Irish alone was just about forgiveable; to be Irish *and* Roman Catholic verged on the brazen, or, as a historian has put it: 'Victorian England looked upon Roman Catholics and Irishmen as inferior to themselves, and when Irishmen turned out to be Roman Catholic, as they generally did, the Englishmen regarded them as doubly inferior.'[1]

The hatred and fear of Catholicism was deep-seated – it was, indeed, one of the few sentiments which all classes held in common – and it was not so long since the cry of 'No Popery' raised by the demented George Gordon had nearly set London ablaze. A succession of books and pamphlets poured from the presses on the iniquities of the Roman Catholic Church, and Foxe's *Book of Martyrs*, with its lurid tales of Catholic persecution, first published in the sixteenth century, was one of the most widely read books of Victorian England. There was almost a shrinking dread of the Jesuits, who were regarded as a dark and sinister brotherhood, and tales about sexual orgies and perversions in convents and monasteries had a ready sale. 'In the days of Henry VIII', began one breathless epic, 'when the monasteries were fully explored, the abbots, priors and monks kept as many women each as any lascivious Mohammedan could desire, and their crimes renewed the existence of Sodom and Gomorrah.'[2]

The press gave great prominence to reports of mis-government in those parts of Italy still under Papal rule and built up a picture of Catholicism as oppression tempered by incompetence.

In the early years of the nineteenth century, the Catholic church in England, still shaken by memories of the Gordon riots, was timid and unobtrusive, and between 1820 and 1830, although Irish immigration was on the increase, only one new Catholic church was built in the London area. Anti-Catholic feeling slowly abated, and a Catholic Relief Act became law but, when in 1850 Pope Pius IX re-introduced the Catholic hierarchy to Britain, there were widespread cries of 'Catholic aggression', a cry taken up volubly by the man in the street, even though he had only the vaguest idea what it meant. 'I have little harrut to go into a public house to sill oranges', a penniless Irish street vendor told Mayhew, 'for they begins to fly out about the Pope and Cardinal Wiseman, as if I had anything to do with it.'[3]

But the Irish had their admirers and there were many people who felt that there was little wrong with them which a prompt conversion to Protestantism couldn't cure. The Reverend S. Garrett, a well-known nonconformist minister, complained that the Irish were being neglected and that there was thus left 'in the very heart of London a population, living in the midst of us, but estranged from our religion, our laws, our manners and our government.' 'I see not', he declared, 'how the young men of this city should better employ themselves than in working among these priest-ridden masses, and bearing a message of peace and liberty and hope, to those over whom Satan has thrown the spell of this fatal witchcraft.'[4]

Such work, he warned, was slow and often unrewarding, and one was never sure whether an outward readiness to convert was an honest change, for 'there is no industry and there is no truth where the Church of Rome has sway'. Yet persevere one must, for the Irish had 'fine natural susceptibilities, more capable than their Saxon neighbours of intellectual development, debased, crushed, dwarfed, unable to stand erect, as men always are when ages of oppression have done their work'. And he went on:

Rome's religion unmans a nation. It produces a slothful, indolent, and improvident character. It either divests the man of the sense of personal responsibility, and plunges him into a hopeless despair. . . . Hence the crouching spirit, and the untruthful spirit. . . . It is not being a Celt that makes the

Irishman in London what he is. There is nothing in Irish air
or Irish birth that is unproductive of energy, or industry, or
truth. Wellington was an Irishman. . . . It is nothing else but
the withering curse of that anti-Christian system which blights
where it falls, and through the soul itself crushes and tramples
on the man.[5]

The Catholic Irish, he believed, were naturally prone to insurrection for they were 'bound by no tie of affection or loyalty
to our Queen and country. England is to them but a foreign
land'. Only when they turned Protestants did they become loyal
to king and country, staunch soldiers, brave fighters, good men.
Snatch the Irish from the thraldom of Rome, and you create a
new class of being:

No longer clothed in rags. . . . No more to live in the dark
back rooms on which the day never shines. . . . Never again
despised and trampelled on . . . and instead of dark alleys in
which they now live, where nothing meets the eye but blackened walls and smokey chimneys – they shall gaze with rapture
on the Golden Streets of the New Jerusalem, and drink of its
living fountains.[6]

The Established Church may have reconciled itself to the
thought that the Irish were unlikely to be won over to Protestantism, but the Evangelists never abandoned hope. They
saw in the dreadful results of the famine a proof of divine wrath,
and new opportunities to win souls.

In Ireland where a man was on his own soil, among his own
people and under the scrutiny of his own priest, he could withstand the importunities of missionaries with their soup-bowl in
one hand and the Gospel in the other; but in London, where
the Irish formed small Catholic enclaves in a Protestant or
pagan universe, they were very prone to adapt to the ways
of their neighbours. The working classes were nominally Protestant. They were buried in Protestant churchyards. They got
help from Protestant charities. Where their children received an
education, it was from Protestant schools, but their actions were
unaffected by their creed, and they tended, on the whole, to be
cheerfully pagan. 'The working classes of East London', declared
the *Spectator*, 'do not go to church or care about religion in

any way.'[7] The Irish who lost their faith rarely went over to an active espousal of Protestantism, but merely lapsed into the non-religion of their neighbours. This did not, however, deter the Evangelists from trying – their very presence was a challenge.

There were numerous church schools in the working-class areas of London, but they expected their pupils to be washed, reasonably dressed and shod. Sometimes they even demanded fees, and held their lessons at hours when a boy could gainfully be employed. The 'ragged schools', which organised themselves into a Union in 1844, suffered from no such handicaps and adapted themselves to the hours and circumstances of their pupils. They met usually in the evening, offered shelter and warmth and perhaps a bun, and were gathering places for ragamuffins and street urchins, or 'Arabs' as they were called at the time. They also offered a rudimentary education plus hymns, prayers, tales of moral uplift, the usual Sunday school fare, without which free buns and shelter were unobtainable in East London.

Here, by way of illustration, is the story of one 'ragged school' pupil, told in his own words:

> When I got there the masters was very kind to me. They used to give us tea parties, and to keep us all quiet they used to show us the magic lantern. I soon got to like going there and went every night for six months. We used to begin school at seven o'clock at night and came out at nine. There were about forty or fifty boys in the school. The most of them were thieves. They used to go thieving coals out of the barges along shore, an cutting the ropes off the ships and selling it at the rag shops. ... After we came out of school about nine o'clock, and from that to eight would go out in a gang together. ... All the whole of the gang would be together while waiting outside the school doors before they were opened. We used to plan up where we would go to after school was over. I think I learnt more good than harm at the school, but I have planned up many times at the ragged school to go thieving with the gang. If it hadn't been for the school we shouldn't have met together so often of a night, and I don't think we should have stolen so much.[8]

Some missionary groups were content to maintain a passive

role, but the City Mission, a nonconformist organisation, adopted a more aggressive policy, singled out the Irish as 'a special class', and appointed seven Irish missionaries to work among them. They ventured into Rosemary Lane, by Ratcliff Highway, the very heart of the Irish East End, and described by one of them as 'one of the most filthy, abandoned, ignorant and wilfully depraved places in the metropolis'. The work, Dr Sheridan Gilley, a perceptive Catholic historian, has observed:

> brought a delicious and dangerous excitement into lives dulled by the sullen passivity of the English poor: Irish urchins banging kettles, throwing excrement and ferocious abuse, Irish women and their husbands flourishing bricks, tiles and bottles, and in the background, the skulking, black-browed, priest.[9]

In Spitalfields, where Jews and Irish lived crammed together, missionaries were attacked by both. Well-to-do maidens from respectable homes, who taught at the ragged schools, had to be escorted to and from work, otherwise they could be assaulted and spattered with mud. Any 'toff', which is to say, anyone respectably dressed, might be taken for a missionary, and many an innocent passer-by, who had nothing more sinister to him than a stiff collar and shiny boots, suffered indignity and assault.

The material inducements, the meal tickets, the bread, soup and coal were eagerly accepted, even solicited, and there could be trouble where they were not produced. As Catholic priests customarily charged a high fee for weddings, many Irish Catholics married in an Anglican church, and often brought children, baptised by their Priest, for christening by the vicar to obtain the customary gifts of swaddling clothes and a florin. Some, in spite of dire warnings from their priest, sent their children to Protestant schools in the hope of better company or a better education, and even where neither was likely, there was usually the promise of better pickings.

Some might become professional Protestants and through habit come round to an acceptance of its rituals and creed, but at times of crises or the approach of death they generally took no chances and came back to the priest.

Catholicism was too deeply ingrained in the Irishman and was, indeed, an essential part of his Irishness. To lapse from the faith was one thing, but to forsake it for Protestantism was to forsake Ireland, one's family, one's friends, one's neighbours. Indeed, oneself. The occasional Irishman adopted Protestantism for that very reason: it was a once-and-for-all endeavour to shake off his old world and to start anew. But, for most, their fellows, their workmates, their drinking chums, were too much a part of themselves. It was the need of the Irishman for Irish company that in part kept him at least nominally Catholic. A man could be non-religious, an incorrigible backslider, even a blaspheming atheist and still be a more or less acceptable member of Irish society, but once he actually turned Protestant this ostracism would be complete. His children would be teased, his wife molested, his presence shunned. Every back would be turned on them, and the open doors, the neighbourliness, the mutual help, the conviviality, the gossip, the cheerful badinage, the thousand little occasions that made life in the mean Irish streets tolerable, would come to an end. To survive as an Irishman one had to be a member of the club and Catholicism, or at least non-Protestantism, was a condition of membership.

Catholicism contributed both to the virtues and defects of the Irishman. At the least it meant that even at his most brutish he was open to the chastisement of the priest; if he feared no man, one could at least invoke the fear of God. It made him a more charitable creature, a more thinking, if not always more considerate creature, and withdrew him for the occasional hour from his sordid surroundings to a more exalted form of existence. It brought him solace in harsh times, and as his times were almost always harsh, it was almost always necessary. It widened his horizons and brought in the next world to redress the balance of this. It added to his optimism. Usually ignorant and unable either to read or write, his religion at least brought him into contact with civilisation in the form of his priest. And the priest, being without wife or children or family responsibilities, regarded his flock as his immediate family and could take risks – as during the frequent cholera and typhus epidemics – which would have been irresponsible in a family man. On the other hand, it was argued that the virtues of Catholicism could, and in the hands of the Irish did, become defects. If it offered solace it was perhaps too consoling, so that the Irish never felt compelled to come to grips with reality. If it tended to invoke the next world, he was inclined to shrug off too casually the responsibilities of this one. If he could be chastised by the priest, it was the libertine nature of Catholicism with the forgiving balm of the confessional which invited chastisement, and if it was the priest who brought him into contact with his civilisation, it was the priest, or so Protestants argued, who kept him ignorant and dependent. Reverend Garret stressed this point:

> The native Irishman does not share the Saxon's love of independence. He must lean on some other arm. Like the ivy he needs support and cannot stand alone. – This may be in part national, but in a great degree it results from an entire subjugation of mind to his priest. So long as he remains a Roman Catholic, he never thinks of questioning his priest's authority. It seems a relief to him to transfer, as he supposes, the whole responsibility of his soul's salvation to his spiritual guide.[10]

But the ready answer to all such criticism, and it was readily borne out by all the available evidence, was that the Irish without religion were infinitely worse. One well-known priest warned his congregants that anyone who sent his children to a Protestant school was in danger of his mortal soul:

> ... at death, the Extreme Unction shall be denied to them, and their bodies refused burial in any cemetery belonging to the Church. The curse of God shall rest upon them, body and soul, living or dead.[11]

Such threats often fell upon deaf ears, and they found that the most effective way of countering the attractions of Protestant institutions was to match them with Catholic ones. The Protestants started ragged schools, so the Catholics started theirs. The Protestants established a Boot Black Brigade to find employment for street urchins, the Catholics followed suit. Soup kitchen was met with soup kitchen and dispensary with dispensary. As Sheridan Gilley observed:

> So militant Protestantism had one unintended result: the slums were policed by the Catholic priest and his lay allies, while Catholic missionary effort took form in the 'forties on an almost Protestant scale, employing methods – district visiting, ragged

schools, selfhelp societies and bread and soup charities – pioneered by the Protestants.[12]

However, the Poor Law institutions, the workhouses – and few Irish were ever far from them – the prisons, the army, the navy, all of which had a large Irish Catholic intake, were all run on Protestant lines. There were complaints in the East End press that Catholic paupers had Protestantism thrust down their throats, and that 'an immense number of Catholic children were being brought up in the principles of the Church of England against the wishes and desires of their parents'.[13] The Irish, it was argued, paid poor-rates like everyone else and were entitled to the benefits of their own religion. In 1865 a number of leading Catholics laid before the Government a list of twelve grievances on the operation of the Poor Law. They complained that the law did 'nothing whatever to provide Catholic paupers with instruction in their own religion', or to allow them to attend Mass on Sundays and Holidays. Priests were discouraged from visiting them and were sometimes rudely excluded. In some workhouses Catholics were banned from retaining 'Catholic books, even catechisms and prayer books'.[14] Catholic pauper children were 'unprovided with instruction in their own religion', and Catholic orphans and foundlings were brought up as Protestants even when it was known that their parents were Catholic. From 1862 Poor Law guardians were empowered to transfer Catholic pauper children to Catholic schools and pay for their keep (which aroused the ire of a great many Protestants who argued that Irish pauperism and crime were the fruits of the Catholic faith), but Catholics felt that the law had not gone far enough. Government grants to Catholic schools had been made since 1848. In 1854 Lord Shaftesbury's Bill to establish Reform Schools for young offenders included a clause which enabled Catholics to establish their own reformatories, which they did. In 1854 Catholic Chaplains were appointed to the army and navy, and in 1862 to the prisons.

The Roman Catholic church, certainly in the East End, appears to have been chronically short of funds. In 1816, when the Irish in London were still comparatively few, the Vicar Apostolic of the London District complained that his resources were wholly inadequate to his task. The old, aristocratic, pre-Reformation

Catholic families felt no particular moral responsibility for the Irish poor, and indeed shared much of the English antipathy to them. A prominent North Country Catholic, when overhearing a conversation about Catholic criminals, felt compelled to point out that there were Catholics and Catholics: and that 'there was all the difference in the world' between English Catholics and Irish ones:

> English Catholics are responsible beings who are taught right from wrong, whereas Irish Catholics, belonging to a yet savage nation, know no better and are perhaps excusable on that account.[15]

When some priests in Spitalfields addressed an appeal to two hundred titled Catholic families for funds for a new church, they received a handful of replies and a total of £5.[16] Father Hearsnip, of the dockland parish of Poplar, who cast his net wider and addressed four hundred titled families, received twelve replies and an equally paltry sum.[17] 'English Catholics', lamented a priest, 'are not a self-denying body in pecuniary matters and are nearly insensible to the privilege, to the blessedness, of *sacrificing* this life's riches for higher gain.' 'O', declared another, 'that our rich brethren in faith would emulate the generosity of the poor.'[18] Old Catholics were not even willing to accept the newcomers as servants in their homes.

Sporadic help was received from the Embassies of Catholic powers like Spain, Portugal and Belgium. One dockland church had its origin in a shrine for foreign sailors paid for by the Portuguese Embassy, and when a famous temperance reformer was brought over to tackle Irish drunkenness he came at the behest of the Chaplain of the Bavarian Embassy.[19] The Jesuits complained that the East End was being neglected, but when they raised money in Rome for a church, it was for Farm Street, Mayfair. It was perhaps little wonder that Cardinal Manning, in a moment of disillusion, was to complain that Catholics had no sense of duty.

The situation improved in the second half of the century when Victorian England experienced something of a Catholic revival and middle-class converts began to flock into the Church. These converts, wrote Sheridan Gilley, were 'a Godsend in more senses than one, and in the first flush of enthusiastic faith were an easy touch, building votive chapels in poor missions and paying the cost of furniture.' But, he added, they came too late:

> For the Irish of the pre-1840 migration, the Catholic revival came ten or twenty years too late, and however readily the priest might call upon the recent immigrant's traditional piety, he also had to reclaim the Irish Cockney, whose faith had all but died away.[20]

There were sometimes complaints that the participation of ex-Protestants in Catholic causes introduced Protestant methods of raising money by charity dinners, outings, bazaars, balls and other functions. Some incurred the displeasure of the Catholic press!

> Fiddles, speeches and alcohol charm the gold from our costive moneybags; and upon ... every congregation is imposed the burden of helping to prop up an hotel; to keep the musician's elbow in grease, to maintain the production and dissemination of bad port ... and champagne ...[21]

But what created even greater concern were the Protestant sentiments behind them. Monsignor George Talbot, English Secretary and Chamberlain to Pope Pius IX, who kept in close touch with events in England, thought it wasn't the function of the Church to 'raise' the poor in the sense of improving their material status:

> I have always taken the greatest interest in the poor of London, but always in order to save their souls, not merely to make them more respectable members of a society, which is the Protestant view of such matters, with which I am sorry to think many Catholics sympathise ...[22]

This was a revealing utterance and seemed to confirm the Protestant view that Rome was anxious to keep its flock poor in order to keep it loyal, but the Church recognised that the pursuit of respectability and material gain – the two invariably went together – even towards a higher end, soon became ends in themselves. The soul needed a certain material sufficiency on which to flourish, but too much was as bad as, if not worse than, too little. The idea of holy poverty was not merely a means of making a virtue out of necessity (if you can't help it, sanctify it!) – it affected the very habits of Catholics, especially Irish Catholics.

'The Irish Roman Catholics', wrote the Reverend Garrett, 'neither love labour nor love cleanliness, and Irish converts would take hard work and its accompanying social advantages as a duty rather than a boon.'[23] Given the erratic (and sometimes poisonous) supplies of water in the East End and most other working-class areas, cleanliness was the mark of the 'toff', but it is certainly true that the Irish rarely regarded hard work as something beneficial in itself. If it had any 'social advantages' at all, it lay in the fact that it enabled one to accumulate enough money to ease off after a while. For all his belief in the next world, the Irish Catholic took infinite pleasure in this one, and preferred the actualities of the here and now to the prospects of tomorrow, let alone the hereafter. He was less inclined to save for a rainy day than anticipate a sunny one. This did not make him entirely improvident.

'The Irish street-folk are, generally speaking, a far more provident body of people than the English street-sellers', wrote Mayhew. 'To save, the Irish will often sacrifice what many Englishmen will consider a necessity, and undergo many a hardship', but not, he added, 'from any wish to establish himself more prosperously in his business':

They will treasure up halfpenny after halfpenny, and continue to do so for years, in order to send money to enable their wives and children, and even their brothers and sisters, when in the depths of distress in Ireland, to take shipping for England. They will save money to be able to remit money for the relief of their aged parents in Ireland.

But, he added:

they will *not* save to preserve either themselves or their children from the degradation of the workhouse; indeed they often, with the means of independence secreted on their persons, apply for parish relief, and that principally, to save the expenditure of their own money. Even when detected in such an attempt at extortion, the Irishman betrays no emotion – he has speculated and failed.[24]

Every instinct kept the Irish of the East End together and their mutual concern was great. A newcomer could always find people who could help to find him a job or give him credit. Where an Englishman might resort to a usurer, the Irishman resorted to his friends – and no interest was charged. And it was not as if the lenders were better off than the borrowers. All could go through hard times, but not all went through them at once. Where the Spitalfields appeal to the Catholic rich in 1852 yielded only £5, the Catholic poor raised £600. As there were only about nine thousand Irish living in the Spitalfields area at the time, most of them poverty-stricken, the sum represented immense sacrifices.[25] Mayhew found that even where an Irishman earned as little as 5/- a week, he always laid aside a penny a week 'for his religion'. One East End priest, Father John Moore, had a corps of five hundred honorary collectors, each of whom extracted a penny a week from his five thousand parishioners.[26] Father William Kelly, his successor, used the same means and raised as much as £50 a week, though by then the parish had grown to some fifteen thousand. His mainstay were the dockers in regular jobs (earning about sixteen shillings a week), artisans, petty traders, and foremen in the local docks and factories. The poor paid their pennies when employed, and his register of contributors was like an index of trade conditions. If the Catholic Church in the East End had no plutocrats, it had numbers, and in one slum area after another churches were built which rivalled the local gin palaces in their grandeur.

In Wapping alone, there were some fifteen thousand Irish and they paid for the upkeep of two chapels, five schools and five priests. In 1857 their old church was demolished to make way for an extension of the London Dock. Within ten years they raised the £20,000 necessary for a new one.[27]

Priests were on occasion too sanguine about the sums which they thought they could raise and were sometimes imprisoned for debt. 'We are pleased to learn', *The Tablet* announced one morning, 'that the Reverend Mr O'Moore has been liberated from prison, and that Mass is now said at this mission every Sunday as usual . . .'[28]

While in some areas towering piles rose to the sky, like the Church of St Mary and Michael, which Father Kelly built, and which still stands in Commercial Road, in others, services were held in private houses, a former sugar factory, a decaying theatre, the garrett of a stable, an ex-mortuary. And still the room for prayer was unequal to the numbers who sought to pray.

'The Holy Father is ever receiving most pitiable accounts of the spiritual destitution of the poor Irish Catholics', complained Monsignor Talbot in a letter to the Cardinal Archbishop of Westminster in 1855. 'You cannot conceive how it pains him to hear that there are 50,000 Catholics in London who cannot go to Mass, and 20,000 who never go to school.'[29]

The figures certainly in the first instance and probably in the second were exaggerated, but the Irish were sometimes excluded from some churches by the need to pay pew rents, and kept away from others because they were massed like cattle at the back and could neither see nor hear. One priest urged that rich and poor were all equally children of God, and should be united in worship, but another felt that one had to recognise that 'nothing less than the virtue of Saints will enable a person of refined and sensitive feelings, not habituated, as priests are, to such trials, to endure the repugnance ... created by the proximity of our squalid poor ...'.[30] He suggested instead a church divided into free and paying places separated by a central aisle, so that poor and rich might be within sight and sound of the altar, without the one transmitting fleas to the former. In St Anne's, Spitalfields, worshippers were expected to pay door money and even seat rents. In Wapping, Father Kelly dispensed with an entry fee and passed plates round instead.[31]

There were difficulties over school fees. In the schools attached to St Mary and St Michael in Commercial Road, for example, there was an elaborate scale dividing the respectable from the ragged poor, with fourpence a week in the better grades, threepence in the lesser, and so on, down to free classes for the destitute, but some Irish found that even the fourpenny classes were not good enough, and sent their children to Protestant schools. An exasperated priest explained that if 'you continue cleanliness and regularity' and demand 'shoes and clean faces', the ragged won't come.[32] And, of course, if one didn't, the others wouldn't. In St Anne's, Spitalfields, there was less trouble about the fees, but there were frequent complaints of disorder and indiscipline.[33] It seems fairly clear that even Catholic Irish associated Protestantism with order, which did not, of course, mean that they went overboard for it. However, many were prepared to risk exposure to alien doctrines and the ire of the priest for a better education.

Catholic poor schools multiplied throughout the 1850s, and the number of pupils north of the Thames rose from eight thousand in 1857 to eleven thousand five hundred in 1865 when Manning launched a scheme to provide a further twenty thousand school places, but it was one thing to get the boys to school and another to teach them to read and write.

Henry Edward Manning, an Archdeacon of the Church of England, was received into the Church of Rome in April 1851. Fourteen years later he became Archbishop of Westminster and Primate of the Roman Catholic Church in England. He was much concerned with social problems and sought to improve the conditions of the poor who formed so large a part of his community. He regarded drink as the root of their misery and looked upon drunkenness 'not as a single sin', but 'the prolific cause of a whole progeny of vice and crime'.[34] From 1868 onwards he devoted his main energies to the temperance cause. Although he was abstemious and ascetic himself he yet recognised the causes which turned the Irish to drink. 'If I was an Irish hodman', he told a Parliamentary committee with pardonable exaggeration, 'I should be a drunkard.'[35] It is unlikely that any of the committee members, viewing his gaunt face, took him literally, but he made his point. The nature of the Irishman's work, his circumstances, the fact that the public house was often the employment exchange and pay-office, all tended to draw him to drink. However, Manning also said,

> I must say one thing, I believe that the Irish working men are tempted into public houses and habits of drink more from companionship, and from a certain lightheartedness and joviality of character than any other race I know of; that they do not set about it with the gravity which we Englishmen show, that I am quite sure of; and that they respond readily to any effort to correct them.[36]

Not that he was prepared to reconcile himself to Irish drunkenness. He was haunted by the recollections of a visit he once paid to the Irish on Ratcliff Highway: 'I saw there figures and

faces deformed and defiled by the sin of drunkenness, and, therefore, by every other form of sin; a population horrible to look
upon, and that is the creation of drink.'[37] When the Irish took
to drink, they took to it with Irish abandon. The excise wharves
at the docks, for example, were a temptation to all who worked
there, but when the Irish got at the drink, they sometimes, quite
literally, drank themselves to death.

In an effort to combat drunkenness the Metropolitan Roman
Catholic Total Abstinence Society was formed in 1840, and it
enlisted the services of Father Mathew who was one of the most
eloquent and persuasive priests of his day. The larger his audience, the more spellbinding was his effect, and he became something of a legend among temperance workers. His open-air
meetings attracted vast crowds and excited great enthusiasm.
Thousands – seventy thousand was one estimate – rushed to
take the pledge and for a time a strange peace reigned in areas
given over to brawling and confusion. It did not last and the
Total Abstinence Society fell into decay. In 1872 Cardinal
Manning himself took charge of the Catholic Temperance
Movement with the formation of the League of the Cross. He
had no hesitation in borrowing useful ideas, whatever their
source: from the Nonconformist, the sober application; from the
Salvation Army, the bands, the flourish and sense of spectacle;
and from the Irish themselves, the sashes and uniforms.

Whit Monday was the great day of the League. They formed
up in broad array on the Thames Embankment and walked in
procession to the Crystal Palace, preceded by banners and bands,
generals, majors and captains, heading the contingents, each
wearing a broad red sash, and forming between them the Cardinal's 'Bodyguard'. The day ended with a great binge which,
needless to say, was not an official part of the programme, and
when Manning put it to the Palace caterers that they might
close their bars for the day, they replied it was quite impossible:
they did better on that day than on any other in the year.[38]

The Cardinal obtained a special Indulgence from the Pope
for all abstaining from drink on St Patrick's day and the days
preceding and following, a period which usually saw a great
deal of drinking and drunkenness. His scheme came to be known
as 'the Truce of St Patrick',[39] and proved highly effective.
Nothing dramatic happened. The Irish areas of London were

never to be known for their sobriety, but slowly and inexorably, Manning's efforts bore fruit, and his biographer was able to note: 'The police reported that whole districts, especially the courts and alleys where, owing to the state of drunkenness and riot, it was unsafe for strangers to enter, were now to a large extent reformed by the Temperance Movement.'[40]

Manning was criticised for laying undue stress on the drink problem. It was said that he had raised abstinence to the level of one of the Ten Commandments, but in retrospect one can see that his priorities were right, and nothing could be done to reform the Irish while Irish drunkenness was rife. But did he, in fact, achieve his larger aim of integrating the Irish into the wider British community? An article which appeared in *Blackwood's Magazine* in 1901, suggested that their basic situation had changed little:

> The Irishman counts the more in London as you near the bottom of society ... they lack purpose and thrift. Jewish competition has hit them hard, yet they persist in 'doing a Mike' or idling, and in objecting to overtime work .... The bulk of the race lives in typical working-class neighbourhoods such as the East End. ... Unskilled and casual labour supports them for the most part – work demanding little more than a brawny arm and a square pair of shoulders ... managers complain of their unfitness for work on Monday mornings ... for a few hours' exertion at high pressure Irish navvies have no superiors ... When the Tower Bridge was a-building, many Irish Londoners were engaged at the outset. They soon fell away and were replaced by steadier men from the north of England ... the bright alacrity of their manner carries with it no purpose of will; they are charming to the casual stranger, but they break their overseer's heart.[41]

They revolted against long, monotonous jobs and were still inclined to those occupations where they could make good money in short spasms, such as the docks or markets, or in chance occupations like street-trading. They had also cornered the haddock-smoking trade, but, warned the writer, 'of Irish cured fish, as of Irish purveyed vegetables, it may be said without libel that the customer should not inquire too closely into their preparation for table'.

His description of Irish flower girls could have come straight out of Mayhew:

> They undeniably use the fowlest language in their altercations with the police and each other; when the evil spirit seizes them they will sit for hours swilling beer without the slightest perceptible enjoyment. Yet they patiently stand all day and in all weathers, after having been to market for flowers as early as six o'clock, and that often to see their earnings spent before their faces by their drunken crone of a mother or an idle lout of a husband.[42]

It was reckoned that about seventy per cent of the London-born Irish, Irish Cockneys, as they were sometimes known, were descendants of the famine influx. They were not improved by their London experience, and employers, where they had to choose Irish at all, preferred the Irishmen off the boat to the Irish Cockney. A docker newly arrived from Cork, it was said, could discharge five tons of cargo against the ton discharged by the Irish Cockney.

The Irish lower middle class, he believed, formed but 'an exiguous fraction of the Irish-born and Irish-descended in London', and with the exception of boxers he did not know of 'a single instance of a London-born Irishman who has risen much above the condition of his parents'.

It is true that boxing was a skill which was particularly attractive to the Irish, and one in which they gained some renown, becoming in some cases, the subject of song:

> Pray haven't you heard of a jolly young Coal-heaver,
> Who down at Hungerford used for to ply;
> His daddles he used with such skill and dexterity,
> Winning each mill, Sir, and blacking each eye.
>
> He appeared so neat and fought so steadily,
> He hit so strait and won so readily;
> And now he's a coal-merchant, why should he care,
> Tho' his dealings are black, his actions are fair.[43]

Boxing, however, as the Jews also discovered, was one area in which being a newcomer and a stranger was no handicap, but it was not the only avenue to advancement – though, of course, it was unlikely that any Irishman who became a dock foreman or manager, or a publican, or a prosperous shop-keeper, would be immortalised in song. The Irish immigrant who began by renting a street-barrow for a few shillings often saved up to buy the barrow, and from there – if he did not drink his surplus – rose to the dignity of shopkeeper. There were many Irish publicans who, in spite of the condemnation of drink as the source of all (apart, that is, from England) Irish troubles were pillars of their church and community. Some Irish families no doubt prospered sufficiently to move out of the East End, possibly dropping the 'O' from their patronymic, and if their rise was unnoticed by the social observer, it may have been because they were accepted as English. The torrent of Irish pouring into London slowed down in the 1850s, eased further in the 1860s, and was reduced to the merest trickle in the 1870s. By the turn of the century the number of Irish-born Londoners was reduced to sixty-six thousand. It was said, as had been said of the Huguenots, and was to be said of the Jews, that the Irish were shy of public attention and had falsified their census returns, and their actual number was much larger.[44] It may have seemed larger because, in areas like East London, the poor were sometimes taken to be Irish through the very fact of their poverty.

In 1856 an Irish writer lamented that his countrymen 'are to the English what the Gibeonites were to the Israelites . . . that is to say that they have become by cruel misfortune and hard necessity, hewers of wood and drawers of water to the proud Anglo-Saxon race'.[45] By the end of the century one found a more cheerful picture: 'With a fair wind and no favour Irishmen are bound to come to the front', wrote John Denvir, and that 'despite persecution and innumerable proselytising influences', they were 'permeating in numerous ways the religious, social and political life of Britain'.[46] This was perhaps too sanguine a picture. A capacity for civil and public action, as Manning observed, needs 'a training and education, but it springs from a love of our country. The Irish have this intensely for Ireland, but can hardly have it as yet for England.'[47] The Irish question dominated British politics in the nineteenth century and the Irish national interest cut across the class interest. Where the Irish in East London were active in politics at all it was on behalf of the Republican cause.

There were a number of Fenian outrages in England in 1867 culminating in an attempt to blow up Clerkenwell prison in which twelve people died, and anxious eyes were turned to the Irish areas of London. In the East End a large body of men were sworn in as special constables to guard against further out-breaks,[48] but none came, and a number of Irishmen, indeed, wrote to the papers to denounce the outrages. There was a block of buildings in Limehouse known as the Fenian Barracks into which the police could venture only in companies, and even then at their peril. The men there, wrote Booth, in his *Life and Labour of the People of London*, 'are not human, they are wild beasts',[49] but there was no political significance in the name. The Irish 'are Fenian in sympathy', said another observer, 'but their Fenian-ism is mostly talk'.[50] When Gladstone was won over to Home Rule towards the end of the century, one found them active in the Liberal Party, and after 1918 in the Labour Party. By then they had assumed a dominant role in East London politics, a dominance which has continued to this day. In 1958 there were ten councillors with Irish names on the Stepney Borough Council.[51]

The Irish were the bane of the trade union movement. Their arrival *en masse* depressed wages, and they were notoriously difficult to organise. Footloose, independent, they wandered from job to job and took what terms they could get. And even where, as in the docks, they formed a settled community, they were not inclined to join a union, and until the great 1889 strike the dockers were amongst the most exploited body of men in Britain. This gradually changed. Ben Tillet, who led the 1889 strike, was the son of Irish immigrants, James Towmey, Presi-dent of the Strike Committee, was Irish[52] and so was Tillet's friend Fleming – who had changed his name from Flannagan 'during the anti-Irish times when the advertisement "No Irish need apply" was supposed to be the motto of loyalty and Christianity'.[53]

A survey held one Sunday in 1903[54] showed that something like twelve thousand East End Catholics attended Mass which, in view of the number of Irish and 'Irish Cockneys' known to be living in the neighbourhood, suggests a definite lessening in religious loyalties, but there was more to being Catholic and a great deal more to being Irish Catholic than the Mass. Dr Sheridan Gilley has written:

> Superstition survived in its own peculiar forms without much benefit of its clergy, and could only be destroyed with the culture of which it was part, and church attendance was but one criterion of that vague respect of traditional things which might linger through 3 generations of a family which had never been to mass. [55]

One is reminded of the old stall-holder who told Mayhew: 'Ah! God knows Sir, I ought to attend Mass every Sunday, but I haven't for many years, barrin' Christmas day and such times. But I'll try and go more rigular, please God.' [56] In a sense, even where the Irishman no longer held on to his religion, his religion held on to him, and it affected his actions long after he had discarded his creed, and if the influence of the priest diminished with every succeeding generation, it never entirely vanished. It is untrue that the Irishman never rose from his class, but he was slow to rise, and even where he rose he was sometimes inclined to stick to his old friends and his old haunts, and wherever the Irish congregated in any number the Holy Ghost, so-to-speak, moved among them, so that even where they were away from church they were kept aware of their religion, of the cycles of the religious year, the bustle of Christmas, the dark mood of Lent, the quickening of religious feeling round Easter, the young girls in confirmation dresses, the nuns – a hurried rustle of black – on their visits, the priest bearing sacraments. The priest always the priest, they continued to believe in him long after they ceased to believe in God. He could separate the warring factions which were part of the social life of Irish neighbourhoods, and warring husband from warring wife. He was an ubiquitous Solomon, acting as umpire, settling disputes and deprived local solicitors from a rush of litigants. He found jobs, fed the hungry, clothed the naked, raised the fallen, cheered the lonely, cured – or so it was said – the sick, comforted the dying, and if he didn't actually raise anyone from the dead, it was probably because he thought they were better off where they were – and who should know better? There was something almost idolatrous in the very faith they inspired, especially among the young.

Mayhew described a visit to an Irish neighbourhood with a priest:

> Everywhere the people ran out to meet him. . . . Women crowded to their doorsteps, and came creeping up from the cellars through the trap-doors merely to curtsey to him. One old crone as he passed cried, 'You're a good father, Heaven comfort you', and the boys playing about stood still to watch him. A lad . . . was fortunate enough to be noticed, and his eyes sparkled, and he touched his hair at each word he spoke in answer. . . . Even as the priest walked along the street, boys running at full speed would pull up to touch their hair, and the stall-women would rise from their baskets; while all noise – even a quarrel – ceased until he had passed by. [57]

Only the National Anthem could have had a like effect on the English.

That was in 1851. Some fifty years later a reporter on the *Pall Mall Gazette* visited St Mary's and St Michael in Commercial Road and drew much the same impression:

> I slipped out and stood in the rain watching the hosts of children come pouring through the porch, presently bearing with them the priest, all smiles, though he was so crushed and jostled. . . . They clung to his cassock . . . they hung round his legs, they fastened to his arms, crying 'Father! Father!' to attract his beaming eyes. 'Bless you! Bless you! Bless you! Now get away home, you'll be wet through.' 'Why Patsy, where are your boots? Got none? Oh well, be good and they'll come soon enough. . . . How's your mother Teddy? Has your father got any work yet? No you can't come; you must go to bed. Haven't got a bed? Well you must stop indoors or your cough'll get worse. Good night, good night. God bless you my children, God bless you.' And he hustled them out gently, now with his hands, now shooing his cassock at them . . . [58]

Whatever changed in the intervening years, the affection and reverence for the priest had not.

Dr Gilley has written that the 'Irish religion seemed both more or less than the official creed of the Church, a compound of ignorance, tribal hate, perversion of orthodox Catholicity and idolatrous trust in the mother of God. Many Irish knew their Pater and Ave and little else.'[59] Some did not even know their Pater or Ave, but their very Irishness helped to keep them Catholic, even as their Catholicism kept them Irish.

# SEVEN

# Christmas Day in the Workhouse

In 1766 Benjamin Franklin, a future American President, visited London and was appalled by what he saw. There was, he wrote, no city where the poor were 'more idle, dissolute, drunken and insolent', and no country:

> where so many provisions are established for them, so many hospitals to receive them when they are sick and lame, founded and maintained by voluntary charities; so many almshouses for the aged of both sexes. In short, you offered a premium for the encouragement of idleness; and you should not now wonder that it has its effects on the increase in poverty.[1]

Franklin touched on a dilemma which was to trouble churchmen and politicians for over a century. At what point did charity increase the ills it sought to soothe? Until the sixteenth century the Church accepted its duties to the poor unquestioningly and every religious house was a refuge for the needy, but all that changed with the dissolution of the monasteries and, in the words of Sidney and Beatrice Webb, the Tudors and Stuarts provided 'for the relief of destitution within a framework of repression'.[2] Under an Act of 1601 each parish was required to look after its own poor. The law did not even contain poverty, which, as time wore on, was seen to have its uses. New industries, the growing size of the army and navy, needed a large mobile labour force and destitution helped their needs. 'It seems to be a law of nature', wrote the vicar of Pewsey, Wiltshire, in 1785, 'that the poor should be to a certain degree improvident, that there may always be some to fulfil the most servile, the most sordid and the most ignoble offices in the community.'[3]

The demobilisation of the army and navy after Waterloo, and the rise in prices, overwhelmed the old Poor Law, but a new one was slow in coming, and it was finally passed in 1834. Under this law the fifteen thousand or so parishes in England and Wales were regrouped into six hundred Poor Law-Unions answerable to a central board of Commissioners. The law was dominated by the ideas of Malthus, who argued, much as Franklin had done before him, that relief to the poor increased their number and their poverty. Relief in future would be available only in 'well-regulated workhouses', whose conditions would in no circumstances rise above the level which the lowest class of labourer could earn for himself. It was to be at once a support and deterrent, and it may fairly be said that it deterred.

As a result of further legislation Poor Law Guardians were appointed for each Union, composed mainly of local farmers and tradesmen elected by a voting system which largely excluded the wage-earner, and they saw to it that the rates burden – which they after all carried – was kept as light as possible. The amenities of a typical workhouse were only slightly above those of a typical jail, and sometimes not even that. They were stern, cheerless places. Husbands and wives, parents and children were kept rigorously apart, and the grief of their inmates seemed to rise like a sigh towards heaven. The poet Thomas Crabbe caught their mood well:

> There children dwell who know no parents' care,
> Parents who know no children's love dwell there;
> Heart-broken matrons on their joyless bed,
> Foresaken wives and mothers never wed;
> Dejected widows with unheeded tears,
> And crippled age with more than childhood's fears;
> The Lame, the Blind, and, far the happiest they!
> The moping Idiot and the Madman gay.

The various parishes of East London were grouped into five Unions, St George's in the East (which included most of the riverside parishes), Stepney, Mile End, Whitechapel and Bethnal Green. In the 1860s they had about five thousand inmates in their workhouses with perhaps twice as many on outdoor relief.

On average one East Ender in fifty was an inmate of a work-house, and one in twelve was on outdoor relief, but as the workhouse population was transient – many remained for no longer than two or three days – it may be reckoned that perhaps one person in ten must have experienced the inside of a work-house at some time in his life.[4]

The workhouse regime eased a little during the festive seasons and every year the papers, to reassure their readers that even the poor were not forgotten at times of good cheer, printed long reports on Christmas Day in the Workhouse. In St George's in the East, in 1857, for example, 'inmates were regaled with roast beef, plum-pudding, one pint of porter, tea, sugar, etc. children, fruit in lieu of beer'. In Whitechapel: 'Breakfast and tea, 6 oz. bread and butter, and one pint of good tea; dinner, half-pound roast beef, 1 lb. baked potatoes, 1 lb. plum pudding, 1 pint porter.'[5] Less reassuring were the reports which appeared elsewhere in the papers describing deaths from starvation or exposure. A cold night could result in a score of fatalities, and despite all their workhouses and their guardians, and the indoor-relief and outdoor-relief, more than four hundred people died of cold or hunger in 1857 alone.[6] The majority of workhouses were such that even the destitute hesitated to approach them. Many people, especially those who had known happier times, would quite literally be seen dead first.

The story of a widow, Mrs Emma Snellgrove, who died from starvation in the summer of 1862, at the age of fifty-eight, shocked Londoners. She had lived with one of her sons, who was out of work, and once the small legacy from her husband was spent they were confined to their beds with illness and exhaustion. There was only a little dry bread in the house. Two days before she died Mrs Snellgrove became delirious and con-tinued raving from hunger throughout the night. The son, too weak to stand up, crawled downstairs on his hands and knees, found a few grains of coffee and made her a drink. This soothed her a little, but going to her bed in the morning he found her dead. He crawled downstairs again and with his remaining strength scrawled a note to a neighbour:

My dear Mrs Cook – My mother is dead; my brother has left; and we had nothing to eat since Friday. Do come.

Mrs Cook called the doctor. He was an experienced man, familiar with conditions in the East End, but he had never witnessed anything as appalling as this:

> The house was in an indescribably dreadful state, it not having been cleaned for a length of time, and there was hardly anything in the place, which had the appearance of the most abject poverty. Mr. S. Snellgrove (the son) was in such a state of prostration that he did not seem to know in which room his mother lay. He found her body in such a state of emaciation, and he thought she must have been at least eighty. The post mortem showed the stomach and intestines to be completely empty, and not only all trace of fat, but all muscular tissue had disappeared.[7]

Under the Poor Law each Union was responsible for the relief of the poor in its area, which meant quite simply that the burden of a district was in opposite ratio to its means. Thus, for example, the rich and fashionable area of St George's, Hanover Square in the West End which had a rental value of over £1 m. supported only seven hundred and fifty-two paupers, while St George's in the East, whose rental was worth only £185,000, supported three thousand six hundred and sixty-six.[8] In parts of East London poor rates were so heavy that many traders could not afford them, and others, like the great dock companies, though able, were reluctant to do so. The vestry of St Paul's, Shadwell, for example, had assessed the London Dock Company's properties in its area at £25,000. The company objected, proposed a value first of £8,000, then of £10,000. Independent assessors were finally called in and valued them at £26,200.[9] The fact that East London carried such an outrageous burden meant that the local overseers of the poor were particularly anxious to keep expenditure at the lowest possible level. The success of an overseer was measured by how little he spent, and the Chaplain of the Stepney Union protested that the local Guardians acted as Guardians of the ratepayers and not of the poor.[10]

Each overseer was, of course, anxious to limit his intake, and each applicant was closely questioned on his means and his movements over the past few years to see how far he had established residential rights. Some could be jostled from Union to Union for months on end. The Bethnal Green Union in particular was a byword for all that was mean, bone-headed and harsh. A builder dropped unconscious in Hackney one hot summer's day and was rushed to the nearest workhouse hospital, which happened to be in Bethnal Green. The overseer wouldn't accept him and urged that he be taken to the Hackney workhouse a mile away. The argument continued for twenty minutes and, when the man was finally admitted over the still protesting murmurs of the overseer, he was found to be dead. 'Prompt assistance in such a case would probably have saved his life', said the Coroner.[11]

Mere need, no matter how acute, did not in itself assure a man relief. First he had to satisfy the relieving officer that he was worthy of it, and prove his worth by entering the workhouse labour yard to break stones, sew sacks or unravel old rope, a task which was known as 'oakum picking'. As one morning paper wrote:

> It would seem that with these poor law officials, a constant contact with misery blunts the perceptions, hardens the heart, and at last leaves them with no sensation for any suffering not their own. They seem to acquire the notion that hard dealing with the poor which may spare the rate is an epitome of all the excellencies . . .[12]

Another paper commented that it was 'a grievous reproach to the Poor Law that men and women are from time to time allowed to lie down and die of starvation in this great city, which is regorging with wealth'.[13]

Such cases were not uncommon. The Coroner added his word of censure and the jury theirs, but no action was taken against the officials involved either by way of dismissal, demotion or even reprimand.

One particularly bad case forced the Poor Law Board to hold a public inquiry. In March 1861 Sarah Ann Smith, a seventeen-year-old girl, who had been in domestic service, was admitted to the Bethnal Green workhouse. She remained there for some weeks. Nine months later she bore a bastard child and alleged that Theobald Meyrick, master of the workhouse, was the father. At the inquiry which followed she alleged that one

Sunday morning before chapel Meyrick beckoned her to his room, locked the door and raped her. Whether she was in fact raped is open to doubt, for she did not appear to have put up much of a struggle, and in cross-examination she admitted that she had screamed only once and then not loudly. What is not open to reasonable doubt is that Meyrick did use his position to take advantage of her, did seduce her, and was the father of her child. His defence depended on blackening the girl's character and he called as witnesses various inmates and employees of the workhouse, who stated that she had had intercourse with them. Their evidence did not stand up to cross-examination. Even more damning was the fact, established beyond all doubt, that £27 had been paid to the girl by friends of Meyrick in order to keep her quiet. Then the master of the Mile End workhouse, where Sarah had been admitted shortly before her confinement, gave evidence. He related how Meyrick had called on him to ask about the girl and in a man-to-man conversation asked if she could not perhaps 'be got out of the way'; he was willing to pay as much as £50 to have this done. Other employees at Mile End described how various figures posing under different names had tried to have a word with the girl, and one tried to bribe the porter to let him see her.

When the hearings, which lasted ten days, were over, few who followed the evidence had any doubt of the outcome. A month passed before the inspector made his report and before the Poor Law Board delivered its verdict. It was received with stupefaction. It did not vindicate Meyrick, for that would have been impossible, but neither did it find him guilty. Instead it declared that as the evidence was conflicting, it found that the charges against Meyrick had 'not been substantiated'.[14]

Meyrick did not use the occasion to resign and vanish quietly from the scene; nor did the Board of Guardians use it as a means of dispensing with his services. They merely 'concurred'[15] in the findings of the Poor Law Board, and Meyrick continued as master of the Bethnal Green workhouse. It was clear that the Poor Law had brought into being a ring of office holders, honorary and stipendiary, whose first loyalty was to each other. If Meyrick had not indeed raped or seduced Sarah Smith, then his workhouse, on the evidence of his own witnesses, was being run like a brothel. But he was not even reprimanded on that. All institutions in the end evolve their own methods of self-preservation and tend, where unchecked, to become conspiracies against the public. The Poor Law was sometimes just that.

Meyrick was in the news again a few months later when one hundred and forty-two 'aged and infirm' male inmates of the workhouse, their years ranging from sixty to ninety-five, petitioned the Board of Guardians against an order laying down the amount of oakum they must pick in a given time, or else their food would be cut down and they wouldn't be allowed out on Sundays. Meyrick denied that he had laid down any such rule, and added that in any case the old people enjoyed oakum picking as a 'game'. And the Guardians nodded their heads and agreed this was so.[16]

About four months after the Meyrick verdict elections were held for a new Board of Guardians. Both the hearing and the verdict had aroused a great deal of anger in the neighbourhood, and one might have presumed the old members of the Board would have been routed and new ones installed, but the old Board was returned almost to a man. The people most affected by the decisions of the Board, which is to say, those who spent their lives within the shadow of the workhouse, did not have a vote. And those who did, the shopkeepers, the publicans, the merchants, were more concerned about the level of the rates than the conditions of the poor.

If the workhouse was no paradise, life outside it also had its drawbacks. 'It would be very hard if a poor creature like me would go to hell', an old East End Irishwoman once told her priest, 'I'm sure we has got our hell here.'[17]

Although the middle decades of the nineteenth century saw a spate of sanitary legislation, local officials were helpless to enforce it in the face of incompetence, laziness or greed, and the local authorities were often themselves serious defaulters. The Thames was an open sewer and the stench during the hot summer and sometimes even during the spring was insufferable. The chemical works towards the eastern end of the area in Poplar and Bow emitted fumes which killed plants in the surrounding gardens and affected horses and people. One company specialised in the manufacture of manure from blood by boiling it in open cauldrons. Another manufacturing sulphate of ammonia spluttered up a poisonous cloud which, according to the local health inspector, 'depressed the nervous system, produced nausea, head-ache, loss of appetite and general debility'. A woman who lived near the works complained that she and her children were ill, that their drinking-butt water was discoloured and had an acid taste, and that there was continued fog and steam from the works all around the area. A man about a hundred yards from the works said that every article in his house was discoloured, his silver blackened, and the plants in his garden dead. A spokes-man for the firm, the Albion Chemical Manure Company of Old Ford, Bow, said that the emission of some sort of smell was unavoidable in a works of this sort, and that in any case some people liked the smell. The company was fined £5, the heaviest penalty the court could inflict, with two guineas costs.[18]

Rothschilds, who had a mint comfortably distant from their offices in New Court, but uncomfortably near Whitechapel, were frequent and impenitent offenders. The emission of sulphuric acid gas from their gold refinery was a constant source of com-plaint causing irritation in the throat and smarting in the eyes. Each time the local authority issued a nuisance warning, the refinery explained that steps were in hand to abate it, and all was quiet until it became perfectly clear that nothing, or not enough, had been done, and the process was repeated, almost on an annual basis. In 1864, finally, the Medical Officer for Whitechapel, Dr Liddle, who conducted what was almost a one-man campaign to make East London a more habitable place, called at the refinery in person. The manager of the plant was at breakfast and Liddle was kept waiting an hour before he came down. Was he aware, Liddle asked, of the escape of gas? He didn't know, he said, and suggested that Liddle might like to climb to the chimney top and have a sniff for himself. The local parish vestry, which as forerunner of the borough council, had charge of such things, was either helpless, or felt helpless, and the nuisance continued.[19]

The supply of water was often both inadequate and tainted. In some areas the water was stored in butts which obstructed the narrow courts and sometimes flooded them. 'A proper cover to these butts', Dr Liddle complained, 'is the exception and not the rule, and from the want of this cover the water soon acquires a layer of soot and dust, the sight of which is so offensive that few persons would be induced to drink it.'[20]

A more frequent source of supply was the stand-tap, which would be open for about twenty minutes daily for six days a week, and this, as Dr Liddle pointed out, also had its disadvantages:

> During the time the water is running, the inhabitants of the courts and sometimes the inhabitants of other courts, where the water supply is equally scanty, crowd round the stand-tap with jugs, buckets and such other vessels as they have for holding water. At these stand-taps scenes of quarrelling often occur, and in most cases where the supply is very short, the strongest only get their vessels filled, the water being shut off before the weaker can get to the stand-post.[21]

And those women who had to go out to work were unable to get to the stand-tap at all.

The East London Water Company, a commercial concern, which was the principal supplier of the area, was both incompetent and largely indifferent to public needs, and its erratic service was the cause of constant complaints and even large-scale demonstrations. But even where supplies were available, landlords sometimes fell behind with their water rates. Then whole courts could be left without water for months – and there appeared to be no law compelling landlords to make water available. Dr Liddle for his part confessed that 'many of the poor have been so long accustomed to have a very scanty water supply that they make no complaint of it'.[22] If a climb down four rickety flights of stairs to the stand-tap or water-butt and then the climb back carrying a heavy bucket meant the difference between cleanliness and squalor, many people were content with squalor. The parish of St George's in the East, near the river, was referred to by one writer as 'St George's in the dirt'.

Dr Liddle laboured on tirelessly, bringing attention to this defect or that one, but no action was taken until they assumed the proportions of a national scandal.

In October 1863 there was a public outcry after twelve children, five of them from one family, died in a small area of Bethnal Green known as Holybush Gardens. There were two hundred and twenty-two houses in the area of which only three had an adequate water supply. The rest obtained water from a usually defective pump and a static tank which, when dredged about a month before the fatalities, yielded three or four pailfulls of black mud. At the post mortem it was found that the children's kidneys had been diseased by the fetid atmosphere and blood-poisoning had set in, resulting in death.[23] The Morning Star described the deaths as 'a clear case of child murder'. There had been frequent complaints about conditions in the area to the local authorities, but they had been laughed at or ignored. One woman who complained that her house was uninhabitable was urged to move to something better near Victoria Park. Another who said she was sickened by the residue of filth in the water was told that she looked very well on it. Most pathetic of all was the woman who did not complain. She had lost five children but her landlord had allowed her a remission of rent and she was silent with gratitude.

'The sanitary conditions of London have been greatly improved in the past twelve or fifteen years', wrote the Morning Star. 'But there are districts in which neither the fear of retributive epidemics, nor the actions of sanitary legislation, is sufficient to bring the changes demanded by humanity and prudence. Bethnal Green is one of these.'[24]

These 'retributive epidemics', usually in the form of cholera, came at regular intervals. There was a serious outbreak in 1848, another in 1855, a third in 1866. On 7 July, nine deaths were reported in the East End and in the following week thirty-four in the whole of London. It then spread rapidly with many fatalities, three-quarters of them in East London.[25] 'The morbidity is overwhelming in some of these districts', wrote the Registrar General:

> In Poplar alone one hundred and forty-five, in Bow one hundred and eighty-eight, died last week. The people are falling ill every hour; you see them of all ages, children and adults, lying in their beds like people under the influence of a deadly poison; some acutely suffering, nearly all conscious of their fate and of all that is going round them. Here the doctor is called in by a husband to see his wife now attacked; there the husband lies in agony; here is an old woman, dead with her eyes wide open; there lies a four year old boy, his curly head dropping in death.[26]

If the East End as a whole was ravaged, the area most deeply affected was St George's in the East. The vicar of St Peter's, London Docks, worked amongst the dead and the dying with no thought for his own safety. 'No wonder', he wrote, 'that when the cholera broke out amongst us it should prove so fatal.' He described the area as a putrid slum, 'where during the hottest part of the day we have fermenting a large manure factory in which are collected, in a very mountain of impurity, hundreds of tons of the refuse, of the streets, the stinking sweepings of the markets, and rotten fish . . .'.[27]

The London Hospital in Whitechapel Road, which was at the heart of the epidemic, gave over a third of its beds to cholera cases. Three hundred and sixty-five were admitted within three weeks, of which one hundred and sixty-two died.[28] The epidemic raged on through August and September and finally began to burn itself out with the onset of colder weather in October. It killed nearly eight thousand people in London, over half of them in the East End.[29]

But the miseries of East London were not over. The epidemic of the summer months was followed by a slump in the winter which continued into the following year, and there was heavy unemployment in the docks, among the ship-builders, in the small workshops of Spitalfields and along Commercial Road. Only the breweries were busy. In Poplar, the home of a great many waterside workers, the number of people on outdoor relief at the end of 1866 was nearly six thousand – a high enough figure. Twelve months later it rose to eight thousand. In Stepney, where the number jumped from two thousand three hundred to over four thousand, applicants were given a shilling a week. In Poplar they received 1/6 or even 1/9 and there were murmurs that the 'generous' doles were attracting paupers from other districts. The help mainly took the form of bread. A Stepney cooper, with a wife and four children, who had been out of work for months, was given three loaves of bread and a quart of oatmeal to see them over the weekend. They began on the bread on Friday evening, by Saturday night most of it was gone, and they disposed of the rest and the oatmeal on Sunday. By about five on Sunday there was no food in the house, no fire in the grate, no candle for light, and they crept into their rags and went to sleep. Their beds and bedding had been pawned weeks before, and the other articles of furniture, as well as their coats, jackets, shirts,

D

vests, boots, shoes, and the wife's wedding ring, all to pay for food, fuel and rent.[30]

Bouts of unemployment and hardship were taken to be as inevitable as bad weather or visitations of a plague, but no long-term remedies were sought. There were demands that the government introduce large-scale public works projects, but these were generally regarded as impractical. An East End emigration fund was launched to help the poor settle in the colonies, and as the slump continued through 1869 and into 1870 the emigration movement grew apace. Over one thousand people a year were sent out from the East End to Canada and other colonies.[31] There was careful vetting of applicants and they tended to be the more earnest workers with useful skills.

The middle classes had abandoned the East End long ago, and with the coming of the railways the lower middle class also began to filter out. Now, with the emigration movement in full swing, the East End was being deprived of the best and the most venturesome elements in the working class. However the area was never entirely forsaken. There were always the shop-keepers, publicans, resident mechanics and foremen, and clergy-men who had, so to speak, to live above their shop; and in the later years of the century, there was an inflow of men and women, all of them connected in one way or another with the Church, clergymen and clergymen manqués who came to realise that one didn't have to go out to Africa to spread goodness and light; that they had a dark continent right on their own doorstep.

# EIGHT

# Home of Good Causes

If the Poor Law was inhuman and harsh, as it often was, it was tempered by a host of voluntary charities attracted to the East End by the constant reports of distress. There were other needy areas of London, but the East End had an immediate emotional appeal; the very name seemed to sum up every component of hardship.

Churches, churchgoing, religion, even sermons, were taken seriously in England as perhaps at no time before or since, and although there were schisms and factions and the denominations multiplied, all accepted charity as the most palpable expression of Christianity and all were engaged in one way or another in offering comfort to the poor. There were Ragged Schools, and Shoeblack Societies, Institutes for Sailors, night refuges for prostitutes, Oddfellows and Rechabites and Philanthropic societies, dispensaries, relief societies, the Limehouse Philanthropic Society, the Bow Benevolent Society, the Bethnal Green Philanthropic Pension Society. There were larger groups operating on a metropolitan or national scale, like the Society for the Relief of Distress, the Metropolitan Visiting and Relief Association, the Stranger's Friend Society, the Society for the Suppression of Mendicity, the Parochial Mission Women's Fund and the Society for Improving the Conditions of the Labouring Classes.

There were in all over five hundred charities at work in the East End spending over £3,500,000 a year between them, with much overlapping of effort and duplication of expense.[1] And worse than the waste of money or effort was the emergence of a class of professional scrounger who, by hauling a hungry, un-washed, barefoot child before a dozen different committees, could come away with a dozen loaves of bread, and perhaps as many pairs of shoes.

An attempt to bring order out of the chaos led to the formation of the Charity Organisation Society, whose leading spirit was Miss Octavia Hill, high-minded, strong-willed, often dictatorial, with calm certitude on her own role to lead the deprived to a better life and with firm ideas as to how it should be done. Henrietta Barnett, a co-worker, who otherwise admired her deeply, confessed that she sometimes demanded a little too much of the poor: 'She expected the degraded people to live in dis-reputable conditions, until they proved themselves worthy of better ones.'[2] She was stern, without a sense of humour, and she was painstaking to the point of being masochistic. Her own strength limited her understanding of the infirmity of others and she seemed to approach her task out of duty rather than com-passion. Nor did she understand that hardships which were voluntarily assumed and could be easily discarded were of a different weight from those which were, so to speak, part of one's birthright.

Cardinal Manning, who worked with Octavia Hill for a time, admired her devotion and integrity but was unhappy about her methods. Because she insisted on the most searching inquiries before allocating relief, which was precisely the fault with the Poor Law, he finally resigned from the Charity Organisation Society in protest. 'The good Samaritan', he said, 'did not delay to pour oil into the wounds of the man half-dead until he had ascertained whether he was responsible for his own distress.'[3] On the other hand, Frederick Mocatta, a leading Jewish philan-thropist and broker who was, so to speak, the Jewish representa-tive on the COS, adopted her methods wholeheartedly. Although he was a man of charitable instincts, he held the Victorian belief that one had to be cruel to be kind and that nothing so hindered a man as help too freely given.[4] This view was shared by a young Anglican clergyman, the Reverend Arthur Barnett who, with the possible exception of Dr Barnardo, did more to change the East End than any man before or since.

Barnett, member of a prosperous Bristol family, came to know Octavia Hill when he was a curate in Bryanston Square and worked for the COS. Amongst her helpers was a wealthy young woman called Henrietta Rowland, to whom he began to pay attention. At first she did not know what to make of him, for he looked much older than his twenty-six years and she regarded him as 'a kindly old gentleman'. He dressed badly, bought his clothes from out-of-work tailors, and his hats by post, so that they never fitted, and he always carried a baggy umbrella. He wore flannel shirts with a large white collar and ready-made ties. He was generous in big things but parsimonious in small ones and carried his money in a cheap purse which he rarely opened. 'Insignificant as were these externals', she later wrote, she found them 'peculiarly unattractive'.[5] However, his eager protestations of love eventually won her over. She came to admire his qualities and his persistance and agreed to become engaged. They spent an afternoon by the river together, and the next day, to her surprise, he left for a holiday with his brother. He had arranged the holiday some months before, and plans were plans and not to be broken by the mere fact of an engagement. This punctiliousness, Henrietta later confessed, 'was a frequent small trial to me'.[6] To an extent it summed up the man.

In 1873 he was offered the living of St Jude's, Whitechapel. 'Do not hurry in your decision', the Bishop of London told him. 'St Jude's ... is perhaps the worst district in London containing (with a certain number of respectable and well-to-do tradesmen) a large population of Jews and thieves.' The population was about six thousand, the income about £300. Barnett did not hesitate; it was precisely what he and Henrietta had been looking for.

The parish, which was bounded on the west by the City and on the south by Whitechapel High Street, consisted of one large street, Commercial Street, and many dark, crowded, insanitary alleys which branched off from it. They contained filthy delapidated lodging houses where rooms were let out at a few pence a night. Broken windows were stuffed up with rags and paper; the paper hung from the walls and the rooms crawled with vermin. Many of the inhabitants were casual dock labourers. Most were out of work, cadging, borrowing, hawking, stealing, but somehow surviving. The church, a brick building with crumbling stone copings, was cheaply built, badly maintained and begrimed with dust. The Vicarage, hard by the main road, was dark, without pantry or bathroom, and the kitchen was a dungeon. The newly-wedded couple moved into it on 7 March 1873.

Barnett was less concerned with suffering than sin. 'In my eyes', he wrote, 'the pain which belongs to the winter cold is not so terrible as the drunkenness with which the summer heat seems to fill our streets, and the want of clothes do not so loudly call for remedy as the want of interest and culture.'[7]

He importuned the famous and the talented to give their services to the East End and, on one occasion, even induced Madame Clara Butt to give a song recital, and in 1879 he formed the People's Concert Society. He organised lectures on Socrates and Milton and annual art exhibitions which attracted great crowds and which led eventually to the opening of the White-chapel Art Gallery. He held annual flower shows which were even more popular, and he arranged adult education lessons in French, German, Latin and Arithmetic. He could, it seemed, make his parishioners do almost anything, except come to church.

Dr How, the Bishop of London, had told him at the outset that East Enders thought of religion 'as belonging to a wholly different class from themselves',[8] and his own experience soon confirmed this. He was depressed by his inability to pack his church and found no consolation in the thought that most East End churches were empty. 'We might as well face the fact that our forms of worship have ceased to express the religious wants of the people,'[9] he said. What he could not face was the possi-bility that the people did not have religious wants. It was perhaps the very recognition that he would never bring about a religious revival in Whitechapel that made him and his wife devote more and more of their energies to social and educational work. Between them they organised day schools, Sunday schools, evening classes, visited people in their homes, helped them with their children. The pupils were often foul-mouthed, ill-smelling and verminous. Sometimes they ran riot, turning out the gas, tying up the teachers and turning over furniture; but they were 'pure gold', Mrs Barnett kept insisting, 'their hearts were good, full of tenderness, quick to respond to what was kind'. She would have the girls cleansed, deloused and put in new clothes, and used her many contacts to put them out in service, not always with the happiest results. One girl was dismissed because she drew a knife at her mistress, another because she threw the baby at her. Yet another went through forty-nine jobs within a few years and finally concluded: 'It's no use ma'am. I've tried hard, but mother always comes, upsets missus, speaks something cruel, and I'm out again.'[10]

In 1881 they cleared a site near the church for a garden, and on warm summer evenings they provided music from a small bandstand, with benches all around for people to sit and listen. Instead they came and danced. Mrs Barnett watched them with dismay:

> I am not quite certain whether pleasure of this sort is worth providing; the noisy horse-play which passes for dancing does not create the desire for another class of pleasures, the enjoyment of which might add so much to the lives of the poor.[11]

On one occasion the dancing developed into what she called 'a Bacchanalian scene'. The music was hurriedly stopped, the band dismissed and the playground cleared. The crowd protested loudly and showered Barnett and his wife with stones. 'And it's us as pays you', shouted an angry voice, which hurt even more than the stones, for, of course, they did nothing of the sort. If something had to be done, Barnett did it, whatever the consequences. When he had to correct a sinner, wrote his wife, he would always confront him face to face and such interviews were particularly painful where the offence was carnal:

> To him, so daintily sensitive on sex relationships, were brought at different times no less than four cases of unnatural vice. One sinner he drew to repentence, another to justice, a third he comforted in his crippling sorrow, the wife of a fourth he induced to remain with him.[12]

This was perhaps a part of their work which troubled them most, for they kept stumbling upon sex at every turn. They were surrounded by brothels and one approached their home of an evening through a gauntlet of whores. They were always in dread that one of the girls in their classes should fall among them, and thus they built round their church a host of societies: the Girls' Club; the Evening Home; the Band of White and Good; the St Jude's Guild; the Guild of Hope and Pity; and a guild for working girls and servants 'to purify life and help the weak and the fallen'. Mrs Barnett, who was childless, followed the careers of her girls as if they were her own, and when one of them vanished – to fall into the hands of white slavers – she was ill for a week.

She used some of her own jewels to acquire three nearby properties which were used as a brothel, and used the rent to rehabilitate the prostitutes. On one occasion she and her helpers went beyond the law and abducted an eleven year old child living with her mother in a brothel and sent her to friends in the country.

The Barnetts worked closely with Dr Liddle, the Medical Officer for Whitechapel, to raise the standard of housing. In 1881 they formed the East London Dwelling Company to provide improved accommodation for working men. The Peabody Trust had been involved in such work for some time but demanded proof of good character and regular employment, which meant in effect that they excluded those who needed help most. Barnett made no such rules. By 1886 he was able to write: 'The rebuilding of the houses of the poor has been going on apace. In the broad streets with their clean, tall buildings it is almost impossible to recall the nest of squalid courts and filthy passages that went by the name of streets.'[13]

The first of the blocks, known as Katharine's Buildings, near the St Katharine Dock, was a five-storey edifice consisting of one-roomed, cell-like apartments, without sink or toilet, and with a tap on each landing. They were not exactly palatial but, as Miss Octavia pointed out, they were good enough for the workers, and the workers were certainly glad enough to have them.[14]

An important part of the scheme were the personal contacts maintained with the tenants by 'the Canon's Ladies', who acted as a corps of honorary rent collectors, a task which called for a certain daring.[15] The tenants were 'a rough lot', said one of the the ladies, 'the aborigines of the East End'.[16]

This mingling of classes was central to Barnett's efforts. 'More and more I felt called to preach the duty of the migration of the rich to dwell among the poor', he said. He and his wife held a monthly entertainment for their parishioners at home and suffered with Christian fortitude 'greasy heads leaning against Morris wallpapers and dirty garments ruining furniture covers. ... Too often are the poor invited for an evening's entertainment, and then sat down in rows to be entertained with songs and parlour tricks which chiefly entertain those who perform,' she wrote. On one occasion, after a visit to Egypt, the vicar amused his guests by appearing 'draped and turbanned in Oriental fashion, and bearing on his head a tray of gifts'.[17]

'At first', Mrs Barnett confessed, 'the people behaved badly. They pushed and scrambled, pocketed the viands, picked the flowers, stole the fruit, and rudely frolicked. They also brought people who were not invited, told glib lies as they invented impromptu relations and unexpected lodgers and smuggled their children in, but gradually they improved.'[18]

Out of such occasions grew what was perhaps Barnett's most lasting contribution to the East End, Toynbee Hall. He was convinced that nothing could be done for the poor that was not done with them.

'It is the poverty of their lives which makes the poor content to inhabit "uninhabitable houses" ', he wrote. 'Such poverty of life can best be removed by contact with those who possess the higher life. Friendship is the means by which the knowledge, the joys – the faith – the hope, which belong to one class may pass on to all classes.' He began to pull in more and more of his young Oxford friends and acquaintances into his East End work, including Arnold Toynbee, Sidney Ball, A. L. Smith, Arthur Sidgwick and the Reverend H. Scott Holland. They were a lively and gifted group, and though several were agnostics they brought a sort of holy dedication to their work. Out of their efforts there was born, in November 1883, the first of the East End Settlements, and it was named after one of their number, Arnold Toynbee, who died at a tragically early age some months before. The memorandum of association showed the wide nature of its aims:

To provide education and the means of recreation and enjoyment for the people of the poorer districts of London and other great cities; to inquire into the conditions of the poor and to consider and advance plans calculated to promote their welfare. To acquire by purchase or otherwise and to maintain a house or houses for the residence of persons engaged or connected with philanthropic or educational work.[19]

Premises were bought for £6,250 (one Oxford man giving

£1,000), with room for sixteen residents and classrooms for three hundred students. It was designed with a quadrangle and covered walks like an Oxford College. There were classes in everything from astronomy to zoology, University extension lectures, a library and reading room, antiquarian clubs, sports clubs, chess clubs, literary clubs. The most popular was perhaps the travellers' club with two hundred members whom Barnett, on occasion, took on trips abroad. Once established 'the Hall' sent out workers to Limehouse, Poplar and other parts of London. They served on the local school board, Boards of Guardians and local authorities. One of Barnett's successors as Warden of Toynbee Hall, Clement Attlee, began his political career as mayor of Stepney. They acted as unpaid solicitors to deal with complaints against landlords. They organised a tenants' defence committee, and in 1896, after a diphtheria epidemic which was partly attributable to the water shortage, they forced a reluctant East London Water Company to buy water from an adjoining board. They acted as arbitrators between employer and workers and had a hand in settling the 1889 dock strike. They were, to use an expression not known then, ombudsmen at large.

The immediate success of Toynbee Hall encouraged others to establish similar settlements. In 1884 the Warden of Keble College, Oxford, disturbed by the fact that 'the Hall' was non-denominational and in effect non-religious, established Oxford House in Bethnal Green, which was run on Church of England lines. Other settlements quickly followed, the Canning Town Women's Settlement, founded in 1892; St Mildred's House, Isle of Dogs (founded in 1897); St Hilda's East, Bethnal Green (1889); St Margaret's House, Bethnal Green (1889); Presbyterian Settlement, Poplar (1899); the Dockland Settlement, Cooper Street (1905), and the Dame Colet House, Stepney (1912). Several others were founded between the wars, all of whom took their lead from Toynbee Hall, and all stemming from the basic idea of Samuel Barnett.[20]

Barnett retired from St Jude's in 1893 and from Toynbee Hall in 1906 and became Canon and sub-dean of Westminster Abbey. He died in 1913 in his seventieth year, and instead of the memorial service in Westminster Abbey to which he was entitled, he preferred something more simple in St Jude's, Whitechapel. He did 'perhaps more than any other single man', wrote a local paper, 'to elevate in the best and most enduring way the poor and working classes to a sense of independence, self-respect and hopefulness'.[21] Like many other social reformers, he had an absolute belief in his own rectitude. He held that there was only one Kingdom of Heaven and that he had the true vision of it, and knew how to reach it. It may be fashionable to smile at it now, but some such belief is a necessary point of departure for any reformer. To the extent that he was a failure, it was perhaps because he was too little of a visionary, too slight a mystic. His eyes had not seen the Glory – as had Booth or Barnardo – he had arrived at it by calculation. He was an intensely good, but rather dry, cerebral man, so in command of himself as to check even what was possibly his strongest impulse – to do good, as Mrs Barnett showed in this telling example:

> On a freezing night, with the north wind tearing down Commercial Street, human brothers, and worse still, human sisters slept on the clean hearth-stoned Vicarage steps, and one dared not give them fourpence for the doss-house bunk, or even twopence for the rope lean-to. If we had only been poor it might have been easier, but to possess the money and to have to withhold it! – The 'principles' made life difficult, but Mr. Barnett never wavered.

He did not seem to respond to the same sensations as the man in the street and did not understand the small pleasures which could brighten a bleak life. One of the things which made life tolerable for East End children, for example, were the annual treats organised by the different churches and charities, a matter of lemonade and iced buns, and perhaps a whiff of sea air. Barnett was against them: 'At such treats the pleasure, such as it is, is given by drink. The children lose their self-control, they shout, they scream, they quarrel and fight for the best places in the carriage, they ill-treat the donkeys, frogs and crabs, and they return home dishevelled, cross and ashamed.'[22] He was wholly in favour of excursions and established the Children's Country Holiday Fund, but he wanted them to be instructive, uplifting.

When the Lord's Day Observance Society protested that the art exhibitions which he organised annually, and which attracted great crowds, remained open on Sunday, he called them kill-joys, but it never dawned on him that he may have been something of a kill-joy himself. Despite all the concerts and oratorios that he organised and the flowers which he brought to church, he made Christianity seem a dour and stern thing. But he was a man of ideas and energy and it was his organising ability coupled with his religious zeal which made him such an inexorable force.

The East End is full of monuments to his endeavour. His improved dwellings have given way to more improved dwellings still, but it was he who spread the idea that society was responsible for the housing of its poor. There is the Whitechapel Library, and the Whitechapel Art Gallery, and Toynbee Hall itself, now grown larger than before, and with paid staff rather than voluntary workers, but as essential as ever to the progress of the neighbourhood. And beyond the buildings is the tradition of public service.

About the time that Samuel Barnett left the East End there died a woman whose influence on the area was less lasting, but whose name is perhaps better remembered, Baroness Angela Burdett-Coutts. Born in 1814, she was the heiress to a great banking fortune and lived long enough to have known both Wellington and Lloyd George; but perhaps the greatest influence on her life was Charles Dickens, who introduced her to the misery and degradation of working-class London.[23] She began to interest herself in the ragged schools and erected a block of model dwellings in Bethnal Green out of her own pockets at a cost of £9,000.[24] In 1864 she built a folly, called Columbia Market, whose full cost eventually reached £200,000; it looked like a Gothic cathedral, complete with cloisters and crypt, but it was intended as a fruit and vegetable market. East Enders had come to accept fruit and vegetables in the later stages of decay – there was an actual market in rotten fruit – as part of their daily diet. Angela Burdett-Coutts wanted to provide a building whose proportions and character would add a certain dignity to the locality, which was yet functional and assure it a ready supply of fresh food. Unfortunately the distributors were unhappy with it and it failed to be viable.

In 1871 Queen Victoria made her a Baroness in her own right, a rare distinction. The title suited her. She was a tall, rather gaunt woman with a big nose, and deep-set eyes. With her large coach and outrider footmen, she was the East End's idea of lady-bountiful, and indeed behaved like one. During the 1866 cholera outbreak she travelled among the poor of East London and distributed 1,850 meal tickets in a day.[25] This was what East Enders meant by charity. She was greeted like visiting royalty and recalled with affection. Towards the end of her life she became a mildly ridiculous figure. Always afraid that men were after her money – and in truth it was unlikely that they would have sought her for her looks – she finally married at the age of sixty-seven an American forty years younger than her.

'Silly old woman', said Queen Victoria.[26]

Another scion of a wealthy family whose eccentricities took a rather different form was F. N. Charrington, heir to a brewery fortune. The East End has seen many changes in the past hundred years, but one series of landmarks common to this century and the last are the three great breweries which form an almost continuous line from Spitalfields in the west to Mile End in the east and which tower over the surrounding neighbourhood. The oldest and westernmost is the great Black Eagle brewery of Messrs Truman, Hanbury and Buxton, founded in Brick Lane in 1666 and still producing great rivers of beer. In the middle, opposite the London Hospital, and next to the Blind Beggar tavern, stands the Albion brewery of Messrs Watney Mann, founded in 1708, and in Mile End there is Charrington's Anchor brewery founded in 1759. The families who owned them, Truman, Hanbury, Buxton, Mann and Crossmann and the Charringtons served on the local authorities, on the Board of Guardians, on the board of the London Hospital and on a score of local charities. They were all good churchmen and zealous Christians and the Black Eagle brewery was patron of the living of Christ Church. Fowel Buxton, who joined the Black Eagle brewery in 1808, was a notable Member of Parliament and active with Wilberforce and others in the anti-slavery movement.[27] Spencer Charrington was also an MP and one can find the names of all the brewers on plaques and foundation stones around East London. As individuals they were widely hailed as local benefactors; as brewers they were often assailed as malefactors, and by no one more vehemently than F. N. Charrington.

Frederick Nicholas Charrington was born in 1850 and already at the age of nine he showed something of his disposition by burning a bundle of banknotes.[28] As a young man of twenty he renounced his share, worth £1¼ m., in the family brewery. This came about because of an incident he witnessed outside a squalid little East End tavern, where a wretched-looking woman was standing, with her children tugging at her skirts crying for food. As he was passing, a man, presumably her husband, staggered through the doorway, and she pleaded for some money to buy bread. He grunted and knocked her to the ground. Charrington was horrified by the incident but was about to go on, when he noticed the name above the tavern: CHARRINGTONS –

> ... it suddenly flashed into my mind that that was only one case of dreadful misery and fiendish brutality in one of the several hundred public-houses our firm possessed ... It was a crushing realisation. ... What a frightful responsibility for evil rested upon us.[29]

Thereafter he acted as a man possessed. He left the family mansion, and found himself cheap rooms in Stepney Green. It is perhaps impossible for a very rich man entirely to renounce his fortune for it would also mean renouncing his relatives and friends. Indeed, although Charrington, once out of the brewery, never held a paid job again, he never seemed to be short of money and never experienced any difficulty in raising huge sums for the many charities with which he was associated. His was one of the best known names in beer and his conversion to the temperance cause and his renunciation of the brewery fortune caused a sensation. When he came to address a meeting at Essex Hall, the nonconformists' headquarters in the Strand, roads for miles around were made impassable by the crowds eager to see him.[30]

And there was more to see than to hear. Tall, fair, erect, with a soldierly bearing, blue eyes, and a handsome profile, he was everyone's idea of the good-looking young Englishman; but he was a poor speaker, and he was to an extent choked by his fanaticism and the powerful feelings which welled up in him. He tended to find expression in action, rather than words, yet he never failed to attract large audiences, especially on his own home ground in the East End. Charrington was a household word. It was emblazoned all over the working man's world, and to have a man bearing that name among them, was like having a legend within sight and sound. And the fact that he was not only rich but had renounced his riches added to his curiosity value. They had all, of course, been told that the poor would inherit the Kingdom of Heaven and that wealth was nothing, but such messages were the stuff of sermons. To have among them a man who had actually treated wealth as nothing was a revelation. Here was a sermon come to life, and they crowded to listen to him and receive his message, and even where they found him incoherent, his very sincerity shone through his words.

He set himself three aims, to spread the word of Christ, to check the torrent of alcohol and to make Britain in general and East London in particular a 'purer' place to live in. He did not prepare any scheme of priority and worked on all three fronts at once. He was no theologian and seemed to believe in the blinding flash of inspiration, that one had only to confront people with the truth at the right moment and salvation was theirs. Thus he crowded the hoardings with large posters proclaiming: CHRIST DIED FOR US . . . I AM THE LIGHT OF THE WORLD . . . I AM THE WAY, THE TRUTH, AND THE LIFE. He also used army friends to enrol Guardsmen from Wellington Barracks who had, so to speak, 'seen the light' to preach on a Sunday evening on Mile End waste, an area of rough ground between the roadway and the shops. They were poor speakers, but they came in full uniform and the sight of a giant in scarlet and busby, proclaiming the word of God, however incoherently, often had a stirring effect, and invariably attracted a crowd.[31]

Charrington was at pains to point out that his methods were always sober because, as he said, 'in late years some have despaired of reaching the masses except by using certain unseemly and sensational methods'.[32] He was referring to the work of William Booth and the Salvation Army whose Halleluiah and bang-the-drum approach had revolutionised revivalism in the East End. The truth, he felt, had its own appeal, though it had to be proclaimed often enough and persistently enough. At the same time, whether he wanted to or not, he featured in the headlines almost as hugely as Booth himself.

In 1886 he opened the Great Assembly Hall in Mile End Road, the largest prayer hall in Europe, with room for five thousand people. He built it with the help of John Cory, the colliery owner, the Duke of Westminster, Lady Ashburton, and other wealthy supporters. The foundation stone was laid by Lord Shaftesbury, prince of all Protestant charity without whom no evangelical effort could prosper, and it was packed almost every Sunday.

Before that Charrington often hired out the local music halls for special Sunday night services. They included Lusby's, then the largest music hall in London, and Wilton's; and to make sure they were filled he and his friends toured Ratcliff Highway, stopping in at Paddy's Goose, the Jolly Sailor, the Kettle Drum and other 'such dens of iniquity', as he called them, to distribute handbills announcing the services. The landlords, who had seen some rare sights in their time, had never seen anything like this and were too astonished to protest. And the crowds came. The meetings opened with: 'Stand up, Stand up for Jesus', a chorus which sounded uncommonly odd inside a music hall. It was not taken up with great enthusiasm by an audience consisting largely of sailors and their girl friends, and one occasionally saw sights which went ill with a prayer meeting. Charrington later turned upon these self-same music halls in a campaign which brought him some ridicule, a great deal of notoriety, and occasionally before the courts.

He was a bachelor, a celibate who, to use the words of his friend and biographer Guy Thorne, was leading a life of 'self-denial and personal asceticism'. He had numerous men friends, some of whom regarded him as a little too holy and nicknamed him 'Doyk' – from his tendency to be gripped by spasms of religious fervour and to proclaim in a loud voice: 'Down on your knees!'[33] He does not appear to have had any women friends at all, and possibly because of the very depths of his denial, he was obsessed with the ideal of purity and the evils of sex.

In his campaign against brothels and prostitution, Charrington rushed in where policemen feared – or were at least reluctant – to tread. Near Mile End Road there were two adjacent lanes known as Lady Lake's Grove and Cottage Row, which contained about a dozen houses between them, all of them brothels. Charrington later described them in a report:

> In none of these houses are there less than ten girls and women carrying on their nefarious trade, and in some of them there

are as many as twenty. The scene on every night of the week
... is one of the most unqualified bestiality. ... Worse than
all, an extensive system of procuration has been carried on at
some of these houses for a long time past, the agents of
Continental houses finding at the 'Grove' their largest and
cheapest supply of goods.[34]

Where the police failed to raid such places he took out a private
summons to close them, and where that did not work, he raided
them in person. His biographer wrote: 'The blackest scoundrels
in London trembled both at his footsteps and his name. ... They
hid themselves like frightened birds at the mere rumour of his
approach.'[35] By the end of his campaign he claimed to have
closed over two hundred of these little back street whorehouses.

He once invited the habitués of one brothel for breakfast.
It was not the sort of invitation with which they were familiar.
After exchanging puzzled glances they arrived to find tables
laden with ham and beef and steaming urns of coffee and an
organ playing 'Auld Lang Syne'. 'It cannot honestly be said',
wrote Thorne, 'that the talk and the general remarks indulged
in were of the most carefully chosen or elevating character, but,
bad though it was, Mr Charrington and his friends bore it, nor
ventured to protest when matters went considerably further, and
the coarsest of jokes were cut.'[36] Nor was a rendering of hymns
at the close of the meal treated with particular respect. The girls
clearly did not know what to make of Charrington – which is
something they shared with a great many people in higher walks
of life – but some of them came to regard him as a friend rather
than a foe and they were particularly useful in the litigation in
which he was shortly to be involved.

It is unlikely that Charrington had ever been inside a music
hall, otherwise he might have hesitated to hire them for Sunday
night prayer meetings. He had heard that they were 'centres of
evil', but had not quite realised what form the evil took. When
he discovered they were a recognised venue for prostitutes he
applied to the local Quarter Sessions to have the licence of the
most notorious of them revoked. (All music halls had to be
licensed as fit places of entertainment.) Unsuccessful in this, he
then prepared an illustrated tract on the horrors of prostitution,
which he passed around town and which he distributed in person

outside the music hall in question. The illustration depicted a young man tugged by the devil on one side and an angel on the other and carried the message:

> A time is coming when God will say, 'He which is filthy, let him be filthy still; and he that is holy, let him be holy still, but "Now is the accepted time, now is the day of salvation." '

> 'Faith cometh by hearing, and hearing by the word of God', therefore come and hear the Gospel at the great Assembly Hall, Mile End Road, open every morning.[37]

The tract did not succeed in filling the Assembly Hall, neither did it empty the music halls. However the proprietors of Lusby's in the Mile End Road, found his nightly presence outside the door a nuisance and took legal action to restrain him 'from annoying them in their business, and from making representations, by the distribution of tracts and otherwise, to the plaintiff's injury'.

Charrington's principal witnesses were two prostitutes whom he had befriended. Both claimed that they had plied their trade on numerous occasions in Lusby's with the definite knowledge of, and without hindrance from, the management. One of the girls added that it was not uncommon for them to have intercourse on the music hall premises themselves – in the boxes. She had seen it done and had done it herself. Charrington spent more than four hours in the witness box relating the story of his crusade, saying that he was no more responsible for the commotion which sometimes whirled about him as a result of his work 'than a target that is shot at', a claim which the judge substantially upheld.[38]

If the interventions of Charrington in the brothels and music halls were dramatic, they were nothing compared to the work of William Booth, founder of the Salvation Army. Charrington prided himself on his 'sober' approach, Booth eschewed it. Drama was part of his stock in trade. 'It is in the interests of the service to be in the columns of the newspapers as often as possible,'[39] he declared, and he was rarely out of them. His very appearance – his great height, white hair, flowing beard, huge nose, shaggy eyebrows and fierce eyes – was dramatic. He looked like a Hebrew prophet come to bring Nineveh to judgement.

His father was an impoverished artisan. His mother was probably Jewish,[40] and if she wasn't, he never dispelled the belief that she was; it somehow helped to give authority to his utterances.

He was born in Nottingham and came to London to work as a pawnbroker's clerk and spent what free time he had in the Methodist church preaching and teaching. But his kind of religious ardour was not in tune with that of the bland, conventional Methodists and in 1861 he broke with them to launch into independent revivalism. His sermons gained him some reputation if not notoriety, and he was invited by a small revivalist group called the East London Services Committee to speak in Whitechapel. It was there, with the Blind Beggar tavern behind him and the London Hospital before him, that he launched his mission to the world.

'There is Heaven in East London for everyone', he began, 'for everyone who will stop to think and look to Christ as a personal saviour.'[41] That was the gist of his message and it never varied. Godliness, piety, merit, all that came later; the point of departure was belief, but before a man's capacity for faith can be evoked, one must first evoke his curiosity, to cause him to stand and stare, and thus Booth's mission came to acquire the nature of a travelling circus. The idea of calling it the Salvation Army came to him in 1878, the quasi-military drill, the terminology, the citadels, the generals, brigadiers and majors, the uniforms, the banners and, of course, the bands followed.[42] He certainly gained attention, but he was also subjected to ridicule and abuse which did not stop short of physical violence; he was cheered by this, for did not the Lord suffer the same? And of course, the fiercer the attacks, the greater the attention, and the more souls within reach. And the louder he was condemned the louder he banged his drum.

Booth was ignorant of theology, prejudiced against science and philosophy, a philistine and perhaps a boor. He did not arrive at his religious beliefs through patient contemplations but through flashes and visions, as if he was in immediate contact with On High. And if there was a surging urgency to his effort it was precisely because of the simple, primitive nature of his beliefs. If he spoke of fire and brimstone, he evoked them so convincingly that a smell of sulphur almost assailed the nostrils. He instilled fear in his fellow men because he loved them and feared for them. And it was the primitive nature of his beliefs that made them so readily and widely accepted and understood. He was sweeping in his indictment of drinking, gaming and even such sports as cricket and football. If in normal society everything was permitted unless it was specifically condemned, in the Salvation Army everything seemed to be condemned except where it was specifically permitted. And yet the Salvation Army was a cheering presence in the East End for it never accepted the Victorian idea of the 'deserving poor'. If a man was poor he was deserving.

Barnett made the most rigorous examination into the circumstances of anyone before he gave them a penny. Charrington was rather more generous, and a notable feature of his Mile End Mission were the Sunday night dinners he gave for several hundred poor, but a picture of the diners with their elaborate bonnets and white collars suggests that they were not amongst the neediest people in the neighbourhood. The Salvation Army demanded no pretensions to respectability and attracted every flea-bitten vagabond in the land.

Booth was not content to feed and clothe the hungry, or even to elevate them to be productive members of society. He argued that one doesn't make a man's soul clean by washing his shirt, and all his social work was but a means of access to the soul. And his efforts in both directions quickly bore fruit. He established shelters for the homeless, an emigration scheme and farm colonies for the unemployed. His influence spread beyond East London to the country at large, beyond the country to America and the empire. As time went on the criticism of Booth became more reasoned and gradually died away. He was applauded by Gladstone and received by Edward VII. He and the Salvation Army became respectable and respected.

Dr Barnardo began his work in the East End – almost at the same time as Booth. He came to Whitechapel to study medicine at the London Hospital in the middle of the 1866 cholera epidemic. He witnessed sixteen deaths in one day, an experience which quickened his feeling that there was little time to be wasted to put the world right.[43] He worked hard as a student but engaged also in preaching and, with the help of fellow-students, he opened a ragged school in a donkey shed not far from the hospital. One evening he was about to lock up for the night when he saw a ragged, shoeless urchin loitering by the fire and told him to run along home. Home? The child looked at him large-eyed, 'I don't live nowhere.' Barnardo questioned him further and found he was without father, mother or friends. Were there, he asked, others like him on their own. 'Oh yes Sir; lots, 'eaps of 'em, more'n I could count.' And he led Barnardo to a huddle of old sheds and warehouses on the edge of the City, in Aldgate, and there he found eleven ragged boys, asleep on an old tin roof, their heads on the slope, their feet in the gutter.

The lad offered to show him more, but Barnardo had seen enough for one night. The experience was a turning-point in his life. He had entered the London Hospital with the intention of going out to China as a medical missionary. Then he wavered between the East End and the East. Now he had chanced upon his true mission. He would devote himself to the homeless child. 'The dread night of discovery', he wrote, 'determined my subsequent career.'[44]

His work came to the attention of Lord Shaftesbury who found it difficult to believe that the stories of misery and squalor put out by Barnardo were entirely true. Social reformers, he often discovered, tended to exaggerate a situation in order to draw help to their cause. Barnardo invited him to come and see for himself. He took him one evening to a cul de sac near Billingsgate fish market, where a high pile of crates was secured under large tarpaulins. Barnardo put his arm in under the flap, seized hold of a naked foot and ankle and roused a young lad from his sleep. Suddenly, the whole tarpaulin began to quiver and seethe, as if it was about to walk away on its own feet and, within minutes, seventy-three children came to light, big and little, old and young, all in foul-smelling verminous rags. The tears welled up in Shaftesbury's eyes at the sight of them. 'All London shall know of this', he said.[45] Money flowed in from all directions with the result that in 1870 the first Barnardo home for working lads was opened at 18 Stepney Causeway.

In 1872 Barnardo opened his first adult mission in a huge tent opposite the notorious gin palace, the Edinburgh Castle and its neighbouring low-class music hall in Limehouse. He wrote:

A roaring drink-trade was going on, and on the stage songs were being sung which won applause in strict proportion to

the filthy double entendres and questionable gestures with
which they were plentifully besprinkled. Round the room in,
niches in the walls, were statues of the nude, which I suppose
would be considered all the more artistic in that they were
disgusting to decent people. No one could doubt that we
were in the presence of a demoralising agency of the worts
description.[46]

On some nights he attracted an audience of several thousand,
and the more his tabernacle as he called it, filled, the more the
pub emptied. Within a short time he was able to buy it and use
it as a mission hall, which transformed the neighbourhood. The
Edinburgh Castle remained the splendid, illuminated edifice that
it was; and it became the first Coffee Palace in the country. Why
should the devil have all the best habitats?

No sooner was Barnardo established as a public figure and
his homes as worthy institutions than all sorts of dark rumours
began to circulate. It was suggested that his children were being
underfed and ill-treated, kept in solitary cells. It was said that
he faked photographs of starving waifs to excite sympathy and
money. There were rumours of embezzlement. All the money
he raised went personally to him and he accounted to no one,
and presented no audited accounts. To answer these charges he
set up an independent board of inquiry headed by the Recorder
of Leeds and including the Reverend John Cale Miller, Canon
of Rochester, and William Graham, a former MP. On the charge
of embezzlement Barnardo was absolved completely, but the
Inquiry found that 'artistic fiction'[47] had been employed in preparing the photographs. On the first charge it found that the
children had been well fed, well educated and well looked after,
but that the solitary cells had existed and that on one or two
occasions boys had been kept in solitary confinement for longer
periods than was advisable. In all other aspects it found entirely
in Barnardo's favour, a verdict which *The Times* applauded:

> The Barnardo Homes are now pronounced to be real and
> valuable charities, worthy of public confidence and support.
> This is really enough. It is just the judgement which the public
> wanted, and we trust it will be accepted as final.[48]

To forestall any future criticism Barnardo appointed public

trustees consisting of figures distinguished in the Church and public life, with the Lord Chancellor, Earl Cairns, as President. Thus reconfirmed in the public esteem, Barnardo launched upon a new period of growth, and by his jubilee year he had twenty-five homes and missions, a village of fifty cottages for girls in Barkingside, a hospital for sick children in Stepney, and various workshops as training centres for boys and girls.

During the twenty-eight years of his mission, he raised over £3,000,000.[49] Once an unknown lady appeared and placed three thousand pound notes in his hand then as he stood incredulous, she vanished as mysteriously as she came.[50] Nevertheless, his homes fell into serious debt and in 1893 he feared that he might have partly to close his doors.

> Never in the history of the Church or the world has an organised attempt been made to rescue the destitute from starvation, the suffering from peril, and the downtrodden and cruelly ill-used little ones from their oppressors and tormentors. Never before have the hands of loving sympathy been held out so widely or so effectively to the orphaned and the helpless. Never before has one man borne so large a share of responsibility in such a case. ... Dare I therefore now in the face of all this, now commence to close my doors in the face of a single homeless child? *I cannot believe that this must really be done.*[51]

His belief in prayer was absolute. The Lord will provide. And the Lord did, but slowly. The crisis continued into 1894 when the Homes were in debt for £6,000. Retrenchments of various sorts had to be introduced, but money began to flow in gradually and the Ever Open Door remained ever open. The slogan emblazoned on all his buildings, remained: NO DESTITUTE BOY EVER TURNED AWAY. In his jubilee year he was able to declare:

> As I walk through the streets I see no more the organised beggary, the universal ingrained ignorance, the systematic neglect, the vicious exploiting of homeless little victims of cruelty and greed which disgraced London in the 'sixties.[52]

Part of this, he believed, was due to changes in public attitudes: 'In 1866 the child was the property of his parents, be they never so brutalised, so gin-soddened, so bestial. Short of murder the

child was his father's or mother's chattel. . . . The Acts for the
Prevention of Cruelty to Children have thrown their aegis over
the little ones in a multitude of households. The extreme meaning
of the words "parental authority" has been pared down to more
reasonable limits.'

At his death in 1905 *The Times* expressed the national sense of
loss:

> It is impossible to take a general view of Dr Barnardo's life-
> work without being astonished alike by its magnitude and by
> its diversity, and by the enormous amount of otherwise hope-
> less misery against which he has contended single-handed with
> success. He may be justly ranked among the great public
> benefactors whom England has in recent times numbered
> among her citizens. With no adventitious aid from fortune or
> from connections, with no aim but to relieve misery and to
> prevent sin and suffering, he has raised up a noble monument
> of philanthropy and usefulness. [53]

His body was moved to the Edinburgh Castle where it lay in
state for several days. About ten thousand people lined the roads
at his funeral and the looks on the faces that day suggested a
very personal sense of loss.

Barnardo adopted several generations of deprived children as
peculiarly his own. He was manic in his possessiveness and
missed his charges painfully when abroad. In 1904, a year before
his death, when some of the girls at Barkingside were preparing
to emigrate to Canada he wrote to their housemother:

> I feel so jealous of you all, YOU mother all my children and
> they are *mine – mine – mine*, not yours. I love every one of
> them, and I feel it so terribly that I cannot be with them on
> occasions of this sort . . . [54]

He regarded the children as 'the solemn gift of God to me',
    he was not using mere rhetoric. As a result once he acquired
charge of a child he fought tooth and nail to retain it. He brought
frantic energies to bear on any problems he tackled, partly
because he was a man in a hurry, partly because he was appalled
by the scale of human need and human deficiency. He believed
himself to be divinely appointed to perform the work in hand,
and he tended to display much of the arrogant bigotry which

goes with profound belief, and like many primitive Protestants, especially of the Irish strain, he had a contempt for Catholicism.

Many of the children he round running wild round the street were Catholic, or at least of Catholic origin, but the Catholic church, he argued, showed no interest in them until he had reclaimed them. He was involved in prolonged and bitter exchanges with the hierarchy as a result. When these came into the open and reached the Courts he was taken aback by the amount of criticism which he incurred. He could not believe that anyone, taking an honest view of his efforts, could have a word to say against him. To an extent he suffered from paranoia and saw himself as the victim of a national Catholic conspiracy.

He was a powerful writer and speaker and excited even the admiration of Booth who told him: 'You look after the children and I'll look after the adults, then together we'll convert the world.'[55] His approach was, of course, much more sober than Booth's but both men combined unworldly belief with worldly administrative ability. From Scotland Barnardo borrowed an idea as yet unknown in England, the practice of boarding out children. He took great pains in selecting the right family for the right child, and established a corps of visitors to watch their progress to maturity. Again, once a child was placed in his trust he expected almost absolute control over his future and all correspondence between the relatives of children and their foster parents had to pass through his office. He tended to regard parents as something of a nuisance. His ideal charge was someone like Jim Jarvis, the small boy he had found loitering by the fire in the donkey sanctuary, who had led him to his 'dread night of discovery', and who was without any family ties whatsoever. Parental rights, he believed, vanished where they were unsupported by parental obligations.

He could, as the 1877 inquiry showed, be stern, even brutal, and in that respect he was perhaps the typical Victorian father, but the overwhelming quality he brought to his work was love and he was able to gather round him people moved by this same force. It was this which, more than anything else, distinguished his homes from the homes ·and orphanages run by the local authorities and even the churches.

By concentrating his efforts on children, Barnardo avoided the dilemma which faced other social reformers – whether, by helping, he was not in fact hindering. If the poor were the cause of their own poverty, their children were at least innocent, they were still young enough to be saved for a happier life, a better life, a fuller life, and very many were saved. The story of Barnardo is the story of the triumph of environment over heredity, and one of the most comforting reflections to be gained from a study of his life was how much good can arise from the efforts of one man.

The same can be said of the lives of Barnett or Booth or even Charrington. It is reassuring to discover that 'do-gooders' – a term of abuse nowadays – can in fact do good – at least on a personal level. One is not, however, quite convinced that they left the East End as a whole a better place than they found it.

For, in spite of the determination of Barnett and others to set their face against casual doles and easy handouts, the East End became known, if not as the land of milk and honey, at least as the land of the ever simmering soup cauldron, and the feckless, the useless and the helpless descended upon it from every corner of the kingdom. In 1896 over eighty per cent of the poor seeking help from the Spitalfields Poor Law guardians had no homes in the neighbourhood, or, for all one was able to discover, homes at all. [56] Brick Lane, one of the main thoroughfares of the area, was described as 'a land of beer and blood', and there were letters to the press appealing for help to cope with the destitution, misery and squalor. There was – there still is – much to darken the eye and wring the heart in the East End, but that was no reflection on the work of the men and women who made it their particular cause. In a sense it was a measure of their success. As people moved up in life they tended to move out of the East End, as they declined they moved towards it. Here was one place where they could always be sure of sympathy, understanding and help.

# NINE

# Jacob the Ripper

On 8 August 1888, the body of Martha Turner, a common prostitute, was found savagely mutilated outside George Yard Buildings, a group of Model Dwellings in Spitalfields. Violence was a daily occurrence and the occasional murder was not unknown in this still squalid area of crumbling tenements, low lodging houses and brothels. However, what distinguished this particular killing was the extent of the mutilation. The woman had thirty-nine stab wounds in her chest and had been disembowelled. 'It is one of the most terrible cases that one could imagine', said the coroner, 'the man must have been a perfect savage to have attacked the woman in this way.' There was nothing to establish either the identity of the killer or the motive for the killing.

Four weeks later there was another murder, equally savage and equally inexplicable. The victim was Polly Nicholls, a married woman in her mid-forties, who was separated from her husband and had taken to the streets. She too was disembowelled, her uterus had been ripped out and her throat had been cut so deeply that she was almost beheaded. A week later a third victim was found in Hanbury Street, not far from the scene of the second murder. She too was a prostitute, she too had been disembowelled, but more roughly and hurriedly and her intestines were strewn about the street. The first murder had occasioned little more than curiosity. With the second there was unease and alarm. With the third something like panic set in.

Jews in their thousands had begun to crowd into the district in the past few years. They were secretive in their ways, kept themselves to themselves, spoke a strange tongue, had strange habits and struck the local population as furtive and sinister; the belief spread that one of them must have been responsible for the murders. If few people now ventured out into the streets during darkness, it was for a time unsafe for Jews to show their face in the streets at all.

'Without doubt the foreign Jews in the East End have been in some peril during the past week owing to the sensationalism of which the district has been a centre', wrote the *Jewish Chronicle*.[1] A local paper went into fuller detail:

> On Saturday in several quarters of East London the crowds who had assembled in the streets began to assume a very threatening attitude towards the Hebrew population of the district. It was repeatedly asserted that no Englishman could have perpetrated such a horrible crime, and that it must have been done by a Jew – and forthwith the crowds proceeded to threaten and abuse such of the unfortunate Hebrews as they found in the streets.[2]

However, special squads of police had been drafted into the area as a result of the murders and they were able to prevent a threatening situation from degenerating into an outright pogrom.

In the meantime, in the continuing absence of any clue to the killer or motive, there was wild speculation in the daily press. The Central European correspondent of the *Standard* drew attention to the fact that each victim had been disembowelled and had had her uterus removed and wrote that in parts of Germany there was a belief that candles fashioned from the uterus gave out fumes which rendered people unconscious and that they were used by criminals to render their victims helpless.[3] Equally bizarre, and far more mischievous, was a report from the Vienna correspondent of *The Times*. A Jew named Ritter had been arrested near Cracow and charged with the ritual murder of a Christian woman. The prosecution had charged that the accused, having had sexual intercourse with his victim, believed that he was obliged by Jewish law to kill her. Ritter was found innocent, wrote *The Times* correspondent, 'but the evidence touching the superstitions prevailing among some of the ignorant and degraded of his co-religionists remains on record and was never wholly disproved.'[4]

His case was to an extent supported by a letter from a doctor, Edgar Sheppard, in the same issue of *The Times*:

I cannot help thinking that these Whitechapel murders point to one individual, and that individual insane. Not necessarily an escaped, or even as yet, recognised lunatic. He may be an earnest religionist with a delusion that he has a mission from above to extirpate vice by assassination. And he has selected his victims from a class which contributes pretty largely to the prevalence of immorality and sin.[5]

The doctor did not suggest that the 'religionist' was necessarily Jewish, but taken together with the report from Vienna the inference was unmistakable. The following day there were angry letters in *The Times* both from Chief Rabbi Hermann Adler and from Haham Gaster, the Chief Rabbi of the Spanish and Portuguese Jews. Adler's letter was comparatively brief and emphatic:

I can assert without hesitation that in no Jewish book is such a barbarity even hinted at. Nor is there any record in the criminal annals of any country of a Jew having been convicted of such a terrible atrocity ... the tragedies enacted in the East End are sufficiently distressing without the revival of moribund fables and the importation of prejudices abhorrent to the English nation.

Dr Gaster made much the same point, though he made it at greater length. Such superstitions as were suggested by *The Times* correspondent, he said, 'do not prevail among Jews even in the most degraded position, but that these are superstitions entertained against the Jews from which the Jews turn with horror and disgust'.[6]

Then word spread of a mysterious, foreign-looking figure who had been seen prowling around in a leather apron. None knew who he was, or what he was, or where he lived, and he was nicknamed 'Leather Apron'. The more the name was passed around the more sinister it sounded. He had, it was said, been seen consorting with at least two of the victims near the scene of the crimes. Some claimed to have seen him knife in hand! Police were hampered by the very flood of rumour, but their search was finally concentrated on a Polish Jew called Pizer. He was an insignificant, quiet-spoken man, but he did wear a leather apron and had been acting suspiciously. He was moreover, a book-binder by profession and the owner of several long knives, tools of his trade, which could have been used for slaughter. He was taken into custody and closely questioned, but was able to establish his innocence on every point. At the inquest into the third murder the coroner asked why, if he was innocent, he had kept himself in hiding. Pizer said that all sorts of wild rumours had been circulating in the streets, and for some reason that he couldn't explain his name had been raised as the killer. If he had shown his face in public, he said, he would have been torn to pieces.[7] Nevertheless, people continued to believe that a Jew must have been responsible. The third of the victims had been found near a Jewish cemetery in Brady Street, and one of the men who found her suggested that 'probably some sneaking Yid wouldn't pay for 'is fun, then she cut up nasty like and he did 'er in'.[8] A more serious theory arose out of the nature of the incisions. They had in almost every case been inflicted with a long blade, a bayonet, it was thought at first, or a sword, and suspicions rested for a time on a soldier who had been with one of the prostitutes shortly before her death. He was traced to the nearby garrison in the Tower of London and was picked up for questioning but he too was able to prove his innocence. The police were still no closer to their man.

Attention then turned to the numerous slaughterhouses in and around the East End, and especially the kosher ones. Could not a *Shochet* – a Jewish ritual slaughterer – have been the killer? He had a rudimentary knowledge of anatomy. He had the knives, which varied in size with the size of the animals to be slaughtered, small ones for fowls, larger ones for sheep, and long ones, like single-edged swords, for cattle. A *Shochet*, moreover, was expected to be, and in those days almost invariably was, a considerable Talmudic scholar, and given sufficient fanaticism, he might have read some crazy interpretation into the numerous Talmudic denunciations of harlots and harlotry. That, indeed, was the conclusion of Mr Robin Odell in a recent book on the murders:

A ritual slaughterman steeped in Old Testament law might have felt some religious justification for killing prostitutes. Talmudic law was harsh where harlotry was concerned and in certain cases whores could be punished by strangulation or stoning.[9]

The police themselves entertained this theory for a while, visited the kosher abattoirs and detained two *shochtim*, Reverend Davidson and Reverend Jacobs, for questioning but both had perfect alibis. In addition the City Divisional Surgeon, Dr Gordon Browne, examined the knives commonly used by *shochtim* and satisfied himself that they could not possibly have been used in any of the murders. The *khalef*, as the implement is known, is single-edged and not pointed, whereas the mutilations on all the victims indicated a pointed blade.

But if the *shochtim* were exonerated the Jews were not, for on 26 September, ten days after the third murder, two bedraggled whores were found dead a short distance from one another. Both had their throats cut, both had been disembowelled. The first of the victims was found almost opposite the International Workmen's Education Club, whose members were mostly Jewish leftists and anarchists and who at the time of the murder claimed to be busy debating socialism and Judaism. There was some noise and merriment at the end of their meeting and if the victim had screamed they did not hear it.

Suspicion now found a new focus. Hitherto it had been a religious fanatic. Could it have been an anti-religion fanatic, one of the members of the International Workmen's Club? All who were present at the club on the night of the murder were closely questioned, and all were able to establish their innocence, but from the information the police were able to piece together they now thought they knew what the wanted man looked like, and they sent out the following description: 'Age 37, height, 5 ft 8 in. Rather dark beard and moustache; dress, dark jacket, dark vest and trousers, black scarf and black felt hat. Speaks with foreign accent.'[10]

It was a description which could have fitted about half of the forty thousand or so Jews who were then living in Spitalfields, and as one of the police inspectors leading the investigation later complained, it hampered their search rather than helped:

The trouble is that if anyone talks of a foreigner most people in the East End think of a Jew. And you can be damned sure when it comes to an identity parade, it's the Jew people pick out and that's why we always get the wrong man.[11]

In the meantime the killer announced himself – or so, at first, it was thought – for after the double murder it was revealed that the Central News Agency had received a letter, postmarked 28 September, in which the writer referred to the earlier murders in a grisly and jocular way, announced that some more were in prospect, and signed himself 'Jack the Ripper'. The second followed two days later. It was written on a postcard and read:

I was no codding dear old Boss. You'll hear about Saucy Jack's work tomorrow. Double event this time. Number one squealed a bit; couldn't finish straight off. Had no time to get ears for the police.[12]

A third communication followed in the form of a poem:

> I'm not a butcher,
> I'm not a Yid,
> Nor yet a foreign skipper,
> But I'm your own high-hearted friend,
>            Yours truly,
>                Jack the Ripper.[13]

The name stuck, and reverberates still, but after examining all the letters the police satisfied themselves that they were a hoax and could not be treated in any way as a clue to the identity of the killer.

But with the double murder a palpable clue was found. The woman who had been killed in Mitre Square had worn a coarse white apron which was found left hanging round her neck. Her attacker had torn a piece off to wipe his hands or the knife, and it was picked up in Goulston Street, some ten minutes from the scene of the crime, and nearby a message had been scrawled up on the walls: 'The Juewes shall not be blamed for nothing.'[14]

It was not, of course, certain that the words had been scrawled by the killer. Rumour had ascribed the blame to the Jews almost from the beginning, and this may have been an attempt by a Jew to declare their innocence. Particular significance was attached by some papers to the fact that the word Juewes had been mis-

5a. The Royal Crown, Ratcliff Highway

5b. The People's Palace

6b. William Booth

6a. Canon Barnett and his wife

spelt, or rather that the lettering seemed to be half Hebrew, which was taken as proof that a Jew must have written it, and the Jew could have been the killer.[15]

Sir Charles Warren himself was puzzled by it and he wrote to the Chief Rabbi as to its significance. The reply was immediate and unequivocal:

> Office of the Chief Rabbi
> October 13th, 1888.
>
> Dear Sir Charles,
>
> I was just about to write to you on the very subject named in your note. I was deeply pained by the statements that appeared in several papers today, the 'Standard', 'Daily News', etc., that in the Yiddish dialect the word Jews is spelled 'Juewes'. This is not a fact. The equivalent in the Judao-German (Yiddish) jargon is 'Yidden'. I do not know of any dialect or language in which 'Jews' is spelled 'Juewes'. I am convinced that the writing emanated from some illiterate Englishman who did not know to spell the word correctly . . .
>
> My community really appreciates your humane and vigilant actions during this critical time.
>
> I am convinced that no Jew unless he be a maniac could be connected with the horrible outrages. There is nothing which a Jew is taught to view with greater horror than the mutilation of a dead body, whether it be a Jew or a gentile.
>
> With sincere regards,
> Hermann Adler

Nothing of this correspondence was known to the press and the speculation continued.

The message could then have been a declaration that Jews, who were being harried and hustled all over Europe, could also have their own back. All that was pure speculation. Most comment attached to the fact that the words had been erased by the police.

As murder followed murder, each more grisly than the other, one paper after another joined in attacks on the Home Secretary and on the Commissioner of Police for their failure to keep the streets of London safe. Now it seemed they were 'covering up for the Jews'.[16] This belief was given further credence when, at the inquest on the two dead women, Sir Charles Warren, Commissioner of Police, said he had given orders to have the message erased because he feared a pogrom, and in the tense situation, a pogrom could well have taken place.[17] Sir Robert Anderson, the Assistant Commissioner of Police, writing some twenty years after the event, declared:

> The conclusion we came to was that he (i.e. the killer) and his people were certain low-class foreign Jews and it is a remarkable fact that people of that class in the East End will not give up one of their number to gentile justice. ... In stating that he was a Polish Jew I am merely stating a definitely established fact.[18]

If Jack the Ripper was in fact a Jew, then one can be fairly certain that his fellows would have kept quiet about it for the simple reason that the whole community could have been held culpable for his deeds, and that the menacing mood of hostility which surrounded them would have given way to outright violence.

No other senior police officer, however, shared Anderson's view. Yet some Jewish observers must have followed the pattern of murders with unease, for there was something significant about their incidence. The first murder took place on 7 August, the second on 31 August, the third on 7 September, the fourth and fifth on 30 September.

7 August coincided with the eve of the first of *Ellul*, the month preceding the Jewish New Year and the Ten Days of Penitence, and, as such, it has been traditionally treated as a month of supplication and penitence. The doom-laden sound of the *Shofar* (ram's horn) is heard during the morning service to warn of the approach of the Day of Judgement (which is another name for the New Year). A crazed fanatic, who may have consorted with prostitutes and was obsessed with his sense of guilt, might have ventured out on the eve of *Ellul* on his deadly mission. There is nothing in Jewish law to sanction such an act and everything to condemn it, but an insane man needs no sanctions.

31 August coincided with the 24th of *Ellul*, a point in the month when the pious rise at dawn to say *Selichot*, special penitential prayers on the immediate approach of the New Year. They are days of deep contrition and the worshipper, with

clenched fist against his heart, goes through a prolonged confessional:

> We have trespassed, we have betrayed, we have robbed, we
> have slandered, we have committed iniquity, and have done
> wickedly, we have acted presumptuously, we have committed
> violence, we have framed falsehood . . .

And so on through every conceivable form of trespass. To a
sane man it was a means of correction, but to an insane man . . . ?

The following week passed without incident.

The New Year and the Day of Atonement, which follows ten
days later, are the most sacred days of the Jewish calendar and
are known together as the Solemn Days. The New Year celebra-
tions continue over two days. The first day fell on 6 September,
and it passed quietly, as did the second, but some hours after
the close of the evening service on 7 September, Annie Chapman
was found in Hanbury Street, with her throat cut, her uterus
ripped out, and her intestines strewn about her body.

A dreadful pattern was emerging and it seemed as if a Jew,
overwhelmed by perverted religious passions, had taken it upon
himself to act as an avenging angel in the name of the Lord.
Had the murder at the close of New Year's Day been followed
by another on the most solemn day of all, the Day of Atonement,
the picture would have been complete, and there would have
been little doubt that Jack the Ripper was a Jew. It would not
have proved Mr Odell's case that he was a *Shochet* because,
though a *Shochet* had a rudimentary knowledge of anatomy, the
mutilations practised on the victims were not consummate feats
of surgery, nor did one have to be an accomplished anatomist to
know, in general terms at least, the whereabouts of a prostitute's
reproductive organs. And if the *Shochet* had the knife as a tool
of his trade, so did the Jewish cobbler, book-binder, butcher
and, indeed, housewife.

The Day of Atonement came and went without incident.

The fourth and fifth murders took place in the early hours of
30 September, well beyond the cycle of the Solemn Days, and
on the 25th of *Tishri*, one of the few days in the holiest of Jewish
months to be devoid of any religious significance whatever. And
then some six weeks later, on 9 November came the last and
most hideous of the murders. Mary Kelly was found in an

upstairs room in Miller Court, not far from the scene of the previous murders, a gaping wound in her throat, her nose and ears cut off, her face and body savaged and torn as if an animal had been making a meal of her.

For months thereafter every violent death by unknown hands led to cries of 'Jack the Ripper', but there were no further murders which fitted the pattern of the previous six, and life in Whitechapel, which had been at a standstill at the height of the scare – one publican claimed to have gone bankrupt as a result[19] – returned to normal.

Speculation on the identity of the Ripper has continued and every few years a new book embraces a new theory. One writer suggested that he was the Duke of Clarence, a member of the Royal Family, and another that he was a Russian secret agent, a third that he was in fact a woman, a local midwife.

The latest theory comes from Mr Daniel Farson[20] who believes that the Ripper was M. J. Druitt, a young man of good family, who bore an uncanny resemblance to the Duke of Clarence. Druitt, a qualified barrister, was a teacher at a private school in Blackheath on the other side of the river at the time and could easily have made his forays into Whitechapel via the Thames tunnel. He was found drowned in the Thames a few weeks after the death of Mary Kelly.

The tenability of Farson's theory rests, in part, on the number of victims. Some students of the case have put it as high as fifteen, others as seven, many as six. Mr Farson, drawing on the papers of Sir Melville Macnaughten who, as head of the CID led the investigations into the murders, believes the number to be five.

All the six women murdered between August and November were prostitutes, but if one takes that as the basis one can include a seventh who was murdered in April, but she was also robbed, whereas what baffled the police in the other six cases was the apparent lack of motive. Macnaughten, in retrospect, excluded Martha Turner, who was found on 7 August, from his list because her murder was a comparatively clean one. She had nine stab wounds in her throat, thirteen in her stomach and seventeen in her breast, but her throat was not cut open. But one could as logically exclude Mary Kelly for she was found in a room and not in the streets, and her mutilations were so extreme that the earlier victims had, by comparison, been treated with delicacy.

The murders brought the East End a new notoriety, attracted new floods of social workers and a readier flow of funds. Re-development schemes, which had been languishing, were under-taken with a new sense of urgency. New youth clubs were opened and new university settlements. The East End became the centre for a new type of tourism – slumming. Well-dressed men and women arrived by the coach-load to be taken, eager-eyed and breathless, round the various scenes of murder: 'And here, ladies and gentlemen, is where they found the body of Mary Nichols, known otherwise as Polly Nichols, a fallen woman. Her intestines were found strewn over there, and her head . . .'.

The East End has been the home of many great men, saints, sages, scholars, explorers, trade union leaders, statesmen, but the one name which still lingers in the public mind and is known to every schoolboy is Jack the Ripper. He has entered into song and is the subject of plays in which he is treated not at all unsympathetically. It has even been suggested that he was a sort of messy Robin Hood and that he slaughtered the poor to rouse the rich to their responsibilities. If he is not perhaps the East End's favourite son, he is its most celebrated son. Mr Farson's case that he in fact lived in another part of town has not altered local attitudes to him, for if he did not live in the East End he undoubtedly worked there, and he did things in a style entirely his own. Almost anyone could get away with murder in those ill-policed Whitechapel streets, and many people did, but to get away with five or six murders suggests a rare combination of good fortune and skill. He was a master of his craft and Jack, first a source of horror and then of awe, finally became a sort of folk hero.

# TEN

# Perfect Strangers

Suddenly they were everywhere, *millions* of them or so it seemed. In 1892 Whitaker's *Almanac* claimed that Jews were pouring into the country at the rate of about 140,000 a year.[1] Another publication calculated that there were nearly a million Jews in Britain by the end of the nineteenth century and, given present trends, there could be over seven million within another decade.[2]

When Board of Trade returns and the 1901 Census showed much smaller figures there were ironic chuckles. Jews, said one observer, 'amuse themselves by leading astray either Government or private inquiries'.[3] 'We have no trustworthy means of numbering our uninvited visitors',[4] said another. Arnold White, who led the agitation against the newcomers, regarded the official immigration returns as worthless. An East End Borough Councillor declared:

> I don't care for statistics. God has given me a pair of eyes in my head and as I walk through Mile End or Cable Street, as I walk through your streets, I see the good old names of tradesmen have gone, and in their places are foreign names of those who have ousted Englishmen out into the cold.[5]

The number of aliens entering Britain during the peak immigration years at the end of the century only averaged about four thousand a year, but most of them settled in and around East London, an area which suffered from chronic overcrowding, high unemployment and which, since the middle of the nineteenth century, had become the focal point of a host of social inquiries experiments and philanthropic endeavour.

These aliens, moreover, were not like the Germans who had been coming in considerable numbers over the years to work in the breweries or the sugar refineries, or the Irishmen who settled near the docks, or even the Lascars and Chinese of Limehouse and Shadwell. They were Jews, and everything about them, their language, their garb, their side-curls and beards, their eating habits and non-drinking habits, their way of life, their very manner of speaking set them apart from their neighbours, and they had no need to descend in countless hordes to make their presence felt.

In 1753 when British Jews – of whom there were then a mere ten thousand – sought naturalisation rights, there were murmurs that they would take over the country, and a satirist envisaged that by 1853 one would see the following in the Jewish press:

> This is to inform the public that the good ship Rodrigue, alias Salvador, Emanuel de Fenesca, Commander; 1,100 tons burthen, 50 guns; Jewish built, a prime sailor, having excellent accommodation for passengers, is now lying at Mr. Caneo's dock in Limehouse, ready to take on Christian families that may be inclined to transport themselves into any part of Turkey, as choosing to live under a Mohammedan rather than a Jewish government. It is proposed that this ship will return loaded with a proper number of foreign Jews.[6]

The piece was reprinted in the *East London Observer* during the protracted immigration debate to suggest that the satire was not all that far from reality, at least as far as the East End was concerned.

Jews were expelled from England on All Saints' Day 1290 and were not formally re-admitted until 1656. The first to settle here were mainly prosperous Sephardim, Jews of Spanish and Portuguese origin, whose ancestors had fled to the Low Countries to escape the Inquisition. They attracted a number of less prosperous brethren, and by 1666 they were numerous enough to have their own Sick-Aid society. Ashkenazim, as Jews of German and Polish origin were known, too began trickling in and by 1690 they were numerous enough to have their own synagogue, and six years later their own cemetery. A synagogue is something comparatively ephemeral in Jewish life; the cemetery suggested that Jews were here to stay. Whenever there was persecution of

Jews in Central or Eastern Europe – and it was not infrequent in the eighteenth century – there was a westward flow of refugees, with a slight overflow moving as far as England. They were aided by the old settlers, that is those who had arrived a decade or two before, but by 1771 their number was so large that the Great Synagogue refused relief to those foreign Jews 'who had left their country without good cause'. What was a good cause was left undefined.

Patrick Colquhoun, the Metropolitan Magistrate, estimated that there were about fifteen to twenty thousand Jews in London at the end of the eighteenth century, with a handful of grandees at the top, and the rest, living in or near Whitechapel, scratching around to make a living in any way they could. The Jewish lower classes, wrote Colquhoun, live:

> ... chiefly by their wits, and establish a system of mischievous intercourse all over the country, the better to carry out their fraudulent designs in the circulation of base money, the sale of stolen goods, and in the purchase of metals of various kinds; as well as other articles pilfered from the Dockyards, and stolen in the provincial towns ...[7]

The utterance of forged coins, according to Colquhoun, was something of a cottage industry among Jews who, in this instance, formed an unholy alliance with the Irish:

> ... there is said to be scarce an Irish labourer who does not exchange his weeks wages for base money ... The Jews confine themselves principally to the coinage and circulation of copper; while the Irish women are the chief utterers and colourers of base silver. A vast number of these low females have acquired the mischievous art of colouring the bad shillings and six-pences which they purchase from the employers of Jew-boys who cry *bad shillings*.[8]

Colquhoun was careful to distinguish the Sephardim, who numbered three thousand, from the Ashkenazim or 'German Dutch Jews', as he called them. The former, he said, 'pride themselves on their ancestry and give their children the best education which can be obtained', while the latter, he believed, 'got no education at all'.

The Sephardim, he continued, 'being mostly wealthy are

extremely attentive to their poor, among whom there is said to be not a single beggar or itinerant'. The Ashkenazim, on the other hand, were, with the exception of three or four wealthy families, 'a very indigent class of people, through whose medium crimes are generated to a considerable extent'.[9]

Jewish newcomers, unfamiliar with the distinction, and who had always thought all Jews were one – at least when in need – were given short shrift when they applied to the opulent Sephardi brethren for help. '. . . the charitable institutions formed by the Spanish and Portuguese Jews', they were told, 'were solely directed to assist their brethren, who either fled from the alluded persecution, or were reduced by other misfortunes, and not for the purpose of encouraging German, Dutch or Polish adventurers . . .'[10]

Few callings were opened to the Jewish immigrant. There was the occasional cobbler, tailor, glazier, but most engaged in various forms of petty trade, pedlars, hawkers, orange sellers, and above all, as old clothes men. Where licit means could not bring them a livelihood, not a few turned to illicit ones. Colquhoun was of the opinion that they nearly all did, and he blamed their traditions and upbringing:

> Totally without education, and very seldom trained to any trade or occupation by which they can earn their livelihood by manual labour; their youths excluded from becoming apprentices, and their females from hiring themselves generally as servants, on account of their superstitious adherence to the mere ceremonial of their persuasion, as it respects meat not killed by Jews, nothing can exceed their melancholy condition, both with regard to themselves and society. Thus excluded from these resources, which other classes in the community possess, they seem to have no alternative but to resort to those tricks and devices, which ingenuity suggests to enable persons without an honest means of subsistence to live in idleness.[11]

It would not be long before other social observers were to complain that Jews, far from subsisting in idleness, were working so hard for so long at so low a wage that no Englishman could compete with them, but Colquhoun's remarks were not based on mere hearsay, and the leaders of the Jewish community took urgent steps to set up trade schools. These however did not convert the Jews into a community of craftsmen and artisans. Trade was still the ideal and even as artisans they sought to branch out as businessmen, and gradually, instead of a poverty-stricken mass with a crust of gilded magnates on top, they became a lower middle-class community, all crowded round the few streets extending eastwards from Aldgate, but complaints continued to be made that their neighbourhoods were the last redoubt of the criminal. To this there was added another. London was hit by a serious outbreak of cholera in 1832 and the East End was particularly affected. One writer, signing himself 'Civis', complained to *The Times* that Jews were the source of the pestilence:

> I allude to Rag-fair, and more particularly to Carter Street and Cutler Street, Houndsditch. These streets are choked up with crowds of Jews of the lowest description and filthiest habits; the pavements are strewed with garments of the filthiest kind; in short, if ever the cholera reaches these polluted parts which border upon the heart of the City, the sacrifice of some hundreds will be the inevitable consequence. I will only add that for hours after the night has set in and the crowds have withdrawn, the stench in the streets is beyond endurance.[12]

Rag-fair was the market in second-hand clothes, the poor man's stock exchange, where a man with something to sell might always find another eager to buy, and it always attracted immense crowds. The streets were narrow, the sanitary arrangements slight or non-existent and, as in any place in London where crowds gathered – and homes were so overcrowded that streets were accepted as a natural extension of one's living quarters – there was noise and dirt and smells. 'Civis' was promptly answered by some one calling himself 'Traveller':

> I am not competent to determine whether there is any material difference between Jewish dirt and Christian dirt, but this I will say, that the most healthy part of Rome, and at the same time the most filthy, is the Ghetto, exclusively inhabited by Jews, who, with their heaps of dirt, are carefully locked up every night. It has also been ascertained that in the progress of the cholera through Europe, the Jewish population has suffered little from its effects.[13]

To which the Editor added a footnote: '. . . the Jews, though slovenly in their outward habit, are remarkably cleanly in their persons. Their religious faith demands frequent and regular ablutions, and they are particularly careful to abstain from unwholesome diets.' Their laws required them to wash every morning and before every meal, but the observance of such laws required more than a nominal degree of devotion. The water supply of East London was hopelessly inadequate and therefore dirt was the common inheritance of any East Ender. Indeed, an outward show of cleanliness bordered on ostentation. It was usually the mark of the clergyman or the charity worker. Mayhew found 'the Jew old-clothes men are generally far more cleanly in their habits than the poorer class of English people. Their hands they always wash before their meals.'

By the mid-nineteenth century, a number of East End Jews had prospered sufficiently to find homes in the City or West End. They had acquired English ways, English traditions, English manners, English dress, and if they were distinguishable from Englishmen of their class, it was possibly because they looked more English, but the East End Jew, his numbers continuously augmented by an influx of newcomers, seemed changeless and he excited eager fascination, as may be seen from the following which appeared in Chambers' *Journal* in 1848:

> To the eye accustomed to the polished Judaism of the Quadrant or the Haymarket, these East End Caucasians seem exaggerated Jews. Noses seem more hooked, ringlets more greasily black, and eyes more piercingly lustrous. . . . Unshorn men in their shirt sleeves smoke at the opened windows, children go screaming about the doors; dirty drabs of women shout at each other from house to house, and knots of men, many of them bearded . . . lounge around the thresholds, bargaining and disputing in that harsh, snivelling, Jewish accent. . . . Altogether the scene is a strange but not a pleasing one. Dirt is the prevailing feature – dirt in the streets, dirt in the houses, dirt in the men and women . . .

To which the editor added a hurried footnote:

> Constant readers will readily understand that the writing and publishing of this paper was not prompted by anything like a wish to amuse by ridicule of a depressed and everywhere

unjustly treated race. It has seemed to us, however, that even a somewhat high-coloured sketch of the Jewish quarter in London might have a beneficial effect in leading to improvements in those personal habits and domestic conditions on which health, and even morals, so intimately depend.[14]

It does not appear that such 'high-coloured sketches', and one found them in many papers, helped at all. What did help, though this was to come later in the century, was improved housing and an improved water-supply.

In 1851, as part of his work on the London poor, Henry Mayhew published some detailed descriptions of Jewish East End life which, like his pictures of the Irish, though critical, were tinged with admiration. There were, he gathered from a survey undertaken by the Chief Rabbi, some thirty-five thousand Jews in Britain, of whom about eighteen thousand lived in London, mainly in the East End. The trades most common to them, he wrote, 'are those in which, as they describe it, "there's a chance"; that is they prefer to trade in such commodity as is not subject to a fixed price, so that there may be abundant scope for speculation, and something like a gambler's chance for profit or loss.'[15] The wholesale trade in foreign commodities, including oranges, lemons, grapefruit, dried fruit, shells, tortoises, parrots, birds, curiosities, ostrich feathers, snuffs, cigars and pipes, was, he believed, largely in Jewish hands. There was a time when the slop trade – as the trade in second-hand clothes was known – was entirely Jewish, with Petticoat Lane as the main centre. They also used to have a near monopoly of orange and lemon street selling, and 'in the hopes of sale they followed anyone a mile if encouraged even by a few approving glances'. They were in this respect sometimes a little over-assiduous.

A commercial traveller told me that he could never leave town by mail or stage, without being besieged by a small army of Jew boys, who most pertinaciously offered him oranges, lemons, sponges, combs, pocket-books, pencils, sealing-wax, paper, many-bladed pen-knives, razors, pocket mirrors, and shaving-boxes – as if a man could not possibly quit the metropolis without requiring a stock of such commodities.[16]

In all of these trades, Mayhew believed, the Jews had been outnumbered and displaced by the Irish. The Jews, he wrote, 'the most assiduous and hitherto the most successful of street-traders, were supplanted not by a more persevering or more skilful body of street-traders, but simply by a more *starving* body'. The Irish, he found, could live on less than the Jews:

> The Irish boy could live *harder* than the Jew – often in his own country he subsisted on a stolen turnip a day; he could lodge harder – lodge for a penny a night in any noisome den, or sleep in the open air, which is seldom done by the Jew boy; he could dispense with the use of shoes and stockings – a dispensation which his rival in trade revolted.[17]

The city-bred Jew, moreover, 'required some evening recreation, the penny or twopenny concert, or a game of draughts or dominoes', while the sole luxury which the Irish sought was 'a deep sleep'. He could thus live on less 'than a young denizen of Petticoat Lane, he could sell at a smaller profit and did so sell, until gradually the Hebrew youths were displaced by the Irish.'

The Jews as a whole, he said, were generally 'most exemplary family men. There are few fonder fathers than they are, and they will starve themselves sooner than their wives and children should want. Whatever their faults may be, they are good fathers, husbands and sons', but if they had a weakness, he added, it was 'their extreme love of money'. Many of the street-sellers, he was told, 'were little more conversant with or interested in the religion of their fathers than are the costermonger boys. . . . They are Jews by the accident of their birth. . . .'[18] The youngsters, Mayhew believed, 'were uncontrolled or incontrollable by their parents, who are of the lowest class of Jews, and who often, I am told, care little about the matter, so long as the child can earn his own maintenance . . .'. In the evening they liked to resort to a coffee house for a game of dominoes or cribbage with their friends looking on and betting pennies or halfpennies on who would win. He visited a garret occupied by one of the boys:

> . . . the room was very bare. A few sacks were thrown over an old palliasse, a blanket seemed to be used for a quilt; there were no fire-irons nor fender, no cooking utensils. Beside the bed was an old chest, serving for a chair, while a board resting on a trestle did duty for a table. The one not very large window was thick with dirt and patched all over. Altogether I have seldom seen a more wretched apartment.[19]

He found the lads nevertheless lively and eager, too eager in fact, and were often 'ready to make money by any means' and thus grew up to be cheats, tricksters, receivers of stolen goods. The Jewish boy was 'content to profit by the thief's work, but seldom steals himself . . . Some of these lads become rich men; others are vagabonds all their lives'.[20] Female street-traders were comparatively unknown; and were carefully chaperoned!

> The majority of the street Jew-girls whom I saw on a round were accompanied by boys who were represented to be their brothers, and I have little doubt such was the fact, for these young Jewesses, although often pert and ignorant, are not unchaste. Of this I was assured by a medical gentleman who could speak with sufficient positiveness on the subject.[21]

Whatever they handled, they were, he found, 'brisk traders'.

He thought that the Jews, as a whole, cared little for politics and that patriotism affected them little, for 'the Jew could hardly be expected to love a land, or to strive for the promotion of its general welfare, where he felt he was but a sojourner, and where he was at best tolerated and prescribed', but Mayhew was told that this disinterest was reflected in the attitude of rich Jews to their own people, 'for whom, apart from conventionalities say my informants, *they care nothing whatsoever*',[22] a point on which, as we shall see, Mayhew was clearly misinformed.

He was on stronger grounds when he wrote: 'Among the body of Jews there is little love of literature. They read far less and are far less familiar with English authorship . . . than the poorer English artisans . . . The amusements of the Jews are the theatres and concert rooms. The City of London Theatre, the Standard Theatre and other play houses of the East End are greatly resorted to by the Jews, and more especially the younger members of the body, who sometimes constitute an obstreperous gallery.'

Mayhew had considerable admiration for the Jewish charities 'which allow none of their people to live or die in a parish workhouse', and which contribute 'their quota to the support of the English poor and church'. This, he added, was 'the more honourable and the more remarkable among Jews, when we recollect their indisputable greed for money'.[23]

A Jew who is old, sick or otherwise helpless, Mayhew was

told, 'is either supported by contributions of his friends, or out of some local or general fund, or hospital'. Although the community was small it had a hospital in the Mile End Road, admitting feeble old men and destitute children. Boys were taught a trade and girls were prepared for domestic service. There were a Widows' Home in Aldgate, an Orphan Asylum in Goodman's Fields, and an old age home in Duke's Place and alms houses in Mile End Road and Wellclose Square, near the Tower. There were also three institutions which gave dowries to destitute girls and numerous loan institutions which lent out money to needy Jews, often without security and always without interest. 'If charities are abused, it is usually with the knowledge of the managers, who often let the abuse pass, as a smaller evil than driving a man to theft or subjecting him to the chance of starvation.'[24]

There were, he found, seven Jewish schools in London, three in the West End and four in or near the East End, all supported by voluntary contributions, the biggest by far being the Jewish Free School in Bell Lane which, by the middle of the century, had twelve hundred pupils. This school had been founded in 1817, partly in answer to the charge that Jews failed to teach their children a trade and thus left them vulnerable to chicanery and mischief, and partly in reply to the London Missionary Society which had founded a free school expressly for Jewish children.[25] The Jewish Free School derived its support from the entire community which, by 1850, subscribed some £1,200 towards it, but it enjoyed the particular patronage of the Rothschilds who provided the children with clothing and the school with numerous amenities which made it one of the best-equipped educational establishments in the country. Other members of the Cousinhood of ruling Jewish families also added their help. One of the Goldsmids, a leading banker and broker, would visit the school in person to guide the children in the proper pronunciation of English. As the children were mostly foreign, a master recalled 'they would say 'vich' or 'vat'. Mr Goldsmid would take the lads in class and make them say 'ooich' or 'ooat'.[26] And they learned quickly. It might be said, indeed, that the school became the principal instrument of the old families for converting the new if not into English gentlemen, at least into Cockneys, into English manners and English ways.

Among the boys who attended the school in the 1870s was Israel Zangwill, the son of a penniless Polish immigrant, who became one of the foremost writers of his day. His novel, *Children of the Ghetto*, which he wrote at the age of twenty-eight, brought him instant success. It drew a vivid if sentimental picture of Jewish life in the East End when it was still a small and compact community: 'If you were in Whitechapel sixty-five years ago', wrote George Lansbury of the 1870s, 'I don't suppose you would recognise where you were. First of all you would hardly see any Jews. There was a small Jewish colony between Bishopsgate and Aldgate High Street, but it was not in the least obvious to the eye.'[27]

There were some prosperous families who had their homes further east among the imposing terraces at Bow, some venturesome traders who had slop shops or ship's chandlers among the Irish in Shadwell and Limehouse, but the main community was concentrated in a few streets whose names still ring like a litany in many Jewish ears, Wentworth Street and Middlesex Street, Butler Street and Freeman Street, Lilley Street and Thrawl Street, Fashion Street and Flower and Dean Street, all within the area of Spitalfields formerly occupied by Huguenot weavers. Brick Lane formed the eastern boundary of this universe and Whitechapel High Street the southern one. There was always a trickle of newcomers, mostly from Eastern Europe, which was just about sufficient to replace the number of Jews moving to Hackney or Hampstead or emigrating to America or South Africa, but not so numerous as to alter the character of the colony.

The Polish Jews tended to look down on the Dutch Jews, the Lithuanian Jews on the Polish Jews, while the German Jews looked down on everyone else. The mutual contempt which each group had for the other was not taken too seriously. The Dutch were the old settlers, which gave them a certain edge over the Polaks, but the Polaks, being newer, could claim a greater depth of Jewish learning, a higher degree of Jewish observance. There was always some quality which enabled one group to have some claim to superiority over the other.

Zangwill reflected this in his story of the Ghetto and through the career of Moses Ancell, a Polish immigrant and a widower. He was a bent, unworldly little man, well-versed in the Talmud, who had in his time been a glazier, tailor, presser, rivetter, clicker, laster, finisher. Whether in work or out of work – and he was usually out of work – he could barely make a living, yet somehow the family lived. In fact, the Ancells of East London could always resort to one of the mutual aid societies which lent small sums for short periods without interest, or to a well-to-do neighbour for a small loan. For a large part of the nineteenth century the Jewish rich (though not the very rich) and poor lived near each other, or at least prayed in the same synagogue, so that the former could never be blind to the wants of the latter. As the century progressed, however, there began an exodus towards Islington, Stamford Hill, Bloomsbury, and even beyond to Kensington and Hampstead. This tendency was viewed with regret by one elder of the congregation (whose own home was in Bayswater):

> Formerly when rich and poor lived in close proximity, every man was himself almost a Board of Guardians; he knew and came continually in contact with the poor and, if he inclined to overlook their wants, he could not do so; they were close to his own door and could and did exhort by clamour and absolute and continued solicitation the relief of that distress which to most of us is now known only by report.[28]

It was to make sure that the poor would not be neglected that the rich established the Jewish Board of Guardians in 1859. By then there were already in being a Soup Kitchen in Spitalfields, established in 1854, the Society for Relieving the Aged Needy of the Jewish Faith (established in 1829), the Jewish Blind Society (1819), the Jewish Bread, Meat and Coal Society (1779), and the Norwood Jewish Orphanage, founded in 1795. We encounter all of these institutions in *Children of the Ghetto* in one guise or another. Moses Ancell's eldest daughter, Esther, is on her way to the Soup Kitchen in the opening pages of the book:

> There was quite a crowd of applicants outside the stable-like doors of the kitchen when Esther arrived, a few with well-lined stomachs, perhaps, but the majority famished and shivering. The feminine element swamped the rest, but there were about a dozen men and few children among the group, most of the men scarce taller than children – strange, stunted, swarthy, hairy creatures with muddy complexions illuminated by black, twinkling eyes. . . . Here and there too was a woman of comely

face and figure, but for the most part it was a collection of crones prematurely aged, with weird, wan, old-world features, slipshod and draggle-tailed, their heads bare and covered with dingy shawls. . . . Yet there was an indefinable touch of romance and pathos about the tawdriness and witch-like ugliness, and an underlying identity about the crowd of Polish, Russian, German, Dutch Jewesses, mutually apathetic and pressing forwards. Some of them had infants at their bare breasts . . .[29]

All the children were fed (though Esther was too proud to admit to hunger) and clothed at the Jewish Free School, which was the great welfare institution of the ghetto – the schooling it offered was of almost secondary importance. As they grew up, Benjamin, the eldest of Esther's brothers, is sent off to the Jewish orphanage to be brought up as a young Englishman conforming to the manners and ideas of the older families, philanthropists who paid for the upkeep of the institutions. He forgets, or tries to forget, the Yiddish spoken at home and will talk only in English, and when he returns home occasionally for a day or a weekend he is embarrassed by the appearance and conduct of his brothers and sisters, and especially of old Moses who, for all his years in the Metropolis, seems as alien in appearance and habit as the day he stepped off the boat.

Unlike the orphanage, the Jewish Free School is not residential so that the process of Anglicanisation is less continuous and relentless, though none the less inexorable, and Esther, too, while never forgetful of her past, comes to think of herself as a daughter of Albion:

Esther led a double life, just as she spoke two tongues. The knowledge that she was a Jewish child, whose people had a special history, was always at the back of her consciousness. . . . But far more vividly did she realise that she was an English girl; far keener than her pride in Judas Maccabeas was her pride in Nelson and Wellington; she rejoiced to find that her ancestors had always beaten the French, from the days of Cressy and Poitiers to the day of Waterloo; that Alfred the Great was the wisest of kings, and that Englishmen dominated the world and had planted colonies in every corner of it; that the English language was the noblest in the world, and men speaking it had invented railway trains, steamships, telegraphs and everything worth inventing. Esther absorbed these ideas from the school reading-books. The experience of a month will overlay the hereditary bequests of a century.[30]

But it was to the Jewish world which she returned of an evening, the close, warm huddle of the ghetto. As she grew older she found it suffocating, but in her childhood it afforded her a necessary shelter against a bleak and hostile outside world, a world of barefoot urchins, carousing drunkards and bedraggled whores, where murderous gangs fought pitched battles in streets which the police feared to enter. This world was all about her, but the traditions and observances of Jewish life somehow formed a corridor through it, and came the Sabbath and the boisterous, murky East End receded into outer darkness:

The Ghetto welcomed the Sabbath with proud song and humble feast, and sped her parting with optimistic symbolisms of fire and wine, of spice and light and shadow. All around their neighbours sought distraction in the blazing public houses, and their tipsy bellowings resounded through the streets and mingled with the Hebrew hymns. Here and there the voice of a beaten woman rose in the air. But no Son of the Covenant was among the revellers and the wife-beaters; the Jews remained a chosen race, a peculiar people, faulty enough, but redeemed at least from the grosser vices – a little human islet won from the waters of animalism by the genius of ancient engineers.[31]

The picture depicted by Zangwill, after he had himself fled from the ghetto, was excessively sentimental and in some ways naive, but it was true in essentials. The Jewish drunk was not unknown, neither was the Jewish wife-beater, but the typical Jew was a good family man – to this all observers testify – good, indeed, to the point of being uxurious, and if the burdens he assumed on behalf of his family were such as to drive other men to drink, their very extent kept him sober, and so, of course, did the restraints of his faith. Judaism at once imprisoned and relieved. The drabness of weekday life was always cheered by the approach of the Sabbath and the seasonal festivals like Pentecost, the Feast of Tabernacles and, above all, Passover, where at the festive *Seder* meal every Jew was king for a night:

Simple Ghetto children into whose existence the ceaseless round of feast and fast, of prohibited and enjoined pleasures, of varying species of foods, brought change and relief! Imprisoned in the era of a few narrow streets, unlovely and sombre, muddy and ill-smelling, immured in dreary houses and surrounded with mean and depressing sights and sounds, the spirit of childhood took radiance and colour from its own inner light, and the alchemy of youth could still transmit its lead to gold. No little princess in the courts of fairyland could feel a fresher interest and pleasure in life than Esther sitting at the *Seder*, where her father – no longer a slave in Egypt – leaned royally upon two chairs . . .[32]

But as Esther grew older the alchemy no longer worked and the lead seemed leaden. She is a gifted and industrious child and eventually she becomes a pupil-teacher at the Ghetto school. There she is noticed by a childless patron of the school and adopted by her as one of the family. Her brother Benjamin dies in childhood, and the rest of her family leave for America to begin a new life in Chicago.

A friend and contemporary of Esther's, the son of their local Rabbi, is also able to rise from the ghetto with the help of a wealthy patron. Zangwill seemed to believe that escape was impossible without such outside intervention, but the institutions provided by the ruling Cousinhood of Anglo-Jewry, especially the Ghetto schools, were opening England to the newcomer. Sir John Simon, an eminent Jewish lawyer and liberal MP for Dewsbury, addressing a prize-giving at the Stepney Jewish School in 1881, spoke of the spread of anti-semitism in Europe. How, he asked, were Jews to meet such prejudice? He had a ready answer:

The first step was to educate their children in all the secular requirements of the day, teaching them their duty as citizens in the States to which they belonged, assimilating them in thought and feeling with the interests of the country in which they lived. It was not enough to profess a mere word of mouth loyalty to their country; they must learn to share all the aspirations of their fellow citizens, to take an active part in local matters as well as in the general affairs of the country, to take their place as legislators of the land or in the bodies which administered local affairs – in a word to discharge all the duties of citizenship, and to show their Christian fellow-subjects that, as Jews, they were imbued with the same English spirit which prevailed among their neighbours, and had a common interest in the country and community to which they belonged.[33]

Cardinal Manning was trying to inculcate precisely those same ideas among his Irish flock, but Simon and his fellows were rather more successful, and if the Jew newly arrived from Poland remained immured in the ghetto, his son had every opportunity to gain a foothold in the outside world, and to join the Jewish gentry of Kilburn and Hampstead, sometimes taking his ancestral faith with him, sometimes discarding it as an encumbrance. There was always a trickle of newcomers, but they were unequal to the number of fugitives and, given a few generations, Anglo-Jewry as a viable entity might have ceased to exist.

Then came the deluge.

# ELEVEN

# The Deluge

In March 1881 Czar Alexander II of Russia was assassinated. In the following months there were anti-Jewish riots in the province of Kherson, bloody pogroms in Kiev and Odessa and as the disorders spread to Poland, in Warsaw too. Before the year was over some two hundred Jewish communities had been subjected to murder, arson, pillage and rape. Some of the outbreaks were checked by the Russian authorities, others were disregarded, and in others still, local troops and police joined in the attack. Provincial commissions set up to investigate the causes of the outbreaks ascribed them to 'Jewish exploitation', and in May 1882 the government promulgated a series of laws which expelled Jews from many villages and towns at the western edge of the country and reduced whole communities to ruin. These events shattered Jewish hopes which had been raised during the comparatively liberal reign of Alexander II. A great exodus of starving and desperate Jewish families began.

As the first refugees arrived in London the Lord Mayor and the Jewish Board of Guardians set up a joint committee to raise funds and dispense relief. However, the Board became alarmed when it became clear that the emergency was not a temporary one, but would continue unabated. With the influx the Jews were bursting out of their confines between Aldgate and Commercial Street and pressing eastwards past Brick Lane into Mile End, northwards past Hanbury Street onto the fringes of Bethnal Green, southwards across Whitechapel Road and Commercial Road as far as Cable Street.[1] Beyond this a solid body of Irish dockers impeded further progress. But it became increasingly clear, even outside dockland, that the Jews were not wanted. The cry was heard that the country was being flooded with paupers and the volume of protest grew until it assumed the proportions of a mass movement whose sole aim was to halt the Jewish influx. One charge was that some thirty thousand foreigners a year were arriving in Britain, many of them, attracted by 'the well-known munificence of the wealthy English Jews, who are ever ready to help their poor brethren'.[2] The Jewish Board of Guardians, which consisted of many such people took the charges seriously. Letters were sent to leaders in Eastern Europe urging them to limit the exodus, and advertisements were placed in the Jewish press in Poland, Russia and Rumania warning against the hardships which faced the newcomer. The aged Chief Rabbi, Nathan Adler, warned that newcomers often found it impossible to support their families 'and at times they contravene the will of their Maker on account of their poverty. . . . Some have been ensnared in the net of the missionaries and renounced their religion . . . woe to the eyes which see and ears which hear such things.'[3]

The Board also tried to pass immigrants on to America and was told, even before the flow had gathered momentum, by the Hebrew Immigrant Aid Society of New York that it would accept no further immigrants from England unless the expense of their settlement was guaranteed. Money was found, but Congress passed a succession of Acts in 1882, 1885 and 1891 which restricted entry to the United States so that the flow to Britain increased further.

Early in 1885 Simhe Becker, a recent immigrant who had not risen far above the level of poverty himself, opened a rudimentary shelter for newcomers out of his own pocket. The Board of Guardians came to hear of it. Two of its grandees, F. D. Mocatta and L. D. Alexander descended for a tour of inspection and, not surprisingly, found the premises 'unhealthy'. Such 'a harbour of refuge', they declared, 'must tend to invite helpless foreigners to this country, and is therefore not suitable to exist'.[4] At the Board's instigation it was closed on sanitary grounds. There was a public outcry and towards the end of the year the shelter was re-opened in newer, more sanitary premises. Its sponsors, who included such eminent philanthropists as Ellis

Franklin and Sir Samuel Montagu, were careful to call it the Jews' *Temporary* Shelter, providing a maximum of two weeks' stay to immigrants 'who could prove that they had led respectable lives', and that in any case it offered only a roof 'and food that was little better than bread and water'.

Although the Jewish leaders did all they could to dissuade any more immigrants from coming to this country, their very names were an inducement. No name occasioned more hope in the heart of the Jewish poor than the golden name of Lord Rothschild, English head of the banking clan, and thus, so to speak, the Rothschild of Rothschilds. There was an unexpressed belief that one had only to reach England to share in its bounty.

The principal publicist of the anti-immigration group was Arnold White, who argued that part of the trouble with the Jews was their persistence in their Jewishness. 'Each immigrant foreign Jew settling in this country', he declared, 'joins a community proudly separate, racially distinct, and existing preferentially aloof.'[5] In this, he believed, they were different from the other immigrant groups who had made their homes in England. 'In the case of the Huguenots and Flemings the second generation was a negligible element, because in the course of thirty or forty years they blended with the native population.' It was, he felt, quite otherwise with the Jews.

> Orthodox Hebrew immigrants refuse miscegenation or assimilation, either with the Russians in Russia, with the Arabs in Tunis, or with the English in England, just as rigidly as did their ancestors with the Gentiles in the days of Nehemiah. That this repugnance to assimilate either with English or Russians, so far from being concealed or denied, is both conscientiously felt and openly expressed by the very flower of the people, and especially by the poorer Orthodox Hebrews immigrating into this country or even by those born in the second or third generation.[6]

This was largely true. Generally speaking, the poorer the Jew, the stauncher his Judaism. However, Socialist ideas had spread rapidly among the Jewish masses of the Pale of Settlement in the last decades of the nineteenth century, and especially in the Lithuanian and Polish provinces of the Russian Empire. Some of these Socialist groups later assumed a nationalistic form and they became the leading stalwarts of the Zionist movement. Others formed themselves into the Bund, a Jewish Socialist party, which envisaged Jewish political and cultural autonomy, based on the Yiddish language rather than Hebrew, within a Socialist Russian commonwealth. The readiness of Russian socialists and revolutionaries to applaud the pogroms disillusioned many Jewish radicals with socialism, without, however, necessarily reconciling them to Judaism. Many of them came to London, and if Arnold White opposed the inflow because Jews would always remain Jewish, others opposed it because, they believed, it meant the spread of anarchism.

During the 1890s there were further anti-Jewish enactments and pogroms in Russia. They were small in scale and scattered in incidence, but sufficient to maintain the mood of anxiety and fear. Then, in 1903, came the Kishinev pogrom which decimated a large and thriving community. Forty-nine Jews were slaughtered, over five hundred were injured, countless Jewish homes and businesses were burned and pillaged. Women were raped in front of their children. Over two thousand families were made homeless and destitute. At this the westward flow gathered momentum, growing inexorably from year to year, leaping from about seven thousand in 1894 to fifteen thousand in 1898 to over thirty thousand in 1904. The warnings given by Arnold White and others against 'Alien hordes' seemed finally to be coming true.

An anti-alien group calling itself the British Brothers' League was founded by a City businessman, Mr Stanley Shaw, and it quickly attained a membership of forty-five thousand. Shaw was not from the East End but he made the East End his main base of operations, and he had the eager support of Major William Gordon-Evans, the Tory MP for Stepney, Arnold White and Alderman James Silver, owner of one of the local papers, the *Eastern Post*, which maintained an almost hysterical tirade against the aliens. The first meeting of the League was held in May 1901 in the People's Palace, Mile End. More than four thousand people crammed the main hall and many others had to be turned away. Every Tory MP for East London was on the platform. Major Gordon-Evans, who presided, read a letter from Marie Corelli, the novelist, then at the height of her fame:

There is indeed something grossly unjust in an arrangement which permits useless, incapacitated or meddlesome sections of humanity to be promptly expelled as undesirable inhabitants from their own countries and landed on our shores. Our first duty is to ourselves and for maintaining our position with honour. British work, British wages and British homes should be amongst the first considerations of a British government.

Arnold White moved the first resolution 'that the housing problem in London is insoluble until the immigration of the foreign houseless poor is prevented'. He had, he said, visited the Russian Jews in their own homes in the Pale of Settlement and was convinced that they had not come here to flee from persecution, but 'because they wanted our money' – which brought cries of 'Wipe them out'. Why, demanded White, had not the Government taken action? 'I will tell you the reason. The people who invented key-money in East London belong to the race of whom the majority are poor, but of whom some are very, very rich ... and the very, very rich financiers hold the fate of nations in the hollow of their hands, and are very much against any measure such as you desire.'

Another speaker, Mr Henry Norman, MP, declared: 'This is England. It is not the backyard of Europe, it is not the dustbin of Austria and Russia.' If he had his way he would have a notice at the mouth of the Thames saying: 'No rubbish to be shot here.' It was Mr A. T. Williams, a member of the London County Council, who possibly drew the loudest cheers, his every utterance being greeted with cries of 'Shame' and 'Wipe them out!' Who was destroying Sunday? he asked. 'The Jews', came the cry; Who slept eight in a room? 'The Jews'. Who was debasing our national life? Who was corrupting our morals? 'The Jews!'

The rowdy catechism must have been embarrassing to at least one member of the platform party, Mr Harry S. Samuel, Tory MP for Limehouse and himself a Jew of East End origins. The British Brothers' League was careful to keep the word Jew out of its pamphlets and speeches. The euphemism was 'alien' and Harry Samuel rose to repudiate suggestions that the League was anti-semitic. Its policy was as vital to the Jew as anyone else, he argued, for unless immigration was restricted, the future boded ill for English Jewry. He closed by re-affirming his 'passionate adherence' to the Jewish faith.[7]

The *East London Observer*, which if less anti-alien than the *Eastern Post*, was hardly pro-alien, was disturbed by the vehemence and venom of what it called 'The Shrieking Brotherhood':

> In the last quarter of a century there have been many popular agitations in East London. . . . We do not, however, remember any agitation fostered by greater impropriety, or one having had a quicker descent to the gutter, than the anti-alien movement which has been promoted by the British Brothers' League. It is more than half based on ignorance, bolstered up by prejudice and is justified only by selfishness. . . . As the agitation against the Alien proceeds the more violent become the agitators, the grosser their exaggeration, the fouler their abuse. . . . Notwithstanding suspicious protestations to the contrary, we believe anti-alienism is anti-Semitism in both origin and conduct.[8]

The papers were full of letters on the subject. Perhaps the most damaging and mischievous letter came from some one signing himself Achi-Brith. It purported to be a defence of the Jews, its effect was quite otherwise:

> . . . let me say that I consider it to be a piece of downright audacity and impertinence for any body of British people – and especially the British Brothers' League – to attempt the entry into this country of so-called foreigners. If these British Brothers will read up the history of their country they will find that they themselves are the descendants of foreigners . . . who came across here in times past, and drove the ancient Britons to the hills of Wales. History is but repeating itself . . .
>
> What are the complaints against us? We make money fast. So do the English people if they get the chance. We overcrowd? So do the English and Irish in their own slums. We extract the greatest amount of rent that we possibly can from house property? If that is a vice it is one which has been copied with wonderful accuracy by some of the English landlords. We are dirty in our habits. Can you show me anything more disgustingly dirty than some of the slums in the Irish towns and villages? . . . We don't assimilate with the English people and speak their language? You will pardon me if I say that

we consider ourselves far superior to the English people. If the English government have this question seriously at heart, as you would have us believe, why don't they pass a restrictive measure? They dare not and they know it. The moment such a measure was passed, English credit would go down. You may rail at us as much as you please; but your government is dependent upon our people for its finances. You will, I hope, forgive me if I say that without the brains and intellect of our race the English nation would be nowhere. Who are the smartest, the brightest and most intelligent men on all your local boards – but the people of our race? We dominate the House of Commons; we dominate your daily and weekly press; we shall shortly dominate your local boards and your councils; we are strong enough, powerful enough and influential enough to spoil you if need be, as our ancestors spoiled the Egyptians. Our full power has not yet been put forth against you, but it will, if the necessity arises, and then God help England and the English people.[9]

The letter was a transparent fake. The very pseudonym 'Achi-Brith' was meaningless and the tone of the letter such that no Jew in his senses – certainly none who sought to vindicate his race – could have written it. The letter which appeared in the violently anti-alien *Eastern Post* was designed to cause a sensation and arouse anti-Jewish feeling and it succeeded in both.

Another source of mischief was a mysterious notice, which none could pinpoint but which a great many people claimed to have seen, declaring: NO ENGLISH NEED APPLY. Shaw was even inspired to write a poem on it:

O Spirits of bygone heroes! O souls of England's best!
Can ye in the grave find slumber, can ye in the grave find rest?

Whilst your sons with their wives and children,
Go forth in the winter's cold
At the bid of the stranger's children,
By the power of the stranger's gold.

List now, ye old time spirits,
List to the bastards cry.
In England, O Mother of Nations!
'No English need apply.'[10]

Shaw was challenged to say where he had seen such a notice but couldn't recall it. In desperation he advertised in the local press for anyone who had seen it.[11] None had, or at least none replied, but by then it had become an article of faith. Believing requires no seeing.

The British Brothers' League had the active, if unofficial backing of the Tory party constituency organisations in the East End, but it enjoyed the support of many Liberals too, including Sidney Buxton, MP for Poplar, and one of the most vicious attacks mounted against the aliens appeared in the Liberal *Daily News*:

> From personal acquaintance with those who live in the alien quarters of East London, I learn that these foreigners are the dirtiest creatures and the greatest liars to be found in the whole city. Mr Zangwill may be able to take joy in the domestic affections and the 'holy religion' of these pitiable wretches, but East London can get along without their virtues, and would be better morally and physically for deliverance from their filth and their sweating labour. . . . Let Mr Zangwill stand at the 'Three Nuns' Tavern, near Aldgate on a Saturday night, or take a walk through Houndsditch, and he will see more alien women walking the pavement than he will find in Regent Street or Piccadilly. . . . The English working man has his faults, but he has never fallen so low as this. And I venture to think it is better to be even a healthy, skull-cracking, purse-snatching highwayman than to learn the kind of civilisation and to acquire the moral and religious ideals taught by the daily lives of these unwashed, cringing, lying and wage-cutting aliens, who have elbowed thousands of Englishmen out of their homes and out of their employment.[12]

The *Pall Mall Gazette*, which on other issues had humane and radical sympathies, warned: 'that people in the East End here are maddened to frenzy by the filth, the insolence, and the depravity of this refuse of Europe which is being dumped at our doors'.[13]

There were warnings of impending riots and the fact that they never took place suggests that the local population was unduly quiescent, or that the 'squalor and crime', the superstition and vice, the insolence and depravity were either much exaggerated, or that where they existed the local inhabitants were less aware of them than the special correspondents. The nearest thing to an East End anti-Jewish pogrom, prior to the advent of Mosley, took place during the Jack the Ripper murders in 1888. There was occasional trouble as when a Jewish family tried to move into a street near the docks inhabited mainly by the Irish, as one can see from the following eye-witness account:

> On Sunday about three or four adult Jews and a number of children arrived in a large van to move in. As they did so the inhabitants began to pour forth from every doorway and speedily surrounded the van, climbed up the wheels and into the wagon and in a minute or two the unfortunate foreigners were in full flight down the street with a yelling crowd after them.[14]

The van and its contents were reduced to matchwood and the windows of the house were shattered. Such incidents were not uncommon and, as a result, the area south of Cable Street tended to be free of Jewish settlement. There were also frequent reports of individual Jews being assaulted, and the Jew fresh from Russia could be forgiven for thinking that he was a victim of anti-semitism. The outlandish garb, long beards and side curls of some of the more Orthodox newcomers tended to attract attention, and one party which had reached London via Kings Cross found themselves followed all the way to the East End by a rag-taggle of yahooing men, stone-throwing boys and barking dogs. But incidents involving actual violence were comparatively rare and one could believe that the extent of anti-Jewish feeling in the East End was exaggerated. One is even tempted to conclude that any animosity which did exist was largely stirred up by the press or outside groups like the British Brothers' League.

The BBL was led by outsiders and financed by outsiders, but it was clear from the moment it was launched that its policies had the enthusiastic support of the East End masses. It was helped by external events. The continuing setbacks suffered by Britain in the Boer War aroused a great deal of anti-foreign feeling, especially as the Boers were cheered on by every power in Europe. Nevertheless, the BBL's success was largely confined to the East End of London where it gave expression to deeply felt local grievances.

The grievances were many and varied. It was said that the Jews were dirty, immoral and lazy, that they accepted lower wages and paid higher rents and crowded the Englishman out of his job and his home. They were said to be sweaters and rackrenters; they were devious and without respect for law. Not all the charges were unfounded. In May 1884, before the inflow of aliens had become a torrent, the *Lancet* published a special investigation into the sanitary conditions of 'the Polish colony of Jew tailors', and it found that there were 'close upon 30,000 Russo-Polish Jews huddled together in districts that were already overcrowded', and that their presence had a serious effect on the social and sanitary conditions of East London. It gave some examples:

> In Emily Place ... we found five persons living in one room, while in another house we came upon a Jewish potato dealer who kept his wife, five children and a huge stock of potatoes all in one room measuring 5 yds by 6. There was one bed in the room and probably some of the family slept on the floor.

In Booth Street they found a tenement block with 230 rooms containing some seven hundred inhabitants:

> Here the closets were neglected, soiled and damaged to such an extent that they were ultimately removed to the yard to avoid infecting the houses. Now, however, the inhabitants, many of them foreign Jews, objecting to descend the stairs, simply threw the soil out of the window, according to the practice of the Middle Ages.[15]

The Jewish Board of Guardians took these charges sufficiently seriously to appoint its own corps of sanitary inspectors. This should have been done by the local authorities, but their inspectors were few and inspections infrequent. Moreover, many of the local councillors were themselves owners of insanitary dwellings, so that the sanitary acts were never enforced as effectively as they might have been. The Jewish Board of Guardians' efforts soon had results, and in 1887 it was able to report that 'slowly but surely the sanitary condition(s) of the districts in which the Jewish poor reside is being ameliorated'.[16] This was during a respite when immigration was reduced to a trickle. When the inflow quickened during the following years the Board was almost overwhelmed. There were outcries in the press about the dangers to public health which left the reader with the impression that prior to the advent of the alien the East End was a garden suburb.

There was an editorial on the question in one of the local papers which had the usual obligatory opening:

> We do not in any way share the strong feelings and prejudices of some of our correspondents in regard to the East End Jewish community. Anything like racial hatred is very far from our thoughts.

BUT

> there is the foreign and alien Jewish community whose manners and customs are a distinct menace to the public health not only of East London, but of the metropolis as a whole and the nation in general. Whitechapel, St George's East and parts of Mile End and Bethnal Green baffle description. Here huddle poor creatures who live in a state of semi-starvation; they eat the garbage of the streets, and live in rookeries and cellars. Their dwellings, if such they can be called, are shockingly overcrowded, and to such an extent that those wretched tenements are never empty of sleepers, whilst at night the stairs and passages are the only resting places for the poorest of them.[17]

If these were the living conditions, the working conditions were sometimes worse. Many private houses were used as workshops, and a reporter found eighteen adults working in the top room of a house, amid 'the heat of the gas stacks used for warming the pressing irons, and breathing an atmosphere full of woollen particles containing more or less injurious dyes'. In the circumstances, he concluded, 'it is not surprising that so large a portion of working tailors break down from diseases of the respiratory organs'.[18]

Such overcrowding was illegal, but there was widespread evasion of the Factory Act by both employer and worker, the latter being too glad to find work at all to worry about conditions. If an inspector appeared, workmen would fly to another room or the employer would pretend that he knew no English (which, indeed, was often the case); or he might claim that the extra

7a. Octavia Hill

7b. Dr. Barnardo

7c. Angela Burdett-Coutts

8. Wentworth Street, Whitechapel by Gustave Doré

people in the room were members of his family, and as often as
not he got away with it. The manager of one property in a routine
inspection of his dwellings found twenty-seven people bent over
machines in two small rooms rented as homes. In another room,
16 feet by 12 feet and only 7 feet high, he found twenty-one Jews
cross-legged on their beds, stitching and sewing.[19]

The slum workshop was not the only health hazard. There
were rag-pickers who brought their stock home, worked on
them, lived on them, slept on them, inhaling their decomposing
strands. There were herring picklers and gherkin picklers who
stored goods in their own homes and sometimes processed
them there.

A Whitechapel sanitary inspector had found a house in
Goulston Street in which twenty people lived.

> In a back room, inhabited by a foreigner named Cohen, his
> wife and two children, twelve fowls were feeding under the
> bed. In an adjoining room there were 127 fowls, and there had
> been in the same room 212 the previous week.

The stench from these, said the inspector, 'pervaded the whole
house'.

There was the Jewish penchant for fried fish so that at certain
times of the week whole streets were half hidden from view in a
mist of frying oil.

Then there was the matter of overcrowding. Give a Jew an
inch, it was said, and he put a bed in it; give him two, and he
took in lodgers. Dr Joseph Loan, Medical Officer of Whitechapel, declared that he knew of rooms occupied by ten or eleven
people. They were let and sublet, and sometimes even cupboards
were let as rooms. Everything, he said, was in a filthy state and
some of the newcomers did not have the most elementary ideas
of hygiene.

The administrator of one large housing estate in St George's
said he believed that the Jews came here 'on purpose to bring
fever and pestilence to England', and that he made it his practice
to evict them where there was any proof of overcrowding or
lack of hygiene, but it was, he said, a hopeless task. They crowded
into nooks and crannies which were never intended for human
habitation. In one unventilated cellar he found three beds with
eleven men, women and children sleeping there. 'If I am in one

F

street one week', he said, 'the other street at the other end of the
estate is as bad as the next. They are like rats in holes. If you put
in a ferret and drive them out of one hole, they go somewhere
else.'[20]

Dr Shirley Murphey, Medical Officer of Health for the London
County Council, was puzzled that in view of this the death rate
in Jewish areas was not higher.

> When I came to examine the death rates, which I had expected
> to find very high in view of the conditions of the houses and
> the prevailing conditions of the district, I found them very
> low. I was very much interested to learn how it was that
> people who were living in close courts and crowded alleys
> under conditions which I was accustomed to find associated
> with high death rates wherever I had looked in London, had
> a low death rate. . . . In the end the only conclusion I could
> come to was that the difference in the death rate was due to
> the better care the inhabitants took of themselves and their
> mode of life.[21]

He found that they looked after their children well, that they
had more regular habits of life than was usual in the area and
that they were abstemious. When it was put to him that 'their
wages would hardly admit of intemperance', he replied: '. . . when
people drink, however low their wages are, the money will go
for drink rather than for food.'[22]

The belief that Jews were lazy was entirely without substance
and may have been based on the fact that few of them were to
be found in the more arduous occupations. In the case of the
dockers, for instance, the gangs had, by the end of the century,
become virtual dynasties; and those jobs which were available,
were passed down from father to son, and few outsiders, certainly
few Jews, had a look in. In fact Jews worked rather too hard
and were too eager to get on, and it was this very eagerness
which was at the source of a more serious charge – that they
were a race of sweaters.

In 1887 a Board of Trade report declared that some twenty
thousand workers in East London could be classed as sweated
labour. About seventy-five per cent of them were 'recent arrivals,
and most of the rest were Jews of foreign extraction'.[23] Certainly
sweating was commonplace in those areas where Jews pre-

dominated, like the tailoring trade. A detailed examination of the trade was made by Beatrice Potter, who was one of Charles Booth's assistants in his work on the London poor. She found that in the large purpose-built workshops, where twenty-five or more people were employed, the conditions were comparatively pleasant. But the majority of workshops were small, employing ten hands or less, and it was in them that the worst excesses of the sweating system were to be found.

> The small employer seldom knows the distinction between a workshop and a living room; if he himself sleeps and eats in a separate room, some of his workers will take their rest on a shakedown between the presser's table, the machines and scattered heaps of garments.[24]

In such circumstances the employees might work for days on end without catching a breath of fresh air or a glimpse of the outside world. In the tailoring workshops, the very size of the presser's table and the machines meant an unavoidable minimum of space. Shoemakers and capmakers required nothing so bulky and their employees were often huddled together in cellars. The working day in 1892 was between thirteen and fourteen hours, but at busy times the men might help their masters by working longer hours without extra pay. The masters themselves worked as hard, if not harder, than their hands and extracted an only marginally higher livelihood. It was easy to become a master:

> His living room becomes his workshop, his landlord his security; round the corner he finds a brother Israelite whose trade is to supply pattern garments to take as samples of work to the wholesale house; with a small deposit he secures on the hire system both sewing machine and presser's table. Altogether it is estimated that with £1 in his pocket any man may rise to the dignity of a sweater.[25]

As a result of the intolerably long hours of work, ten thousand garment workers went on strike in 1889. They demanded a twelve-hour day, with an hour for lunch, a half hour for tea and the right to have their meals off the premises. They stayed out for six weeks, held rallies and parades, and at one point marched on the Great Synagogue in Duke's Place where Chief

Rabbi Adler was holding forth and demanded a sermon against sweating. Instead he gave a sermon against anarchism.[26] The workers finally won their demands, but this was before immigration reached its peak. The evils of sweating were to continue.

In 1888 the House of Lords appointed a Select Committee on Sweating which reported in 1890. It recommended, among other things, a more effective inspectorate, but family establishments composed of relatives were outside their survey, and some of the worst offenders operated fly-by-night establishments. Hardly were they traced to one place than they were at work in another. One of Her Majesty's Factory Inspectors described the conditions:

> The taskmaster and sweater is an unprincipled, loathsome individual, whose tyrannical methods and disposition are only equalled by his complete ignorance and open defiance of everything that is moral and humane. He is usually found in a basement or a garret, concealed from the outside world altogether. His workshop reeks with foul smells; the atmosphere is loaded with human visitation; the combustion from burning refuse and the emission of sickly fumes from cheap oil lamps and other implements of work, and from the process of manufacture, together with an absence of natural light, make this particular class of workshop a positive danger to the community. Here the alien is imprisoned day and night, and kept at work in a semi-nude state for a starvation allowance.[27]

Lionel Alexander, the Honorary Secretary of the Board of Deputies of British Jews, giving evidence before the Select Committee, said that the sweating system was neither as extensive, nor as bad as people made it out to be, but at its best it was bad enough. The most that the newcomers could have said in mitigation was that, in the words of one of Al Capone's henchmen, 'we only kill each other'. If Jews were the worst sweaters, then Jews were their worst victims, and Christians the principal beneficiaries.

John Burnett, Labour Correspondent of the Board of Trade, whose report on sweating, though biased against the alien, is a classic study of the subject, told the Select Committee in 1888 that about twenty thousand people were involved in sweating in East London, the great majority of them foreigners, and of the English element nearly all were Jews.

How was it that Jews were able to survive, even to thrive, in conditions which, it was said, would have stifled an Englishman or even an Irishman? It was not superior physique or stamina. A British general visiting the Poor Jews' Temporary Shelter at the turn of the century was impressed by the appearance of some of the immigrants. He had never seen such a fine body of men, he said. 'They were all well-developed, well-fed, big-chested, with legs like moulded pillars', but they were not typical.[28] The average Jew, as is evident from contemporary descriptions and pictures, was slight, short, bent and walked with a stumbling gait as if he carried all the burdens of exile on his shoulders.[29] He was not, perhaps, as slight as he looked, for he was sinewy and had perseverance, but what sustained him mainly were intangibles. First of all he took work and accepted conditions which others would not tolerate, because he had no alternative. If he was Orthodox at all, as were most of the new-comers, and wanted to be free on his Sabbath and festivals, he had to seek work from a Jew. And where he was not Orthodox the competition for jobs was such that no Gentile would have him. The Jewish sweater thus had a captive labour force.

Moreover, bad as things were for the newcomer in London, they were often worse in Russia, Poland or Rumania, and if his employer starved him he could always look for sustenance to a host of Jewish charities, ranging from the Board of Guardians, the Jewish Soup Kitchen, the Boot and Shoe Guild, the Coal and Fuel Society, the Grocery for the Poor Society, a Society for the provision of *Choles* for Shabbat, and many others. Where these did not suffice, there were charity handouts at the local synagogue on the eve of the festivals. His children were fed and clothed at school, and so long as they had enough Jewish parents were content with little for themselves.

The other factor was hope. It was not merely his material condition which depressed the Jew. Coming from the Pale of Settlement, where the prevailing mood was one of despair, he arrived in England full of optimism about the future. In the small bethel in which he assembled for prayers of a Sabbath morning, he could see men who came from his own part of Lithuania or Poland, still speaking Yiddish (unable indeed to converse in English) still conforming meticulously to Jewish observance, who had risen to the dignity of *Parness* or *Gabai* of the synagogue, and were dressed in frock coats and top hats, and had heavy gold-watch chains across their growing bellies, whose wives were clothed in silks and daughters in satins, and who ate white bread and fish even on weekdays. Here was the sort of eminence to which he could aspire, and if he could not make it, his son, possibly attending the Jewish Free School in Bell Lane, almost certainly would.

And then there was his religion. For six days he laboured, his frame weary with fatigue, his clothes bedraggled, his face begrimed, stopping now and then to snatch a bite of black bread or a piece of stale herring. On the seventh he was a different man; his body purged at the local steam bath, his suit pressed, his boots polished, he made his way to synagogue for prayers. Afterwards, as he returned home, the windows were alight with candles, doorsteps were scrubbed, doorknobs polished. Front rooms which might have served as workshops during the week were transformed, white *cholles* on white cloth, and silver *kiddush* cups and polished cutlery, salvaged from some distant moment of prosperity, and perhaps a bottle of raisin wine; all caught in the warm glow of the candles, the smell of candle-wax, floor polish and cooking mingling in the air. And then to a meal of fish and soup and chicken, and the inevitable compote of stewed prunes, and all he yearned for during the week of hunger, with course divided from course by *zemiroth*, table hymns, sung by the whole family with hearts full of gladness. The Orthodox Jew was king for a day. He starved himself for six days to have sufficient on the seventh, and the seventh seemed all the more regal for the privation he suffered on the previous six. But when he resumed his labours on the first he was a new man. The Sabbath was quite literally his recreation.

Not every Jew remained Orthodox and, as competition became more strenuous, he jettisoned one observance after another, but even where he ceased to believe in God he had a sneaking feeling that God still believed in him. Nor was his optimism always justified by his experience. Many innocent immigrants from Eastern Europe suffered great hardships and exploitation, working long hours for minimal wages. In this way the sweaters in dying trades like shoemaking were able to compete for a time with the machinery that was revolutionising the industry. But by the end of the century they were eliminated because the manufacture of shoes was concentrated in places like Northampton and Leicester. The tailoring trade was more fortunate. The subdivision introduced by the Jewish immigrant, and the ready labour, meant the introduction of cheap, mass-produced, ready-to-wear articles. These did not compete with the bespoke tailoring trade, where each man produced a complete and immeasurably superior garment for an entirely distinct market. But they virtually eliminated the old clothes market and the lower class tailoring trade which had been taken up by the Irish. They also competed with German manufacturers who exported their finished goods to England. A German journal of the period complained that the German mantle trade had contracted because of competition from the Jewish garment makers in England.[30] The 'ready made clothing trade is not an invasion of the employment of the English tailor,' Booth declared, 'but an industrial discovery'.[31]

But the people most immediately affected by the press of newcomers was the wave of immigrants who had come before, and who were beginning to think of themselves as *alte gessesener*, old settlers. They welcomed the newcomers – indeed were often instrumental in bringing them over – in one breath and resented them in the other, and the continued influx depressed wages. 'We always did get a wonderfully good living,' said an 'old settler' in the shoemaking trade, 'but since these foreigners have come here, they have got their little money, and they can go and manufacture their goods at such a low rate ... these little men work in cupboards; you don't know where they are.'[32]

If the sweaters came in for much justified opprobrium, their employers, the wholesale clothiers, did not. Of the eighty wholesale clothiers operating in London at the end of the century, only eight were Jewish. George Lansbury, the veteran Labour leader who spent much of his life in the East End, later observed: 'No one had any sympathy with sweaters and sweating, but everybody knew quite well that many British firms not holding the Jewish faith made huge fortunes buying up these goods and selling them at greatly enhanced prices.'[33]

A frequent complaint made about the newcomers was that they were killing the British Sunday. Petticoat Lane had always been regarded as a special licensed area for Sunday trading, but the street markets were spreading northwards to Bethnal Green and eastwards to Mile End, and a local paper felt compelled to voice the sense of outrage which, it said, was being felt by many Christians in the area:

> The suspension of labour on Sunday is more than a religious ordinance in this country; it is a sumptuary law, a social convention, which the older Jews, the Hollanders and the Germans, wisely regarded with respect. The change began with the inrush of Slavic Jews who were on a lower plane of civilisation. The evil of this insolent and defiant disregard for British convenances and customs is freely admitted by all that is best among our fellow citizens. Dr. Adler (the Chief Rabbi) assures the public that his community are as anxious as their Christian fellow citizens to safeguard the observance of the national day of rest.[34]

Because Jews were unable to work on Saturday, special legislation was sought and granted to give them the right to work on Sunday: a proviso was made that 'the workshop is closed on Saturday and is not open for traffic on Sunday'. The second part of this provision was found to be virtually unenforceable and not infrequently ignored. 'The streets of Stepney are precisely the same on Sundays as on weekdays', complained a factory inspector. 'This is one of the gravest symptoms against the Jews. The observance of Sunday has absolutely disappeared from the affected areas.' And he went on:

> While Britishers have extended unlimited and unconditional hospitality and freedom to members of the Jewish persuasion, the repayment consists of nothing less than defiance to what is to our countryman his most sacred possession.[35]

Nor, as the aliens became assimilated and the competition quickened, were they particularly scrupulous about their own Sabbath. Some Jewish workshops began to operate for seven days a week. It cannot be said that Sundays in East London were ever noted for their religious spirit, but this did not mean that Churchmen could watch with equanimity the wholesale profanation of the Sunday by newcomers.

Another charge against the Jews was that they were immoral and even depraved, and that they formed a particularly slippery criminal class, not brutal perhaps, not violent, but underhand. The Jew, wrote an observer in a survey sponsored by Toynbee

Hall, 'is inclined to the subterfuge of the timid. He rarely tries frontal attacks and his methods lead him to be suspected of duplicity.' He went on: 'He has few scruples and sometimes considerable ability in such matters as perjury and swindling . . . It is also well known that he is an inveterate gambler.'[36]

This last criticism at least was well-founded. It was the Jewish vice. Social observers described it, commentators remarked on it, Rabbis denounced it, none could change it. Wherever three or four Jews foregathered of an evening, it was over a game of cards. Gambling was to the Jews what drink was to the Irish, though it never quite assumed the scale to compel anyone to lead a crusade against it. It was at the source, as Mayhew observed, of the Jewish entrepreneurial instinct, so that no sooner was a Jew in regular employment with a steady wage and sound prospects, than he threw it all up to hazard his hand as a proprietor.

There was a large increase in the number of foreign prostitutes plying their trade in East London in the last decades of the century, and in the number arrested. The words foreign and Jewish were used almost interchangeably, but many of the prostitutes charged were in fact French or Italian. This did not mean, however, that none of them was Jewish. The number of Jews involved in white slavery and the number of Jewesses trapped as white slaves was a deep cause of concern and heartache to the Jewish community. Jewish prostitution was to an extent a byproduct of Jewish chastity. Among Jewish women, as amongst the Irish, there was no middle class of the merely libidinous, and if a girl was no longer a virgin she was fit only for the streets. This feeling was maintained by the closeness of family ties and the mutual supervision which went with it. But in the upheaval of mass immigration many young girls found themselves alone or among neglectful relatives; they were easy prey for seducers, and once seduced they were quite easily led into prostitution. In 1885 a number of leading Jews, headed by Claude Montefiore, formed the Jewish Association for the Protection of Women and Girls. They appointed officers to meet unaccompanied girls at the docks and established hostels to house them. The Association also helped to bring traffickers to justice. Some Rabbis were appalled by its work, not so much for what it was trying to do as for the adverse publicity it was bringing to the Jews. Montefiore had a ready answer for them!

If you persecute a people or community from generation to generation, you can produce on the one hand many heroes and heroines, but on the other hand, alas, you can produce some human scum, and when to persecution is added social poverty and evil housing conditions, it is hardly a wonder that a certain amount of this evil should exist.[37]

And he was proved right by events. When conditions improved, the evil gradually disappeared and the Association was able to wind up its work.

Yet another charge against the Jews was that they were depriving local traders of their livelihood, and this was not without substance. Butchers, bakers, grocers, publicans, all complained of this and the inspector in charge of the Riverside division of the Metropolitan Police declared that 'the foreign prostitute in my neighbourhood has practically driven the others away'.[38] Local shopkeepers were unfamiliar with the language and needs of the newcomers. Only a kosher butcher could provide the Jew with his meat. Only Jewish grocers knew his exotic tastes like smoked sprats and smoked buckling, smoked mackerel and smoked brisket, and the hundred and one varieties of salted, pickled, marinated and soused herrings, and the pickled gherkins. Similarly, the baker supplying the traditional English loaf lost his trade to the newcomers who could produce the black Russian Ryes, and the sweet and sour loaves, and the bagels and the pretzels, and the bulkes, and the cholas, and the yeast cakes the Jew ate with his tea, or the matzos to which he was limited on Passover. Publicans suffered too because although not all Jews were abstemious, the Jewish drinker had no taste for ale or porter, or even gin. He was used to the spirits and vodkas of Eastern Europe and where these were not available he was disposed to make his own. Some Jews had no idea that this was illegal; others guessed it might be but pretended not to know, and special posters were issued in Yiddish by the Jewish Board of Guardians:

WARNING

Immigrants who arrive in England are
strictly warned against persons who
offer them employment in connection
with the

MAKING AND SALE OF SPIRITS

These are trades which can in England
only be undertaken by persons authorised
by licence granted under the Revenue
Laws of this country, and any unlicensed
person who distils, or makes or sells
spirits,
IS LIABLE TO A HEAVY FINE OR IMPRISONMENT.[39]

The contraptions employed were usually makeshift and the resulting product was hardly more than pure alcohol, but it had a sharp kick and found a ready sale among immigrants. One man charged with keeping such a still was a dairy farmer in Ilford. He had a pot large enough to make eighty gallons of spirits a week which he carted to Whitechapel in milk churns.[40]

The exertions of the police cut down the traffic, but it did not drive the Jews into the pubs, and every East End public house became a centre of agitation against the immigrant. And the unrest increased, so that the Government felt compelled to act. In 1902 Prime Minister Arthur Balfour, whose name was later to be indissolubly linked with the emergence of the Jewish state, set up a Royal Commission on Alien Immigration. It was headed by Lord James of Hereford, a distinguished barrister and former Attorney General, and included Lord Rothschild; Gordon-Evans; Henry Norman, Liberal MP for Wolverhampton South; Alfred Lyttleton, barrister and Tory MP, who was shortly to become Colonial Secretary; Sir Kenneth Digby, Permanent Under Secretary at the Home Office; and William Valence, Clerk to the Whitechapel Board of Guardians and an authority on the Poor Law. Both Valence and Norman were of Jewish origin, which might have played a part in their selection, but Valence was a known restrictionist and Norman was a speaker at British Brothers' League gatherings.[41] Evans, of course, headed the whole anti-alien movement, so that the composition of the Commission was not entirely fair.

The critical issue which faced the Royal Commission, and which finally led it to recommend restrictions on further immigration, was overcrowding. The average population density in the whole of London at the end of the century was 54 per acre. In St George's, Stepney, it was 279·52. In Christ Church, Spitalfields, it was 286. And in Bell Lane, right in the heart of the Jewish area, it was 600.[42] The Medical Officer of Health for London, defining overcrowding as over two people per room, found that 84·5 per cent of all houses in Whitechapel were over-crowded. The actual situation was even worse than the figures suggested. Even the backyards were filled up with outhouses which served as workshops or dwellings and added further to the grimness of life.

The congestion was not due entirely, or even largely, to immigration, though the high – some said the phenomenal – Jewish birth rate had a lot to do with it. About the time of the mass Jewish influx many companies began to realise the com-mercial potential of the East End. It was well served by railways and roads; it was near the City and the docks; rents at first were comparatively low. Many homes were demolished to make room for factories and warehouses. Some of the breweries pulled down whole streets in the course of their continuous growth. The Model Dwellings being erected all over East London, which sought to reduce overcrowding, often made it worse. The Peabody Buildings, Whitechapel, for example, erected between 1881 and 1889, rehoused two thousand five hundred and fifty-nine people, but three thousand seven hundred and fifty were made homeless in the course of the demolition.[43] With the Jewish influx, there was a dramatic rise in rents, resulting in dramatic opportunities for quick profits. 'When a house is empty on a Saturday', complained an East Ender, 'a Jew tenant secures it on a Sunday, and then he charges even his own people £5 or £10 for key money if they want to rent it. The new tenant borrows the sum from a loan society run for the purpose, and in a week the place is full of a herd of them, often two full-sized families in every room and cellar.'[44]

In 1895 various Jewish philanthropists working through the Jewish Board of Guardians and headed by Lord Rothschild established the Four Percent Industrial Dwellings Company, which provided two- or – 'where the exigencies of the families should need the extra accommodation' – three-roomed tenements, in six-storey blocks at a reasonable rent.[45] They were similar to the tenement blocks erected by other charitable bodies such as the Peabody Trust, the Sutton Trust, the Guinness Trust. A reasonable rent was not, however, always within the means of prospective tenants who often accepted leases first and worried about paying for them afterwards. Then they sublet. Although both the charity trusts and the local authorities had sanitary inspectors there were not enough of them to prevent widespread evasion.

Rents rocketed everywhere in the East End, but they rose faster in the predominantly Jewish areas. In the circumstances the anecdote of Chief Rabbi Hermann Adler about the East End Jew who thanked God that his landlord was a Christian was less than amusing.[46] That such practices were against the tenets of their faith did not worry the landlords. 'When I go to synagogue I'm a Jew,' said one, 'when I come for my rent I'm a goy.'[47]

The newly-arrived Jewish immigrant was helpless in the face of the rack-renter. He arrived in London penniless, without any knowledge of language or craft. He had to find a home near the docks; employment which called for no ready skills, a milieu where there was no language barrier. All these were to be found only in the East End. He also needed a world not too remote from the one he had known – and that too was to be found in the East End. If he was religious – and he usually was – it contained all the necessary institutions, the *Beth Hamedrash* for himself, the Hebrew classes for his children, the ritual baths for his wife, the kosher butcher, grocer, baker, for his family. And even where he was agnostic he still needed the coffee houses and, indeed, the gambling dens in which to find company and spend his occasional free hours. The East End contained all these things. England beyond was too strange a place to encounter without a period of acclimatisation. The East End it had to be, and if he was rack-rented by his landlord, he rack-rented the tenants to pay for it. The fact that the indigent Jew had both a tradition of communal generosity and a host of charities behind him meant that in the last resort, if his own money would not run to it, he would be helped to keep a roof over his head, and as such he was much better able to compete with the indigenous pauper for the available space. This competition, of course, kept up rents.

But all this having been said, one should add that between 1881 and 1901 the population of the newly created Metropolitan Borough of Stepney, which included much of Jewish East London, increased by 5·7 per cent, while the population of

London as a whole increased by 7·3 per cent. But there was this important difference. The latter increase was due mainly to indigenous inhabitants, the former to the influx of foreigners. The alien population of Stepney had increased from sixteen thousand to fifty-four thousand three hundred, which included British-born children of alien parents. Also, while the population of Stepney increased by only sixteen thousand, the number of Jews increased by almost forty thousand.[48] Overcrowding was thus not perhaps the point at issue so much as the displacement of local population. More people might have been tolerable; what was intolerable was more Jews.

The Royal Commission on Alien Immigration called for restrictions and the Government placed a Bill before Parliament to give effect to its main provisions. The Liberals, then in opposition, fought the measure tooth and nail. Winston Churchill, Liberal Member for Manchester North West, poured scorn on the claims that the immediate exigencies of the situation made such legislation necessary:

> To judge by the talk there has been, one would have imagined we were being overrun by a swarming invasion and ousted from our island through neglect of precautions which every wise foreign nation has adopted. But it now appears from the Board of Trade statistics that all the aliens in Great Britain do not amount to a one hundred and fortieth part of the population ... Germany has twice as large and France four times as large a proportion of foreigners as we have. It does not appear therefore that there can be urgent or sufficient reasons, racial or social, from departing from the old tolerant and generous practice of free entry and asylum to which this country has so long adhered and from it has so often gained.[49]

Sir Charles Dilke, MP for the Forest of Dean, made a similar point, to which Gordon-Evans retorted that it was all right for him 'in the sylvan seclusion of the Forest of Dean' to philosophise on the traditions of England:

> Had he seen his friends and constituents driven from their homes and deprived of their work? Will he undertake to house 10,000, 20,000 or 30,000 foreigners in the homes of his con-

stituents ? . . . Sir, the open door is a very fine thing, so long as it's someone else's. [50]

The precedent of England's treatment of the Huguenots was frequently invoked as an example of hospitality repaying itself a hundredfold, and the prime minister, Arthur Balfour, felt compelled to put them in their historical perspective:

> The much quoted case of the Huguenots only meant this –
> that we had just been at war with Louis XIV, and were about
> to go to war with him again, and that there was a body of his
> subjects who disagreed with him and agreed with us whom
> we welcomed with open arms. That kind of policy this country
> always has had, and it did not mean any high standard of
> civilisation or any broad views on the rights of conscience. [51]

The Bill was passed in July 1905 with a majority of ninety and became law in January 1906, but this did not mean a complete end to immigration.

The Tories were routed in the General Election some months later and the incoming Liberal Government interpreted the act in such a way as almost to nullify it. The outbreak of war in 1914 brought the portcullis crashing down. It was to be raised a few inches intermittently to admit a handful of harried stragglers, but the old tradition of asylum was at an end.

# TWELVE

# Men at Work and Play

On Midsummer's Day 1896 His Royal Highness the Prince of Wales, accompanied by his wife and two daughters, opened the East London Trades, Industries and Arts Exhibition at the People's Palace in the Mile End Road. The whole of the East End had turned out to see him as he drove in an open carriage through Whitechapel and Mile End. The long, squat façade of the London Hospital in the Whitechapel Road was draped in crimson and gold. The Royal standard fluttered from the roof-tops while, outside, nurses and staff were, in the words of one reporter, 'grouped very picturesquely', so picturesquely in fact that His Royal Highness was said to have 'expressed very great pleasure at the sight of this company'. A little further, by the Trinity House almshouses, built a hundred years earlier for retired mariners, there fluttered a banner reading: 'The East End welcomes the noble owner of Persimmon'[1] – Persimmon, the Prince's horse having won the Derby a few days earlier, an event which stirred the entire realm, and especially the East End.

East London, especially after the notoriety brought by the Jack the Ripper murders, was regarded as the last redoubt of the hopeless, the helpless and the feckless, a city of dreadful night, and the exhibition was in part an attempt to show the other side of the picture, an assertion of local pride in its many skills, though there was perhaps a melancholy symbolism in the fact that the Thames Iron Works and Shipbuilding Company, Black-wall, whose numerous models of fully rigged men of war domi-nated the exhibition, was approaching its final years. Here they were, all built on Thames-side, the *Vasco de Gama* for Portugal, the *Pervenetz* for Russia, the *Sultan Mahmoud* for Turkey, the *Fujji* for Japan and other ships for other navies which in the coming decades would nearly all be at war with one another. But the congestion of the Thames, the growing size of vessels, the higher wages demanded by London workers compared with those in Scotland and the north, the distance from the raw materials all combined to make it difficult for ship-building to continue on the Thames. It could no longer compete with the Clyde. In 1911 the Government announced that it would not build any more iron-clads on the Thames. Two years later the Thames Iron Works folded and its highly skilled force of metal workers, ship-wrights, caulkers, riggers, fitters, carpenters and others was dispersed.

Other exhibitors included the Telegraphic Construction and Maintenance Company, who put a rather uninspiring coil of cables on display. There were safes from Rathner's, concertinas, pianofortes, and 'a new patent portable harmonium' from George Jones, and there were matches, tapers and boxes 'arranged with skill and taste' from Bryant and May.[2]

Bryant and May had been opened at Bow in 1861 and used a large female labour force, paying them wages ranging from 5/– to 18/– a week, with most of its hands at the bottom end of the scale. The girls had to pay towards the cost of the equipment used in their work and they could be fined sixpence a time for the slightest offence, like dropping a tray. They were compelled to take their meal at their workplace in an atmosphere laden with phosphorous, and many were disfigured by a consumptive dis-order known as 'Phossy-Jaw'.[3] Girls were also required to carry heavy loads on their heads and as a result suffered premature baldness. The low wages and harsh conditions finally became intolerable and in June 1888, in a spontaneous gesture the entire workforce of fifteen hundred girls went on strike. The men, who were mostly in supervisory roles and better paid, remained at work, but there was nothing for them to do and they were sent home.

This was the first strike in the history of the labour movement involving a large number of women, and it excited wide interest and much sympathy. The girls put together makeshift banners and their marches and rallies attracted large crowds. They were not organised in a union, so of course there were no strike funds; but help came from far and near and they were able to stay out for several weeks. Annie Besant, the social reformer, who was one of their leading supporters, addressed letters to the shareholders of the company after they had lately received a dividend of 20 per cent:

> How would you like to start your work at half past five a.m. and reach home again at seven p.m., having been on your feet nearly all the time, and after doing this for five days, with an additional half day on Saturday, to take home 11/2d as a reward? And if you did not reach the average, but only got 5/6d and had been at work for fifteen years, might you not say like my poor friend said to me the other day, 'I'm most tired of it'.[4]

On 16 July, the company, embarrassed by the persistence of the strikers, the length of the strike and the popular support it had engendered, finally capitulated and promised an all-round improvement in conditions and wages.[5]

The exhibition also contained, as a token presence, two hand looms, reminders that the East End had been a famous centre of silk-weaving. As we have seen, the years between 1812 and 1816 had been a time of distress, but in the following years the industry revived until there were about twenty thousand looms clattering away in East London, employing some fifty thousand people, with operatives earning as much as 25 shillings a week. Then, as free trade opened the ports to foreign silks, there came another decline. An 1832 petition to Parliament lamented that wages had been lowered to about 8 shillings a week and that even at this pittance not every weaver could find work.[6] Ten thousand looms were idle and thirty thousand men had been thrown out of work. Spitalfields, which manufactured the best quality of silk goods, was also badly hit by smuggling. By mid-century its plight was desperate, and Mayhew found highly skilled men earning less than 5 shillings a week. One weaver told him:

> The workmen are obliged to take the low prices, because they have no means to hold out, and they know if they don't take the work the others will. There are always plenty of weavers unemployed, and the cause of that is owing to the lowness of prices, and the people being compelled to do double the

quantity of work in order to live. . . . The cupboard gets low, the landlord comes for his weekly rent. The masters are all trying to undersell one another. . . . It's been a continuation of reductions for at least six and twenty years, and a continuation of suffering for just as long.[7]

The Irish went into hand-loom weaving after the English left it and suffered its final agonies.[8] Street collections were held for them, special appeals were made in church, and attempts were made to settle them overseas. By the end of the century what had been a major local industry had been reduced to a handful of small firms producing special silks.

As one moved on through the exhibition one found corks, bungs, shives, rings and cork helmets, aluminium castings, metal valves, coils of cables, cutlery, 'burglar-proof' safes and 'fireproof' safes, brushes and baskets, claypipes and broughams, floor polish and leather polish, medicines, surgical appliances, false teeth and a funeral car.[9]

The breweries, which are still very much in business, were well represented. Truman's was by then one of the biggest brewers in England. With its own cooperage, wheelwrights, farriers, carpenter's shop, paint shop, and artists' studio (for inn signs), it was almost a small town. It had a stable for 130 horses, but for all its great size and massive turnover, it employed a mere four hundred hands.

Watney Mann's Albion Brewery in Whitechapel Road also had huge stables and workshops and, like Truman's, had a small workforce. When Stepney was made a borough in 1900, Edward Mann, chairman of the company, became the first mayor. Charrington's Brewery was likewise a small employer. The larger the breweries grew and the more capital they consumed, the fewer men they engaged.

But they were good employers. An entry in Truman's minute book in 1865 reads: 'Agreed to allow William North a drayman 5/– a week for a year in order that he may go into the country for a change of air.'[10] Senior and middle-rank employees from supervisory grades onwards were treated with great, almost excessive generosity by most large employers, but it was unusual for a drayman to be handled with such care.

An industry which had been important to East London but which was virtually extinct by the time of the exhibition was the refining of cane sugar. The refineries were crowded together in and darkened the skies of St George's in the East. The largest, in Christian Street, had the tallest chimney in London and belched forth smoke at all times of the day and night. The men worked half naked in the intense heat, pouring the boiling sugar into moulds. The bakers were all Hanoverians because, it was said, only they could withstand the fierce heat which rose to a temperature of 140°F. However, the main reason was probably that the sugar companies were all German-owned and they preferred their compatriots as workmen. The bakers lived on the premises to guard against the ever present danger of fire – Matinau's, one of the biggest firms, was burned down twice in thirty years with a total loss of over £600,000. Wages were high and the men lived mostly on beef-steak which they washed down with huge draughts of beer supplied by the company; their average consumption was two gallons a day.

Unfortunately, such a happy state of affairs did not last. The introduction of beet sugar changed the manufacturing process and, after the 1860 Free Trade Act, French and Belgian loaf sugar flooded the country. The refiners of cane sugar were ruined.[11]

The largest and in some ways the worst employers in East London were the colliers and shipping companies using the docks. Their employees were at the mercy of winds, tides, treaties, wars, trade cycles and the continuing intrusion of new machinery.

For example, the coal-whippers who humped $2\frac{3}{4}$ cwt bags of coal from the dark holds of the colliers were badly hit by the growing volume of coal, hitherto sea-borne, which was being transferred to the railways. Whole gangs were thrown out of work without compensation as a result of this change. A local MP, Mr A. S. Ayrton, was scathing about the employers:

When these men get rich in the Tower Hamlets or Wapping, or the waterside, they go to live near the pleasant parks at the other end of the town, and have nothing to do with the poverty that has sprung from their proceedings. They go to live in those favoured regions where poor rates are trifling and leave the misery to others who are compelled to pay out of their incomes the just compliment of wages withheld from the working man.[12]

The coal-whipper was among the aristocrats of the waterside for their calling demanded a combination of precision and brute strength. He would raise the load of coal from the hold and then at a precise moment whip it from ship to shore. A false step and he was in the water or, worse, in the hold with broken bones. Earnings in the 1850s were sixpence a ton and in 1859 they struck for ninepence. They excited considerable sympathy and even poetry:

Oh ye whose bosoms heave with pity's sighs
Who mourn the wrongs which ye would fain redress,
Who list, with throbbing pulse and tearful eyes,
The stories of oppression and distress,
To you we cry, to you our grief express.[13]

Work, when it was available, came in fierce spurts and in a good week a man could make thirty shillings. Some small part of his wages went into a provident fund, but as the men were paid in pubs – often owned by the coal-factors – only a small part of their earnings ever reached home, even in the good weeks.

The growth of the West European ports brought hard times to the London docks, and in 1864 all except one of the companies along the north bank of the Thames were merged into two: the East and West India Dock Co., and the St Katharine's and London Dock. The exception was the Millwall Dock which required special power and skill on the part of the workers, its trade being largely in corn and timber. When the men went on strike in 1872 for higher wages the company imported strike breakers from the Essex countryside. These men – about eight hundred were involved – eventually settled down on the Isle of Dogs. The contractor, who was paid by piece-work, lived near the men and they formed a close knit community, cut off from the influences of the East End, and functioned almost as a cooperative. They were usually members of the same church, with their own clubs and provident societies. The regular men averaged about thirty-three shillings a week over the year, and even the casual men did not earn much less.[14]

The situation was quite different in the two main dock companies which employed over five thousand five hundred men, most of them casual labourers. The shift from sail to steam did little to alter the erratic nature of dock work, and as ships were becoming larger and more expensive it was necessary to turn them round without delay. This meant that frantic spurts of effort were followed by long spells of idleness. According to Beatrice Potter's account, a ship would enter dock in charge of a transport gang, and as soon as she was berthed, the men swarmed aboard and into the holds, running 'up and down like the inhabitants of an ant-hill burdened with their cocoons, lifting, carrying, balancing on the back and throwing the goods on the quay'.[15] At the timber wharves, as a result of continual friction, dockers developed a growth at the back of the neck like a giant collar-stud they called a 'hummie', which came in useful in balancing planks.

Loading was undertaken by stevedores employed by master stevedores and not by the dock company. Stowing goods was a skilled job and stevedores regarded themselves as a craft union. They were an exclusive brotherhood and, until 1963, anyone hoping to join them (other than sons of members) had to pay a fee. There were many categories of waterside workers, tea-sorters, wool-packers, coopers, granary corn porters, steamship workers, riggers, weighers, trimmers, cranemen, winchmen, and coal-heavers. However, the majority of men, the casuals, arrived early each morning for 'call', ready to turn their hand to anything. Amongst them was a group known as 'Royals' who, because of their greater industriousness or strength (or greater readiness to bribe the foreman), enjoyed priority over the mere 'bum casuals', the least favoured, most harassed and largest group in the docks. The earnings of bum casuals over a year might average out at about 3/6 a week. One could not feed a family on that in the latter decades of the century, and therefore they were dependent on the earnings of their wives, on poor law relief or charity, or on a bit of pilfering to make ends meet. Often they were involved in all four.

Most of the casuals were of Irish origin, a generation or two removed from their homeland but still recognisably Irish. 'The cockney-born Irishman', wrote Beatrice Potter, 'as distinguished from the immigrant, is not favourably looked upon by the majority of employers. In a literal and physical sense the sins of the forefathers are visited upon the children, intensifying the evil of a growing Irish population.'[16]

Miss Potter found the system utterly demoralising:

> Rise early and watch the crowd at the St Katharine' or the West India gates. The bell rings, the gates open, and the struggling mass surge into the docks. The foreman and contractors stand behind the chain, or in the wooden boxes. The 'ticket men' pass through, and those constantly preferred are taken on without dispute. Then the struggle for the last tickets. To watch it one would think it was life and death to those concerned. But Jack having secured a ticket by savage fight, sells it to needier Tom for twopence, and goes off with the coppers to drink or to gamble. . . . The honest worker, not yet attracted by the fascinations of East End life, will return to his home with a heavy heart. There he will mind the baby while his wife seeks work . . .[17]

The casual system was a godsend to the men with a casual attitude to life, the men who liked to work when the mood suited them, to rest when it didn't, to lounge around, gamble, drink, or even sleep, and keep their wits ready for any dubious act which might bring in a quick shilling. They tended to pass on their disposition to their children and there emerged a class of hereditary casuals:

> These men hang about for the 'odd hour' or work one day in seven. They live on stimulants and tobacco, varied with tea and bread and salt and fish. Their passion is gambling. . . . They have a constitutional hatred for regularity and forethought and a need for paltry excitement. They are late risers, sharp-witted talkers, and, above all, have that agreeable tolerance for their own and each other's vices which seem characteristic of a purely leisure class whether it lies at the top or the bottom of society. . . . Socially they have their own peculiar attractiveness; economically they are worthless, and morally worse than worthless, for they drag others who live among them down to their level. They are parasites eating the life out of the working class, demoralising and discrediting it.[18]

The existence of this mass of unskilled labour, plus the many grades into which the skilled hands were divided, made it difficult for them to act in unison to improve their conditions and raise their wages. The fact that they were often Irish or of Irish origin made it even more difficult – if not impossible. But the impossible was achieved by Ben Tillet, himself of Irish origin, a thin, ascetic, rather scholarly man, who worked in a tea warehouse. But in 1889 he managed to bring all the waterside workers in all their variety out in one concerted strike. It proved to be a watershed both in the history of the docks and the trade union movement.

It began on 13 August over a small local issue – a dispute over the bonus payments for handling difficult cargo in the South West India Dock. Tillet, backed up by Tom Mann and John Burns, his associates in the Social Democratic Federation – the forerunner of the Labour Party – organised meetings at the dock gates. Within a week his tiny Tea Operatives and General Labourers' Union was reorganised into the Dock, Wharf, Riverside and General Labourers' Union. One of its first acts was to send out a strike call to all its members and by 20 August the docks were at a standstill and the great Port of London, for the first time in its history, was closed to shipping. The strikers' basic demand was a minimum of 6d an hour – the 'dockers tanner' – regular hiring to avoid the savage early morning battle for jobs, and the abolition of contract work.

The newly formed union had only a scratch organisation and 7/6 in strike funds, but money came pouring in from other working men at home and abroad and from places as far away as Australia. By the end of the month they had nearly £50,000,[19] and were able to offer relief tickets to strikers' families. They held frequent marches to maintain their spirits and keep their case before the public, now along the riverside from Tower Hill, now through the City and into the West End with banners held high, and fife and drum playing. They had help from local churchmen and from Toynbee Hall. Karl Marx's daughter, Eleanor, acted as an honorary secretary to the strike committee. Tillet complained that they had an embarrassment of helpers, and 'some of them had to be firmly told to quit'. At first the strike was slow to have an effect but after nearly a month, when the whole economy of the country seemed threatened with paralysis, the Lord Mayor of London set up a conciliation committee consisting of Sidney Buxton, a dockland MP, Bishop

Temple and Cardinal Manning. Most of the dockers were Catholic and Manning's role proved to be crucial. The authority attaching to his office, his own personality, the saintliness of his bearing and sincere concern for the working man impressed Tillet and his fellow strikers immensely, even where they were agnostic or, in some cases, anti-religious:

> The meeting at the Catholic schools in Poplar will be ever remembered by me for what it meant. The old man bent with his years, saintly and almost bloodless, his tall figure stooping while his hands rested on the school desks, age appearing to have vanished almost as his eyes looked steadfastly at the crowd of men brought together to listen to what he had to say after he had acted as the 'go between'.[20]

Differences were resolved, the docker got his tanner and even more important, as Tillet believed, he gained a new standing:

> From a condition of the foulest blackguardism in directing the work, the men found a greater respect shown them; they too grew in self-respect, and the men we saw after the strike were comparable to the most self-respecting of the other grades of labour. The calls worked out satisfactorily ... the work was better done; the men's lives were more regular as their work was – the docker had in fact become a man.[21]

But the unity and euphoria did not last. A few years later Tillet was complaining with despair that the Port of London was the great unmanageable. The very militancy of the dockers and the high wages they earned meant that shipping was often diverted to other ports and that the introduction of new machinery was speeded up. Nor had the unions established themselves as effectively as they thought.

In 1910 Tillet led his dockers into united action with other transport workers and formed the National Transport Workers' Federation. In London the Port employers headed by Lord Davenport and the Port of London Authority refused to recognise the Federation, and a series of conflicts ensued which came to a head when the Thames lightermen went on strike against the use of non-union labour. Tillet called out the rest of the port in sympathy, but the employers had prepared themselves for this

and brought in outside labour. Tillet, addressing a rally on Tower
Hill, asked his men to remove their hats and join in prayer asking
God to 'strike Lord Davenport dead'.[22] The prayer remained
unanswered and, after the strike had dragged on for two months,
it collapsed.

The First World War brought many benefits to the docker,
and a body of men hitherto regarded as feckless ne'er-do-wells,
or revolutionaries, were suddenly cherished as part of the nation's
front line. Many of them flocked to the colours, and for a time
the casual vanished from the docks. Demobilisation brought
them back but there were periods during the inter-war years
when over a third of the dock labour force was out of work.

A great gulf divided the rank and file of casual dockers from
those who had secure employment in the management structure,
even at its humblest level. Beatrice Potter noticed this already in
1887:

> The foreman is distinctly the official. Directly the day's work
> is over he hurries from a disreputable neighbourhood back
> into the odours of respectability which permeates a middle-
> class suburb. There, in one of those irreproachable houses
> furnished with the inevitable bow window, and perchance with
> a garden, or at least with a backyard wherein to keep and ride
> his hobby, he leads the most estimable life.[23]

The permanent labourer, too, were tending to move eastwards
into Forest Gate or West Ham. What remained was a solid,
inbred, working-class community. They were cheerful, stoical
people, ready to help each other, inclined to roister and riot at
times, but not devoid of respectability, as one can see from the
following recollection of a woman brought up in the heart of
dockland in the early years of this century:

> Our house was one of a long terrace of houses stretching out
> in an endless procession as like as peas in a pod, with no
> individuality whatever. Each front window was draped with
> lace curtains looped back sufficiently to reveal an aspidistra in
> an art pot. . . . Each front door was exactly like its neighbour.
> The street was deadly monotonous in appearance . . . the
> houses were huddled so closely together that there was little or
> no privacy at the back, and with only a small patch of dried-up

earth enclosed within a five-foot brick wall, which not even the most confirmed optimist would call a garden, we lived cheek by jowl with our neighbours, for ever looking out upon the world of bricks and mortar.[24]

The back garden, or rather backyard, was a depository for everything which could not fit into the small house. It might contain zinc baths, copper boilers, clothes lines, washing boards, rabbits, racing pigeons or chickens, and sometimes a man might even try to coax a plant out of the sunless, reluctant earth. Children would play in the streets, for the traffic, though noisy, was slow.

There was something constantly buoyant about the waterside parishes in spite of their poverty, due possibly to the proximity of the river, the presence of ships and sailors, the chandlers' shops, the rope makers and the canvas makers, the smell of tar and Thames-side mud, the hint of distant places. The tangy flavour of the area was beautifully caught in the novels of W. W. Jacobs (for many years a Thames-side clerk) as, for example, in this extract from *A Master of Craft*:

A pretty girl stood alone on the jetty of an old-fashioned wharf at Wapping, looking down upon the silent deck of the schooner below. No smoke issued from the soot-stained cowl of the galley, and the forecastle and the companion were both inhospitably closed. The quiet of evening was over everything, broken only by the whirr of the paddles of a passenger steamer as it passed carefully up the centre of the river, or the splash of a lighterman's huge sweep as he piloted his unwieldy craft down the last remnants of the ebb-tide. In shore, various craft sat lightly on the soft Thames mud; some affecting a rigid uprightness, others with their decks at various angles of discomfort.[25]

Away from the river the scene became more sombre. From the end of the nineteenth century until after the Second World War, when a writer sought a scene of degradation and squalor, he tended to set it in the East End.

Perhaps the most famous of the nineteenth-century novels with such a setting was Arthur Morrison's *A Child of the Jago*, written in 1894. The novel is short and intensely moving, partly

because it is told with great narrative skill, but mainly because
it mostly rings true. This, one feels, is a corner of East London
as it was. 'I resolved', said Morrison, 'to write *A Child of the Jago*
in which I could tell the story of a boy who, but for his environment, would have become a good citizen.[26] The child was Dicky
Perrot who lived in a mean warren of streets called the Jago.
His mother, Hannah, was a boilermaker's daughter, of good
artisan stock, but Josh, her husband, is a weak lout whose intelligence does not rise above the level of cunning. A former plasterer,
he has been unable to hold on to his job, and we find him at the
outset amid the squalor of the Jago, doing an occasional day's
work, but more usually involved in robbery, and sometimes
robbery with violence. Dicky soon falls into his ways and enters
upon a career of crime by stealing the gold watch of a bishop who
has descended on the East End to open a welfare mission. His
father belts him for the exploit and goes off to sell the watch,
and drinks the proceeds.

On most nights Hannah and the children are left on their own
in their wretched room:

> A little heap of guttering grease, not long ago a candle-end,
> stood and spread on the mantelpiece, and gave irregular light
> from its drooping wick. A thin-railed iron bedstead, bent and
> staggering against a wall, and on its murky coverings a half-
> dressed woman sat and neglected a baby that lay by her,
> grieving and wheezing.[27]

The baby is small and backward, and only Dicky is prepared
to give it affection or attention:

> He sat on a small box, and rocked the baby on his knees,
> feeding it with morsels of chewed bread. The mother, dolefully
> inert, looked on and said: 'She's that backward and I'm quite
> wore out; more'n ten months old and don't even crawl yet.'[28]

Hannah, though fallen into the Jago, was not yet quite of it.
'She had soon grown sluttish and dirty, but she was never drunk,
never quarrelled and never gossiped freely. Also her husband
beat her but rarely, and then never with a chair or a poker.
Justly irritated by such superiorities as these, the women of the
Jago were ill disposed to brook another: which was that Hannah
Perot had been married in church.'

Thus, when a quarrel broke out in the Jago, she was apt to be picked on by both sides, and once during a fight between the feuding Learys and the Ranns, she is savaged by one of the Leary harridans. Looey, the baby at her breast is also injured and, a few days later, it dies.

'Hannah felt a listless relief'; Josh felt nothing in particular and took his wife out for a drink to cheer her up. Dicky left alone with the dead child, 'spread about it with outstretched arms, exhausted with sobbing, a soak of muddy tears. "Oh Looey, Looey! Can't you 'ear? Won't you never come to me no more?" '29

Police rarely venture into the Jago whose inhabitants are mostly left to kill themselves and the only intruder from civilisation is Father Sturt, whom they regard with a mixture of affection and fear, as if he might invoke some dark, unearthly force against them.

Sturt is planning to build a church right in the heart of the Jago, but is more immediately interested in the young. Dicky has by now become an expert thief and Weech, a pillar of the church and café-owner, who is also the neighbourhood fence, a mixture of Fagin and Uriah Heep, regards him as one of his most promising suppliers. Sturt intervenes, however, and finds Dicky a job as an errand boy with a local tradesman. He is hard working, imaginative, intelligent, and applies himself with cheerful eagerness. Here at last is a child who might escape the Jago but, through the treachery of Weech, he is wrongly accused of theft and dismissed, and he returns to his old ways and old haunts, trapped. At seventeen he is stabbed in a gang fight and dies.

Morrison was accused of sensationalism, but the Jago was based on a warren of streets in Bethnal Green called the Old Nichol, home of a notorious pack of cut-throats known as the Old Nichol Gang, who were active in the 1880s and who were thought at first to be responsible for the Jack the Ripper murders. Bethnal Green had been the most poverty-stricken part of the East End ever since the decline of hand-loom weaving and the Old Nichol was its most squalid corner. And much of the substance of the book, which was thoroughly researched, was based on the work of the Reverend A. O. Jay, Vicar of Holy Trinity, Shoreditch, who appears as Father Sturt in the story. John Reeves, a School Attendance Officer in the area, wrote that 'there was scarcely a family but appeared to have some reason for fearing the police, and many of the men were on ticket of leave'.[30] Overcrowding was appalling. One house of ten rooms in Old Nichol Street held ninety people. Stairways were dark, doors and windows were broken, the noise was appalling, and the stench poisonous. In 1889 its death rate was forty per one thousand, double that of Bethnal Green, which in turn was double that of London as a whole.[31]

An equally celebrated and very sentimental East End novel of the period was Sir Walter Besant's *All Sorts and Conditions of Men* published in 1882. The novel, which tells the story of an heiress who works in Stepney, was a best seller and touched the hearts and purses of England. It does not have the ring of truth of *A Child of the Jago* and, indeed, one has the impression that Besant made a number of hurried excursions into the area, took the air, did not like it and fled. He thought of it as a place without roots, without history, without sense of locality; whereas of course it had all three. A garrison, he felt would have given it pride in the martial virtues, a greater patriotism, but there was a garrison on the fringe of the East End in the Tower of London, and it brought good trade to the whores of Ratcliff Highway. As for patriotism, there was hardly a corner of the British Isles where it was stronger, as was shown by the jingoism engendered during the Boer War and the First World War, and by the rush of volunteers to the colours whenever a shot was fired.

Nor was it the wilderness he imagined – if only for the oases provided by the many churches scattered about the area, and the warmth, dedication and zeal of the men who worked in them.

(A secondary, though not insignificant factor was the point that the clergy were often among the few people of substance in the neighbourhood who were not in the drink trade. In 1908, by which time the East End was, comparatively speaking, a much improved place, the borough of Stepney, with a population of three hundred and ten thousand, had only three hundred and forty-nine rate-payers whose rental qualified them for a place on the roll of jurors, and, of them, one hundred and fifty-four were publicans. In St George's, twenty were qualified, and thirteen were publicans. In Shadwell seven qualified – *all of them publicans*.)[32]

Not every East End cleric was a saint. There was, for example, the Reverend Mr Lee, Vicar of St Philip's, Stepney, who fled the country in 1853 to dodge his creditors (and had his church living sequestrated for four years to pay them),[33] or the more serious case of the Reverend James Bonwell, Vicar of St Phillip's, who was unfrocked for fathering a bastard child. (What was perhaps more remarkable than the facts of the case was that he continued to minister to his parish after they became known and contested the disciplinary action taken against him right up to the Judicial Committee of the Privy Council.)[34] Reuben Seddon, a Congregationalist Minister, a father of four children, who was involved in a similar case, had better luck in the courts but was disowned by his church.[35] And there was the Poplar curate who abducted the fifteen-year-old daughter of a parishioner.[36]

Apart from actual scoundrels there were also the occasional dotards who thought they had done their duty to God and man by preaching on occasion to an empty church, but what must impress any student of East End life was the extraordinary number of men, and women (the wives sometimes bore the most grievous part of their burden), of all denominations who devoted their lives to the rather thankless task of bringing Christianity to East London. It cannot be said that it became a holy city as a result of their efforts, but one dare not think how much worse it would have been without them.

There were the Catholic priests and nuns who ventured into cholera-stricken households to bring aid to the sick and comfort to the dying and who, not infrequently, succumbed to the disease themselves. (There is the well-known story of the old Irish woman who, upbraided for summoning a Protestant vicar to her sick husband's side, replied: 'but Father, he was down with the plague, and sure I didn't want a dayscent man like you to catch it.') There were many tributes to their selflessness:

Duty! That magic word – that war-cry of Catholic priests – the ensign round which they rally; and despite persecution, ingratitude, incompetent means, and every other obstacle, perish or conquer, no matter which. Careless of the world's smiles, heedless of its frowns, sympathising with, yet above its petty sorrows, they press onwards, until a blighted youth or toilsome old age is rewarded by the martyr's crown and a glorious eternity. Such are the Priests of God's church . . .[37]

These words from a Catholic magazine give the impression of rather too stern and godly a group, descending from on high to minister to the faithful, whereas they were an integral part of the community they served, reproving, chastising, sometimes bullying, but enriching. Theirs, to an extent, was an easier task, for they worked mainly among believers, and even the Irish non-believer had a sneaking reverence for the cloth. Anglican clergy, in that sense, had a far tougher task, but they persisted, and sometimes with remarkable results.

There was the Reverend Osborne Jay, the original of Morrison's Father Sturt, who held services in a disused stable right in the heart of the Jago.

If Jay had a fault it was his excessive faith in churches. A Bishop of London, Dr Bloomfield, in anticipation of a religious revival which never came, had built twelve churches in Bethnal Green – presumably because there were twelve apostles. There was thus no shortage of church building in the area, but Jay regarded the actual building of a church as symbolic of the heights to which a community aspired. With the help of pennies gathered from the poor and larger sums elsewhere, he finally built Trinity Church, and beside it a model lodging house where, for 4d a night, a man could be assured a clean bed and the privacy of a cubicle. He also held Sunday afternoon services which attracted large crowds of costermongers, casual labourers, unemployables and unemployed. They were informal occasions where men might sit and smoke a pipe, but they listened and prayed.[38] It was Jay, also, who was instrumental in having the slums of the Old Nichol surrounding his church demolished and model dwellings raised in their place.

In many cases they were about the only people with any education or culture in their parish, the only people to whom parishioners could turn for guidance or advice, for help with the police or authorities, or when some legal problem arose. And their presence encouraged others who might have had sufficient education to feel that they were above the level of their neighbourhood, to tarry and not to move out. The cliques they formed may have been inbred and sometimes sanctimonious, but they were at the source of every endeavour to raise the level of life in the area. They ran day schools and night schools and ragged schools and Sunday schools; they organised choral societies and floral societies and literary societies, and their small local efforts perhaps bore more fruit than grander designs. The People's Palace, a great cluster of buildings, was hardly built before it was found to be a costly embarrassment, as passing enthusiasms turned to stone often are.

Early in the nineteenth century, Barber Beaumont, painter, engraver, architect, economist who founded the County Fire Office and designed it, sought to bring enlightenment to the East End with the creation of the Philosophical Institute in Mile End. He spent £20,000 on the building and library and gave it a further £13,000 in endowments. At first it engendered some enthusiasm and interest, but the trustees were more intent on preserving their capital than in putting the institute to effective use and it languished for several decades. Then the Drapers' Company, a generous benefactor of East London, bought it with the idea of incorporating the proposed People's Palace.[39] This scheme, launched at a great meeting in the Mansion House presided over by the Lord Mayor and in the burly presence of the Prince of Wales, aimed at creating:

> an institution, in which, whether in science, art or literature, any student may be able to follow up his education to the highest point by means of Technical and Trades Schools, Reading Rooms and Libraries – in fact that the Palace may become the University for East London; but whilst offering such facilities for education, the trustees also desire to provide for those who wish simply for social enjoyment, and to this end propose to establish the Winter Garden, Concert Hall, Recreation Grounds, Gymnasium and Swimming Baths for both sexes, and room for indoor games . . .[40]

The first part of the aim was fulfilled, for in 1896 its educational side was merged with the Bromley and Bow Institute (a centre for adult education) to form the East London Technical College. In 1905 it became the East London College (later renamed Queen Mary College) and a constituent of London University. The second aim, to make the People's Palace a place for social enjoyment, was not achieved for the simple reason that the trustees' idea of delight and fun was not that of the East End. For one thing, it was unlicensed. One could have coffee or tea, but a man couldn't drop in with his friends of an evening for a glass of beer. Sunday was the East End working man's only free day and on that day it was closed. When the Reading Room was opened on Sunday the Working Men's Lord's Day Rest Association protested.[41] Then, again, the building was far too imposing to be regarded as a place of ease and entertainment by the working man. It was the sort of place which called for polished boots and a collar and tie, and a well-pressed suit. It was grand without being flamboyant, a cross between a cathedral and the palm court of a south coast hotel. Perhaps it was the presence of the massive organ in the main hall that gave the Palace its church-like atmosphere. Whatever it was, working men stayed away from it even as they stayed away from church. There were occasions in the year when fairs and circuses, horse shows and donkey shows and military tattoos were held on ground adjoining the Palace and these were well attended. But the fun side of the Palace atrophied as the educational side grew, until it was reduced to a mere concert hall, and even as such it was barely used.

When it was burnt down in 1931 it seemed like a mercy. There rose from the ashes an Odeon-style edifice which promised to bring new life and zest to the East End,[42] but it hardly opened its doors before they were closed by the war. It was one of the few major buildings in the area to survive the blitz, which was regarded by some as further proof that the Germans would stop at nothing to undermine public morale. It was refurbished and re-opened after the war with a gala performance of *The Beggar's Opera*. A season of plays followed, which brought a trickle of visitors from the suburbs but almost no one from the neighbourhood, and a paper complained that poor attendance was due to 'highbrow plays which East Londoners do not want, instead of light entertainment which they do'.[43] The Governors tried music, ballet, light opera, Gilbert and Sullivan, concerts, films, without avail. The Palace continued to lose money even though it was an outright gift to East London and paid no rent. Finally, it bowed to the inevitable and in 1953 the last facility 'for social enjoyment' was sold to Queen Mary College for £95,000.[44]

The College, on the other hand, continued on an unbroken course of expansion and progress, and is now a major institution of international standing. But it is a College of London University which happens to be located in the East End, rather than an East End College. There are attempts to recruit staff who, if not living in the locality, were at least born there, but the student body is as polyglot a bunch as in most other colleges of London University. Few are from the neighbourhood, and as the College is non-residential the students add little to the life and colour of the place. The area does not even derive much from the buildings. They form a drab collection, much asphalt, much glass, no imagination, no grass, and were plainly erected on the principle that the East End can take any heap of masonry. It is quite the ugliest campus in the British Isles, and might well claim to be the ugliest anywhere.

It is questionable how many other institutions launched for the benefit of the East End brought any benefit to it. The Whitechapel Art Gallery which Barnett opened in 1901, and which still flourishes, attracted large crowds to its annual exhibition, but the pictures of some of these crowds, the parasols, the hats, the whole attire, suggested Kensington rather than Stepney. And so it has been almost to this day. The more the reputation of the gallery grew, the less it had to do with its neighbourhood, and gradually what was intended for the East End was given over to the West End. Its previews became festive occasions reported in the gossip columns and the glossy magazines, but any East Ender who might have strayed into one of its exhibitions, went out blinking. The gallery did not reflect the life of the East End, nor anything in which the East Ender could conceivably be interested. It is only in the past year or so that the gallery has, so to speak, reverted to the people. Exhibitions like *This is Whitechapel*, a display of photographs of East End life, attracted considerable local interest and local crowds. A later exhibition, held in the summer of 1973, of trade union banners, attracted crowds from all parts of town.

The one area where the benefits provided for East Enders were undoubtedly beneficial was in the provision of open spaces. (Though even these occasioned fear in some minds. A Spitalfields Priest, addressing a meeting of parents, warned them of 'the dangers to which the children were liable in the summer months in the attractions of parks and other places by which they mixed in the most dangerous occupations which became the occasion of many mortal sins'.)[45]

The very names of the East End neighbourhoods conjure up visions of rustic idylls – Bethnal Green, Spitalfields, Poplar. It had occasional moth-eaten patches of green, usually round the church yards but no large open area until Victoria Park was laid out in 1840. It was on the north east edge of the area and was not readily accessible to the waterside parishes until the cutting of Burdett Road later in the 1860s. During the week it was left to the old and young. (The former were not very numerous, for to be retired and alive suggested a measure of prosperity which was rare in East London.) It came alive on Sundays, especially during the long summer days. A writer, describing the scene in 1868, declared:

> It is no exaggeration to say that on a Sunday Victoria Park would even rival Rotten Row in the height of the season for the latest fashions. It is true, the dresses are not so grand or expensive . . . but the patterns and cut are on a par with them, down to the very latest importations from Paris.[46]

The young men were equally fashion-conscious:

> Just look at their hats – of course in the newest style, namely the 'Champagne Charley'. . . . A sort of low-crowned, broad-rimmed thing . . .

The hair cut short, like a convict, an eye-glass twirling on a string, or twisted, with much contortion of muscle into the face; the jackets short and ending almost where the arse begins; and short too at the sleeves to expose stretches of cuff; the trousers tight, 'which brings out into such bold relief the various leg deformities'. And finally, to complete the ensemble, a lean cigar in the mouth and a short stick in the hand, twirled merrily as one goes.

Were these young swells on a thousand a year? asked the writer. Not at all. They were impoverished clerks and counter-hands playing as swells, and he was distressed by their pretensions:

> The fact is, such aping of fashions amongst the poorer classes, not only in Victoria Park, but elsewhere, is nothing more than an ambitious endeavour to maintain themselves in a higher position of society than their station and attainments warrant.

It maintains a position which begins and ends in hypocrisy. Moreover, it should be remembered that no amount of dressing or fashion makes a man a gentleman.[47]

People in the 1860s were still expected to know their station and to keep to it.

A contributor to a monthly journal venturing into East London late one Saturday night found himself walking down

a long, narrow thoroughfare so crowded both on the pavement and the roadway that the squalid, greasy passengers trod on one another's heels; a road kerb fringed on both sides with the quaintly-lighted stalls of bawling street-sellers; side-paths bordered by dingy publics and dimly-lighted chandler's shops, and gas-flaring opposite butcher-shops . . .

Beyond was a music-hall housed in what looked like a converted chapel, the air heavy with tobacco and gin, while liveried waiters pressed through the throng with laden trays. Drunken sailors chorused and whooped, while performers did asinine little dances on a tiny stage, but their performance was perhaps the lesser part of the entertainment:

What struck me as special in this music hall was the business-like manner in which the sailors were taken in tow by the female corsairs in squadrons about the hall. It is a delicate, or rather indelicate thing to write about, but unless such scenes are at least hinted at, East End night life – and for that matter, day life too – would be very imperfectly described.[48]

The whores were as much a part of the East End as the dockland cranes and a good deal more ubiquitous.

In 1858 the East London Association, consisting mostly of local clergymen, was formed 'to abate the class of public nuisances which consists of acts of Indecency, Profanity, Drunkenness and Profligacy'. It complained of 'swarms of fallen women plying their trade, seamen beset and quarrelled for by rival harpies, words and deeds obscene and disgusting, fights and often stabbings are the daily features of one of our main thoroughfares', and warned that 'the shame of Ratcliff Highway and its outlets will soon become the shame of the Whitechapel Road and of every thoroughfare in the East'.[49]

And as it spake so it came to pass, for in 1862, a similar body, known as the Association for the Suppression of Vice, and headed by the brewer George Hanbury, found that in an area of Whitechapel bounded by four thoroughfares and consisting of 656 houses, no less than 166 were 'houses of ill-fame'.[50] One such house in Bethnal Green was owned by a local worthy. An inhabitant of Oxford Street, at the back of the London Hospital, wrote to the press complaining that 'the scenes of immorality exhibited in this street, not only by night but by day has arrived at such an intolerable degree of infamy as to be unbearable'.

Some of the churches organised regular patrols and men and women would venture out two by two, with meal tickets as bait, to invite 'the unfortunates', as they were called, back for a late night service:

> At half past ten o'clock those invited began to arrive. . . . Very speedily the spacious room was well filled. Now they are all seated, what a picture of poor, fallen humanity do they represent. The majority without bonnets, their hair dishevelled, some without shawls, some with scarcely any boots or shoes, attempts here and there at tawdry finery, some with hardly any clothes on, some with babies at their breasts . . . poverty, disease, dissipation and drink stamped upon each countenance; there they sat, from the mere child of fifteen to the grey-headed woman. . . . While tea was being placed upon the table, it was suggested to give out a hymn, accordingly 'Come to Jesus' was sung, many of them joining. The next hymn was given out as one which they all, doubtless, would recollect singing in their childhood –
>
> > Here we suffer grief and pain,
> > Here we meet to part again,
> > In heaven we part no more,
> > Oh, that will be joyful.[51]

This was sung – nearly all present joining in a remarkably plaintive but sweet manner; it seemed to recall old and fond associations, and tears trickled down the faces of many.

The East End was the home of numerous music halls, some of which were but a step above a brothel and some, indeed, a step below them. The lowest of them all were the 'Penny Gaffs' which were entirely confined to working-class areas and were particularly numerous in the East End. The buildings were usually of bare brick with whitewashed ceilings and lit by candles or, later in the century, by flaring gas jets. These gaffs, declared Mayhew, taught 'the cruellest debauchery', and many girls – some no more than eight years old – were led 'to understand the filthiest sayings and laugh at them as loudly as the grown-up lads'. He was particularly disgusted by the 'performance of a scene whose sole point turns upon the pantomime imitation of the unrestrained indulgence of the most corrupt appetites of our nature'. There were coarse songs with even coarser refrains which were taken up by the audience in lusty chorus, and the applause was so frenzied that the whitewash settled in a cloud upon the throng below.[52] If Mayhew was disgusted by what happened on stage, he was less than charmed by the audience. Boys cursed, smoked, spat, and 'tickled the girls in front who laughed hysterically', and the air was heavy with sweat, shag, whitewash, and, inexplicably, the smell of fried fish.

These gaffs had their golden age in the middle years of the century. After 1870 they were hardly heard of, but by then the music hall proper had come into its own and there were half a dozen in business in a small area of the East End. The oldest of them was perhaps the Royalty in Wellclose Square, which was opened in 1787 and burned down in 1826. The Brunswick, which opened in 1828, collapsed three days later. The Pavilion, opened in the same year, was burnt down in 1856, rebuilt, and continued in use, latterly as a cinema until 1934. The Standard, built in 1835, was burnt down in 1866 and rebuilt in 1867. David Garrick, who was of Huguenot stock, made his debut at a theatre in Alie Street. In 1831 a newly erected theatre in Leman Street was named after him. It was a cut well above the others and was described as a place 'where ladies can seat themselves without rats running over them'.[53]

The fare varied. The Pavilion celebrated its re-opening after the fire with 'a grand Aquatic Spectacle with Water', and 'Bertha Gray – Six Illustrations of Cruelty'.[54] Later it offered something called 'Lilly's Love – at half price'. Towards the end of the century, when the East End filled with Jews, it turned to Yiddish operettas and later became a cinema. The Standard Theatre, its nearest competitor, used to alternate Shakespeare with farces, and sometimes had them together in one package, as with *Hamlet* and *A Chapter of Accidents*. Towards the end of the century it staged Saturday afternoon matinées in Yiddish for the benefit of immigrant audiences.

There was a Yiddish theatre in East London, which had to compete with frequent troupes of strolling players from Russia, none of whom prospered. There was a 'Russian Jewish Opera Company', without a permanent home which staged everything from not so grand opera to vaudeville. The most ambitious effort witnessed by the immigrant community was Feinman's Yiddish People's Theatre, a large hall with accommodation for fifteen hundred which opened in 1912 with a performance of King Ahaz, an opera by the Jewish composer Samuel Alman. It then went on to stage a Yiddish version of Rigoletto. 'Nowhere except in grand opera at Covent Garden', enthused the *Daily Chronicle*, 'could one hear in England a company of such brilliant talents as in this Yiddish theatre in the East End, which has been founded by the subscription of rich and poor Jews, and has been built to fulfil a great racial ideal among these people.' Alas, it closed in the year it was opened.

But the staple fare of most of the theatres was music hall turns. The entertainments were a good deal more robust than those of the West End, and thus they would attract West End audiences. In time, however, the East End came to be regarded as something of a music hall turn in its own right. It became fashionable to go 'slumming' on conducted tours of the toughest, roughest streets, taverns and music halls. Scenes of crime, especially those associated with Jack the Ripper were very popular. It is difficult to say which was the more amused, the West End at the sight of the East End or the East End at the goggle-eyed groups in evening dress and toppers. The formation of a company specifically to promote such tours aroused the anger of the local press:

> Anything more scandalous than the formation of a commercial company to provide West Enders' personally conducted night-tours of East London at a guinea a head cannot be imagined. This newly-formed organisation is doubtless basing its calculations upon the love of new sensations, which is supposed, rightly or wrongly, to exist in a large proportion in the jaded and blasé West End. . . . Experience has long ago proved that

the streets of East London are far safer than Piccadilly, the
Strand, or Drury Lane, but are West Enders to discover that
such experience is dearly bought for a guinea?[55]

Early in 1906 the *East London Observer* published a description
of what it called 'The Real East End'. It did not deny that the
area had its mean streets and black spots, and slums 'through
which a lady might not stroll unattended', but there was another
and happier side to it, as a place of 'prosperous and cheerful
toilers', and the mean streets were relieved 'by stately roads and
pleasant squares and terraces':

> The notorious Whitechapel Road, for instance, is one of the
> broadest thoroughfares in London. It is not beautiful, but follow
> it eastwards until it becomes the Bow Road, and there you will
> find a beautiful road lined with handsome houses and with
> trees that would do credit to the Parisian boulevards .... The
> name of the East India Dock Road conjured up to many people
> a vision of an amphibious Alsatia, smacking of the Spanish
> Main, with low-ceilinged taverns in which sailors are in the
> habit of knifing each other. As a matter of fact it is a pleasant
> road down which trams run with an air of almost painful
> gentility. Its neat terraces alternate with ancient houses stand-
> ing in high-walled gardens with carriage drives. The leafy
> vistas of the East India Dock Road ended by the clock tower
> at the entrance to the East India Docks, and the masts of ships
> is as pretty a picture as London, so full of pretty pictures, can
> show.[56]

The paper was right in trying to correct the balance, but it
could not entirely gainsay the impression created by many of the
stories which crowded its columns:

> Chung Hong, a Chinese subject, and described as the lodging
> house manager at 14, Limehouse Causeway, was charged with
> assaulting Ah Weng. Prosecutor deposed that he went to the
> lodging house shortly after six o'clock the previous evening,
> when the accused, who was smoking opium, struck him across
> the head with a pipe ...[57]
> ... Eliza Holloway, of Pekin Street, Poplar, deposed she made
> prisoner's acquaintance about 3 years ago, and on 22nd March,
> 1907, went through a ceremony of marriage with him at Poplar

Parish Church. At that time she did not know Hunt was a married man . . . last November she heard prisoner had a wife and children alive, but when she spoke to him about it, he said it was not true. Last Saturday week Hunt brought a woman home and said she was 'Nell Street' with whom he had lived for 22 years, and turned witness out. Then after 5 months he turned Mrs. Street out and took witness back. On Saturday week he again told witness to clear out, and she did so. He took Nell Street in, and witness gave information to the police . . . [58]

Frank Nyers, of Lucas Street, Commercial Road, was charged with assaulting his wife, Jane. The latter, who had a plastered head, said that while talking to her daughter on Saturday night the accused smacked her face. . . . He then threw her from the top to the bottom of the stairs, and in consequence her head was cut and she was otherwise hurt. . . . In cross-examination, the witness denied annoying her husband by continually singing 'Our lodger is a nice young man! . . . !' [59]

London was the biggest port in the country, and one of the biggest in the world, and it contained small colonies of mariners from every part of the globe. With one home for German seamen, another for Scandinavians, numerous homes for English seamen, and the 'Strangers' House' for natives of India, Arabia, Africa, China, the Mozambique and the Islands of the South Pacific. The most numerous body of foreign sailors was perhaps the Lascars and Chinese, who were hardier than Europeans, thrived on a cheaper diet and were paid much less. The Chinese tended to be concentrated around Limehouse and their exotic appearance, their particular life-style and their pigtails, excited frequent attention:

Down the West India Dock Road you will find Limehouse Causeway, and there you will see over twenty dingy and decrepit buildings which constitute a Chinese quarter. Half the houses are Chinese shops, and the other half Chinese lodgings, and some of the places originally intended as shops are used as lodging houses. In the shops are Chinese wares, to help remind John Chinaman of the Flowery Land; Chinese books and newspapers, Celestial medicines and ginger, tea and candles, tinned Chinese fish and bad curries, opium pipes and opium itself. [60]

They were an industrious, peace-loving, even timid body of men, who were nervous of attention and outsiders and kept themselves entirely to themselves, to their own few buildings, their own few streets, speaking their own tongue, eating their own food. But their very exclusiveness, their apparent secretiveness, their strange ways, excited curiosity and hostility. They were inscrutable orientals and this was a time when the oriental, as represented in popular literature, was the embodiment of all that was sinister and evil. A popular monthly magazine which, as a rule, devoted most of its pages to religious articles and stories with a moral message, gave this description of a visit to Limehouse:

You may see plenty of Orientals at the Home of Asiatics, and you may see them also, if you can get entrance to an opium den, in the drugged sleep of the opium pipe. As fast as the police close one such place, another starts not far distant. Perhaps it is like a little general shop outside, in a Limehouse street, and if you passed beyond the door the obsequious Oriental would be ready to sell you anything, and perchance offer you a cup of tea from the ornamental teapot on the counter. . . . But in the backroom or upstairs you would see the low couches, made of matting, on which the opium smokers recline. There is a little lamp near, and the opium pipe, long shanked and curiously shaped, lies by his side. The smoker takes the 'chandu', as opium prepared for smoking is called, and places a piece of it about the size of a pea into a small cup at the end. . . . The piece in the pipe being ignited, the opium is 'destructively distilled', and the products come off with the smoke. This is inhaled as the smoker reclines on the settee, and breathed out slowly through the nostrils. A feeling of excitement, both mental and physical, follows in the case of Orientals – but not so much so in Europeans – an artificial sense of contentment supervenes, followed by narcosis, or shall we say drunken sleep?

It is a strange, almost incredible sight, to see this Chinese opium-smoking here in modern London; and the villainous, cut-throat look on some of the narcotised pigtailed Celestials is most repulsive. But hush! there is a terrible clatter of feet down the stairs. You see half a dozen or so Orientals – a set

of as evil-looking men as may be met within a day's march –
hurrying down the steps and along the passage, and so out
into the street.

What have they been doing? You mount the stairs – ah!
Through the open door of one of the rooms you observe a
large square wicker-work basket turned upside down, and the
word 'gambling' rises to your lips. Too often quarrels arise –
a seaman's knife could easily pin a cheating hand through that
wicker-work table, and the cuffs of the 'heathen Chinese' could
be searched. Perhaps worse follows, and while one lies gasping
and wounded on the floor the rest clatter away down the
street, round the high walls of the docks, and lose themselves
among the shipping.[61]

In 1908 there were anti-Chinese riots in the East End. Those
involved were European seamen – not all of them British –
who felt their livelihoods threatened by the increasing use of
Asiatic deck-hands. Several Chinese boarding houses were
attacked and ransacked. But the main trouble was round the
Board of Trade offices in Poplar. It was here that deck-hands
signed on for new jobs, and a large and angry crowd of sailors
thronged the surrounding streets determined to keep the Chinese
out. Sixty policemen surrounded the office and, with their help,
some Chinese managed to get in. However, the police did nothing
to protect them as they came out, and they fled down the street
with several hundred sailors in full cry after them, until they found
refuge among a crowd of about eighty Chinamen in a hostel in
Pennyfields. The crowds milled for a time outside, throwing
stones and shouting threats, but no attempt was made to storm
the hostel. Had such an attack been made, wrote a reporter,
'there would have been murder, for the Chinese were in the
condition of rats in a corner, and had gathered rude weapons of
various degrees of usefulness'.[62]

Chinese Limehouse dwindled in the inter-war years and
vanished finally during the Second War. There are still Chinamen
to be seen in the East End, but as restaurateurs and waiters
rather than as sailors, and they no longer form a compact, exotic
colony.

By the end of the nineteenth century a new and more wholesome East End was evolving, and the *Daily Telegraph*, which a

decade or two earlier had spoken of it as a place of misery and
darkness, was led to confess, 'that the lower labouring classes of
East London are, at the present time, in enjoyment of more than
their fair share of the good things which it is in the power of the
rich to bestow on the poor'.

It was not yet felt that the poor had quite earned the 'good
things', for many of the improvements noted had been provided
by external agencies and not through their own efforts, but they
were everywhere evident:

> ... the aspect of the whole poverty-stricken area, in its length
> and breadth, from the Minories to Mile End, and from Spital-
> fields to Shadwell, has been vastly improved, and the deplorable
> conditions of thousands of toilers who lived in squalor and
> half-starved on bread alone correspondingly ameliorated. They
> have more wholesome dwellings; they are less under the cruel
> thumb of the slop-work agent and the sweater; their religious
> welfare is abundantly cared for; while for their instruction and
> amusement they have their own parks and open spaces, a
> splendid museum . . .[63]

Shipping was thinning out along the Thames and there was
talk of encouraging pleasure steamers to East London by opening
a pier at Shadwell, until recently the site of a fish market. The
idea at first sounded about as probable as Wigan pier, but why
not? asked a local paper: 'There are some people who incline to
think that because they have usually counted Shadwell as slummy
and unsavoury, and have not taken their pleasure there, that it
should remain slummy and unsavoury.'[64] The idea was somewhat premature and is being taken up only in our own time, but
the fact that it could be broached at all showed the extent to
which the East End's view of itself had changed by the end of
the century. People were better housed, better fed, better clothed,
without being more drunk. They were better educated. They were
enjoying life more.

But here and there were indications that things were not quite
as well as they appeared to be. The number of people on poor
relief in Stepney in January 1891 was one thousand and seven.
Twelve years later it was one thousand seven hundred and forty-
two.[65]

The poor are always with us, but they have never been so

ubiquitous as in the East End, not because it was – or is – the most neglected area of London but, on the contrary, because it is the area which has always excited the most solicitude. It was the last resort of the good Samaritan and charities, secular and lay, social agencies, missions, settlements, lined the area as thickly as the whores used to crowd Ratcliff Highway, and the needy will find their way to the charitable, the helpless to the helpful, as naturally as bees are drawn to honey. The East End, which has changed in almost every other respect, remains constant in this one, and its traditional role is perhaps best symbolised by the shelter for meth drinkers opened in the crypt of Christ Church, Spitalfields, in 1965. Here are men so derelict, so devoid of all human dignity, so pathetic and apathetic, so filthy and repellent, so incorrigible in their poisonous habit, that not even the Salvation Army will have them. They are an alarming sight, tousled hair, wild-eyed, faces emaciated and scarred, clothes tattered, reeking of urine and spirits. A casual visitor to the area must think he has stumbled across some preserved corner of the East End of yore, now happily vanished. But if one stops to talk to the men one finds that Irish accents predominate, that a good many are from Scotland, and that actual Londoners seem to be in the minority. They are not products of East End life but are drawn to the East End because there alone can they be sure of sympathy and help.

# THIRTEEN

# The Two Communities

The passage of the Aliens Act removed the Jews from the headlines for a time, but all was not quiet within the Jewish community itself. The established English Jews watched with dismay the arrival of so many Russian Jews who brought with them not only their bedding, their cutlery and their crockery, but also their own way of life. They appeared to pose a threat to English Jewry, who had evolved a parallel denomination to the Church of England through the United Synagogue, with the Chief Rabbi at its head in the role of Archbishop. The clergy below him assumed the title Reverend rather than Rabbi and wore the black coat, broad brimmed hat and dog-collar of the Anglican clergy. The high noon of United Synagogue Anglicanism came during the reign of Dr Hermann Adler, Chief Rabbi from 1890 to 1911. He wore the insignia of the Royal Victorian Order like a pectoral cross and sometimes even sported gaiters, and Edward VII once referred to him affectionately as 'my chief Rabbi'. He was assuredly not the Chief Rabbi of the Russian community, nor was his synagogue theirs. His very office was alien to their experience. In Eastern Europe, one rabbi might be raised above another by the depth of his learning, his piety, his religious zeal, his sagacity, but there was no such thing as a Chief Rabbi. And as for the English synagogues, the newcomers would enter and look around them confounded. The lofty ceilings, the stained glass, the vaulted cupolas, the massive pillars, the very size and spaciousness suggested a cathedral. And, as if the building itself was not alien enough, the decorum of the place made it seem church-like, and it opened and closed at certain hours like a bank.

The typical East European synagogue was more in the nature of a small room which was open at most times of the day and night. It was part bethel and part club-house, and at times of emergency it might even be used as a lodging house (with the Ark holding the sacred scrolls of the law suitably covered up). Its small congregation, known as a *Chevra*, came there to pray, study or chat, or perhaps all three. Above all it was an intimate, friendly place.

Probity was not always the strong point of these *chevras* and their treasurers absconded with funds with distressing frequency, usually to start a new life in America or South Africa. Sometimes they were caught, like Israel Horowitz, who was charged with embezzling £6 to £7 belonging to the Grand Order of Israel Friendly Society, or Harris Greenbaum, Treasurer of the Prince George Hebrew Benefit Society.[1] Greenbaum was charged with embezzling £24, which he claimed he did not take, but which he was, on the other hand, willing to repay.[2]

Beatrice Potter, who wrote on the Jewish community for Booth's *Life and Labour*, visited a number of these *chevras* and was, on the whole, taken with them:

> For the most part the religious minded form themselves into associations (Chevras), which combine the function of a benefit club for death, sickness and the solemn rites of mourning with that of public worship and the study of the Talmud. Thirty or forty of these Chevras are scattered throughout the Jewish quarter.[3]

Different *chevras* sometimes represented different degrees of religious zeal, but more often they represented fraternities from various parts of the Pale. They were formed, wrote Miss Potter, by 'old associations from ties of relationship or friendship, or, at least from the memory of a common home':

> Here, early in the morning, or late at night, the devout members meet to recite the morning and evening prayers, or to decipher the sacred books of the Talmud. And it is a curious and touching sight to enter one of the poorer and more wretched of these places on a Sabbath morning.... From the outside it

appears a long wooden building surmounted by a skylight, very similar in construction to the ordinary sweater's workshop. You enter; the heat and odour convince you that the skylight is not used for ventilation. . . . A low, monotonous, but musical toned recital of Hebrew prayers, each man praying for himself to the God of his fathers rises from the congregation. . . . Your eye wanders from the men who form the congregation to the small body of women who watch behind the trellis. Here, certainly, you have the Western World, in the bright-coloured ostrich feathers, large bustles, and tight-fitting coats of velvet or brocaded satinette. At last you step out stifled by the heat and dazed by the strange contrast of the old-world memories of a majestic religion and the squalid vulgarity of an East End slum.[4]

The *chevras*, though they had undoubted warmth and colour, caused some consternation among the older Jewish families, who feared that they were perpetuating strange, outlandish customs that they themselves had abandoned long ago. The *Jewish Chronicle*, which was their mouthpiece, declared that 'the sooner the immigrants to our shore learn to reconcile themselves to their new conditions of living, the better for themselves. Whatever tends to perpetuate the isolation of this element in the community must be dangerous to its welfare'.[5] The paper went on to urge that the *chevras* should be brought into a federation which would associate itself more closely with the established community, an idea which filled one provincial Minister with horror:

It is because Jews have lived within themselves in other countries on the *Chevra* principle that they have made the existence of Jews in those countries intolerable. . . . Your suggestion would help foreign Jews to do for England what they have done for Russia . . . the sooner the *Chevra* movement is crushed out of existence the sooner we will remove from our midst the only drawback to the advancement of Jews in this country.[6]

Many of the newcomers were barely literate, or if literate did not have a literary style to match their feelings, and amongst the less usual callings introduced by the immigrants to this country was that of the professional letter writer. One, in practice in

Spitalfields, had a notice on his door in Russian, Polish, Yiddish and German, offering to write letters cheaply. He charged a penny a page, he told a reporter of the *Daily Mail*, and at busy times he might write two hundred letters per week. 'I witness many a tragedy and offer a helping hand in many a romance', he said. As a rule he preferred elderly male clients:

> They just tell me what they want to say and in a few minutes they go away satisfied. It is a different matter with young girls, particularly those of them who are love-stricken. I can never find adequate terms to render their feelings to their whole satisfaction. They always insist upon warmer terms and an endless repetition of their protestations of love, until I am fairly on the way to losing my temper.[7]

The newcomers were also easy prey for the unscrupulous. In 1906 a woman claiming to be a sorceress was sentenced at Clerkenwell to nine months' imprisonment and ordered to be deported for fraud. She was a Mrs Rachel Nauhans who offered to charm back an absconding husband to his deserted wife on the payment of a small sum. The sum was paid and, as a start, Mrs Nauhans burned a candle with pins stuck all round it. When this did not bring the man back, she made incantations over an open fire and threw a brick into it. When this in turn failed, she declared that she had to have more money – 'the more you give me, the quicker he will come'. The wife, a poor Jewish char-woman, parted with her life-savings of £5 14s and a quantity of linen which Mrs Nauhans undertook to treat with a special preparation, so that when she woke her husband would be by her side. When she woke and her husband was not, she went to the police.[8]

Neither counsel, nor clerk, nor the police, nor even the judge could keep a straight face as the story, related in Yiddish, un-folded through the medium of an interpreter who, in turn, was convulsed with laughter. However, it was very unlikely that the older community was amused and its members redoubled their efforts to pull their brethren into the twentieth century.

The main agent of this process was a bearded Jew who, but for his great rounded belly and well-cut suit and patrician manners, could himself have stepped off an immigrant boat. He was Sir Samuel Montagu, Liberal MP for Whitechapel. Montagu was born in Liverpool in 1832, moved to London in his youth, made one fortune, married another, joined the radical wing of the Liberal party but remained as conservative in religion as he was progressive in politics. Neither his great wealth, nor exalted connections, nor his titles (he was eventually raised to the peerage as Lord Swaythling) lessened his adherence to Orthodox Judaism. He was sympathetic to the problems of the newcomers and it was principally to him that the old community delegated the task of leading them into England, except that while some of his colleagues were anxious to yank them out of the ghettoes at any cost, he was anxious to preserve them as Jews.

In 1876 he founded the Jewish Workingmen's Club for 'the Anglicisation of the Jews of the East End and the provision of a place of innocent amusement'.[9] It was housed in substantial premises in Alie Street and could accommodate over a thousand people in its main hall, which came to be the scene of many historic meetings. As a means of Anglicisation it was less than a success, for the newcomers were only mixing amongst themselves, speaking their own language, reading their own papers, amusing themselves much as they would have amused themselves in their own country. Montagu also headed a Jewish dispersal committee, which tried to direct immigrants away from the congested East End and into such areas as Chatham and Reading. It also had limited success, for many Jews felt that to leave East London for the provinces was to put one's religion at risk.

He found much to admire in the *chevras* and if there was anything about them to condemn, he believed that could be eliminated through bringing them together into one organisation under his guidance.

'I found that there were different isolated minor synagogues in the East End which were disposed rather to quarrel among themselves and I formed the idea of amalgamating them together – quite a voluntary association – for their general benefit. The chief object was to get rid of unsanitary places of worship, and to amalgamate two or three small ones together, and have a suitable building. We succeeded very well in this respect.'[10] Thirty-nine synagogues with a membership of twenty-four thousand joined his Federation of Synagogues and Montagu himself became its president.

The Federation by no means included all the *chevras* in the East End. Some were too small and unsanitary to qualify for membership, and others broke away from existing *chevras*. These continuing schisms rarely implied any theological or religious disputes – for theology rarely entered into the thinking of the Orthodox Jew. They rose out of a clash of personalities, temperaments, ambitions.

The archives of the Poor Jews Temporary Shelter yield some telling figures. Of the two thousand Jews who passed through the Shelter during 1895–6, no less than four hundred and sixty described themselves as 'merchants', a grandiose title for men who were, and to get accommodation had to be, self-confessed paupers.[11] The description was an expression of hope rather than reality, and many of them did acquire small shops and warehouses and become merchants of sorts. But having become of consequence commercially – which is to say, solvent – they sought to be of consequence in other fields, and stood for public office – not yet on the local councils, that was to come later – but within their own community. An English student of Jewish life has described this tendency most succinctly:

> This strife for personal distinction seems to be one of the main causes of that multiplication of small organisations and institutions which is such a marked feature of the East End Jewry. It appears that the ambition of the well-to-do and rising immigrant commonly soars after some kind of official dignity; and as he is willing to pay for it . . . hence the number of small synagogues or *chevras*, friendly societies and miscellaneous institutions, which spring up like mushrooms wherever the foreign Jews are gathered together.[12]

In 1889 Rothschild, the uncrowned king of Anglo-Jewry, clashed with Montagu when he tried to bring the United Synagogue into the East End. Montagu felt that the East End was sufficiently catered for by the Federation of Synagogues; but there was some feeling among the old families that, in his sympathies for the newcomers, Montagu had himself to an extent turned native. The United Synagogue was represented on the fringe of the East End by the Great Synagogue in Duke's Place. It was now proposed to move into the heart of the area with a larger synagogue which would, like the Federation, include provident societies and funeral benefits, and would also serve as a cultural and welfare centre. If the East Enders would not come into the United Synagogue, the United Synagogue would come to them.

Montagu was outraged by this attempt to poach on his preserve and used all his authority against it. In the end it failed because it was a hugely expensive idea and the old community, while applauding it in principle, was not prepared to pay for it. In the event it proved to be unnecessary, for, while the first generation of emigrants were content to be in the Federation and the *chevras*, their sons tended to gravitate towards the United Synagogue. It was a sign of arrival.

The schools were mainly responsible for the Anglicisation of the new arrivals. They were supplemented by evening classes in English which, towards the end of the nineteenth century, attracted some sixty thousand Jewish students a year. Of the six Jewish day schools in London by far the most important was the Jews' Free School which, with its continuous extensions, became the largest school in the world. It had over three thousand five hundred pupils. Even then, according to an observer writing in 1900, there were 'hundreds clamouring for admission and the sights on a day when vacancies are filled are not easily forgotten. Crowds of anxious parents with equally excited children fill every available place in the streets, besiege every entrance until the regular pupils find it impossible to get in. Formerly some of the weakest were actually trodden underfoot in the rush for educational advantage, and nowadays the assistance of the police is invoked to keep the crowd in order.'[13]

The headmaster of the school for nearly sixty of its most formative years was Moses Angel, a high-minded autocrat, who taxed himself severely and taxed his pupils and staff no less. He had no high opinion of his pupils or their parents. They were, he said, 'ignorant even of the elements of sound; until they had been Anglicised or humanised it was difficult to tell what was their moral condition and many of them scarcely knew their names'. Others, he said, 'knew neither English nor any intelligible language ... their parents were the refuse population of the worst parts of Europe, whose first object in sending the children to school was to get them out of the way'.[14]

At this time, wrote a reporter, more than 95 per cent of the

children at the JFS were the children of foreign parents, 'ignorant
of their own names, poverty-stricken, scarcely robust, and so
accustomed to ill-usage in the lands of their birth that they cannot
at first understand kindness'. And he went on:

> The task of raising such helpless ones from a condition of
> ignorance, training them to adopt English methods of thought
> and life, and freeing them from superstition while preserving
> and cultivating religious beliefs is one of such magnitude that
> neither masters nor committee can for one moment cease from
> their labours.[15]

'The task ... of freeing them from superstition, while preserving and cultivating religious belief' was a phrase which
summed up the dilemma of the school managers and the elders
of the Anglo-Jewish community. They wanted to convert them
into English gentlemen but preserve them as Jews, and there
was an hour and a half added to the daily curriculum for Hebrew
and religion. Even this was not enough for many parents and
they would send their sons after school to small evening classes,
or *cheder*, where they were taught reading and writing, the Penta-
teuch and its commentaries, and perhaps a page of Talmud.

The six Jewish schools in East London had a total population
of about six thousand at the beginning of this century. In addition
to these, there were sixteen Board schools, run by the local
authorities, with some fifteen thousand pupils, who were practically all Jewish. The schools closed early on Friday afternoons
and during Jewish holidays, and taught the Jewish religion during
the periods normally allotted to religious instruction. Even some
of the Church schools had large numbers of Jewish children and
in one, St Stephen's, Spitalfields, where four hundred and ninety-
eight out of the seven hundred and ninety-four children were
Jewish, the Church made special provision to instruct the Jewish
children in their own religion.[16] Out of about ninety-eight
thousand children attending schools in the East London area,
about twenty-five thousand were Jewish, and of these about a
third were born abroad. Mr G. L. Bruce, a member of the London
Schools Board and in charge of the Whitechapel Schools,
declared:

> The Jewish children have proved excellent scholars, far the
> most regular in London, usually well-fed even in poor families,

and bright in school. This is due largely to the excellent domestic character of the parents, never drinking and devoted to their children.[17]

The scholastic successes of the Jewish pupils was the occasion of frequent comment. 'How is it that so many of these Jewish children climb the ladder so quickly, and capturing the scholarships for which all compete, so often passing the Christian children in the race?' asked an East End educationist, Mr Harold Spender. He had his own answer:

> It is because following that great tradition which has brought their race undiminished through so many centuries of exile, they look after their children so well. Watch the playgrounds of the schools at the hours of departure. It is the Jewish mothers who are the first to fetch their children. Go through any class. It is the Jewish children who wear the marks of most careful home tending.[18]

Russel, an English writer otherwise critical of the Jews, found the transformation of the immigrant child 'astonishing'. 'All the children who pass through an English school may be said to grow up into "English Jews" – and in this phrase there is implied a world of difference.'[19]

Boys were compelled to leave school early to earn a living, and the Jewish Board of Guardians tried to encourage them to join one of its apprentice schemes which would have equipped them with a skilled trade and good prospects. However, both boys and parents were averse to a lengthy apprenticeship. They wanted and needed quick returns and they entered one of the overmanned Jewish trades, where the hours were long and the pay was low, but even then they tried to continue their education through evening classes. One such class, run by Christ Church, Spitalfields, attracted many Jewish pupils, and a local churchman marvelled at their industry:

> The Jewish child's idea of time is somewhat remarkable. Our caretaker at the Brick Lane hall tells us that even up to 11 o'clock at night they will bring him to the door to know 'whether there's anything at the school'. They are somewhat unlike other children too in their reluctance to leave a class or meeting. Once they have gained admittance they have literally

to be driven out at the end; they will hide away under tables etc. to escape detection.[20]

The Rector of Spitalfields, the Reverend R. C. Billing, who was sometimes thought to be anti-semitic, once told his parish: 'Go to the Jew thou Christian, consider his ways and be wise.'[21]

The conduct of the Jewish child, however, did not always evoke unequivocal admiration and one headmistress wrote:

> I have never met such memories in any other race. They can learn everything, and apparently without much effort. Little children who have never been to school before come in here to me and pick up the beginnings of an education in two or three days. I never cease to marvel at them. But they have absolutely no manners and no conception of them.[22]

Jewish youth clubs played their part in the process of assimilation. Jewish lads, while rarely resorting to violence, were often self-assertive, noisy, obstreperous, slow to respond to discipline and obstinate, and the Bishop of Stepney once felt moved to write to the Chief Rabbi about their behaviour, suggesting something be done to keep them 'occupied in industrious pursuits for their edification, enlightenment and upbringing'.

Oxford and several public schools by then had established numerous settlements in the East End and it occurred to the Chief Rabbi that Clifton College, Bristol, which had a Jewish house, might be persuaded to start a settlement for Jewish lads, and he put the idea to the Reverend Polack, master of the Jewish house:

> It seems to me that if some magnanimous benefactor, suitably motivated, could be found to provide the wherewithal for this worthwhile and necessary venture, that our boys and past scholars might be encouraged to do their social duty towards their less fortunate brethren in the East End.[23]

The result was the Victoria Club founded in 1901. It was not the first in the field, for the Brady Club and Settlement, founded in 1896, was already doing important work.

The clubs were run by unpaid managers, prosperous young men with earnest intentions from the older families, who kept a detailed progress report:

Bagatels again in great request, but draught and dominoes seem fairly popular. Not so, however the reading room, which was but slightly used.

Have discovered a lad suffering from infectious skin disease. I have returned him his entrance money (4d) and told him to bring a doctor's certificate when he is cured.

I had to send Schneiderman home as he is suffering from some complaint affecting his hair. Says he caught it from a boy at school.

I have noticed an improvement as regards cleanliness of hands and hair.

With time one notices progress in other directions. The reading room is more used, but then an old Jewish complaint raises its ugly head:

Two visitors, J. Finklestein and A. Cohen, introduced the noble game of toss haepenny into the club. We lectured the gentlemen on the iniquities of gambling and thereupon they announced their intention of foreswearing the sport.

Careful attention is paid to the effects of cricket and there, at first, the results were not entirely heartening:

There is till too great a tendency to squabble and play selfishly, also a disinclination to recognise the captain's authority.
The situation improves with time, but not entirely so:
Very successful day of cricket. . . . The behaviour of the boys in the field was good, but there is still a tendency not to accept the umpire's decision as final.[24]

The largest and most successful of the Jewish settlements, Oxford and St George's, was founded shortly before the outbreak of the First World War by the late Sir Basil Henriques (the street in which the club stands has been named after him). Henriques worked for a time in Toynbee Hall and saw for himself the effects which poverty and overcrowding were having on Jewish youngsters in the neighbourhood.

The boys idolised him. Fair-haired and over six feet tall, he was a man of heroic stature, with a commanding presence and a commanding voice, sensitive, yet robust, good and godly without being remote, and in a sense he never grew up. There are photographs of him in summer camp in short trousers, long stockings and boots, bright-faced, eager, ready for fun, a boy among boys. He was perhaps the eternal boy-scout. He loved sportsmen and sportsmanship, fair play and doing his bit (and more than his bit) for others, songs round the camp fire and the team spirit.

His settlement contained a large synagogue in which he preached regularly. He was deeply religious but not orthodox, his Judaism being of a very personal, liberal type. He approached the High Holy Days comprising the New Year and the Day of Atonement with a special sense of exaltation. 'A marvellous day', he wrote after one day of prayer, 'about a thousand present. For one and a half hours at the end, decorum perfect and tension almost unbearable. . . . Preached three sermons during the day. One on sex and gambling, one on Jonah, and one on peace.'[25]

Few Jews in this country have had such an influence on the young as Basil Henriques, though not everyone was convinced that his influence was for the good. The unease which he occasioned among the Orthodox was at first muted by the admiration with which he was held in the East End and beyond, but their feeling soon found expression in protest from both Rabbis and laymen.

'No one appreciates more than I the excellent social work which Mr Henriques and his devoted wife are doing in the East End', wrote one local social worker. 'I am, however, more than ever convinced that Mr Henriques' religious work is resulting in the weakening of the Jewish bond, and consequent cleavages in Jewish families. The very teaching he enunciates sets up differences between parents and children, as what he advocates is the very negation of the ideals so many of us cherish and hold dear.'[26]

Such letters never deflected him from his chosen course. He acted as a man directed from on high. Most of the club members came from religious homes and Henriques therefore did not instil religious feelings where none existed, but merely replaced one form of Judaism with another. His influence was at its height in the 1930s and by then many of the religious traditions and observances which the immigrants had brought with them had lapsed. The extreme left and militant atheism were winning over large parts of the Jewish East End and, it could be argued, he was able to retain thousands of young people within the faith who would almost certainly have been lost to it. He retired in 1948 but continued to haunt the settlement for years after and could not bear to be parted from the boys or the place. He died in 1960.

Colonel A. E. W. Goldsmid, an ex-Indian army officer who stemmed from the same ruling Anglo-Jewish clan as Henriques, founded the Jewish Lads' Brigade, a sort of pre-Baden Powell scout group in 1896. 'We should endeavour to instil in the rising generation all that is best in the English character', he said, 'namely independence, honour, truth, cleanliness, love of active, health-giving pursuits etc.'[27] There was an implication in his statement that the ghetto lad was devoid of such virtues, but also a belief that there was little wrong with him which the influence of Englishmen and England could not put right.

The highlight of the year was the annual summer camp, usually under canvas under an English heaven, with the boys totally removed from the influence of parents, home and ghetto, which gave the opportunity for what Goldsmid called 'ironing out the ghetto bend'.[28] For many of the boys this was their first taste of gentile England, the regimen of clean living, exercise, long walks and long runs, tales of Indian hill-stations round the camp-fire, and songs and comradeship, and games of cricket on warm afternoons, and, in time, the children, while inhabiting the same universe as their parents, came to draw their ideas and feelings from another.

Some parents tried to catch up with them and made strenuous efforts to improve themselves and their English and adapt themselves to their new homeland. Observers were often moved by their zeal:

I would like to take your readers to some of our Ghetto evening schools, the schools where the adult Russian and German Jews, artificially thrust back into darkness by European governments, clutches at his last hope of knowledge. They come to this country like their children, ignorant of the English language, very often unable to read, write or add up. They are at work all day ... very often doubled up in some little sweating den. In the evening they rush from their work, with scarcely a bite for food, straight to our evening classes ... in a few months they will learn to read or write our English tongue, almost as well as the Christian workman who has half forgotten half he has learned at school. I never feel prouder of England when standing in these schools and watching this work. . . . Nothing is more pathetic than the desire of these people to be English, to work for England, fight for England. England is the only Western European nation that has been wholly just to the Jew. And in return England is the only country where the Jew is as proud of his nation as of his race.[29]

If there were at the end of the nineteenth century two Jewries, the old and the new, the one living in the suburbs and the other in the East End, there gradually evolved two distinct Jewries within the East End itself, the one sacred and the other profane, the one reaching back towards Russia and beyond it to the Second Temple, and the other reconciling itself to this world and to England. The former, even after their children had grown to maturity, kept their old world intact and sought to transmit it as received to the next generation. The snow on their boots never melted. It was they who chased their children to *cheder* and tested them on their Jewish knowledge on Friday night, and had them by their side in synagogue or *shtieble* on the Sabbath, on Fast Day and Feast. The stars of their firmament were the great Rabbis of Eastern Europe who might grace their city with a visit. When the Reverend Chaim Zundel Maccoby, a celebrated preacher and sage from the Polish town of Kamenetz, delivered an address in the Duke's Place synagogue, roads on every side became impassable:

> So immense was the crowd, that it was found necessary to close the synagogue doors half an hour before the commencement of the service, and admission had to be consequently refused to a thousand persons. A force of 20 policemen was required not however to preserve order, which was admirable, but to regulate the throng. In the synagogue itself there was not a vacant inch of space.[30]

Rabbi Maccoby confined his speech on that occasion to a mere thirty minutes, though he could keep an audience enthralled for hours. Lesser figures could speak for as long, or longer, and attract equal attention. Their sermons were almost a form of folk entertainment and, among the immigrants, they were given not during the Sabbath morning service – as in the English synagogues – but between the afternoon and evening service on the long summer afternoons when the Sabbath extended almost until midnight.

The *droscho* bore little relation to the dry, phlegmatic, Anglican-type sermon normally heard in the English synagogue. It was part parable, part reproof, part Talmudic exposition, each told with variation of voice and tone, now chanted, now whispered, now lost to hearing altogether, to surface suddenly in a loud cry, and all attended with much swaying of body and gesticulation of hands. It was a dramatic performance, a one-man passion play, requiring great erudition and infinite wind on the part of the performer, and infinite patience on the part of the listener, and both seemed equal to it. A less arduous form of sacred entertainment was provided by the *Chazan* (or Cantor).

The services in a synagogue are led by a *Baal Tefillah* (literally, supplicator), but as synagogues grew larger and congregations more prosperous it became usual for them to employ someone with some pretensions to vocal excellence, who not only led prayers but used them as occasions to display their virtuosity – especially during the High Festivals, when the synagogues were packed and the services continued for five or six hours at a time, or on the Day of Atonement when they went on all day. The Anglicised United Synagogues employed full time Cantors, but the smaller synagogues attended by the newcomers could only import Cantors for the High Festivals, and then with some flourish in the form of handbills, posters and press announcements that 'the famous Chazan Schlossberg has arrived for the solemn festivals. Don't miss this opportunity of hearing him intone the prayers. The only synagogue that can afford to pay a cantor £300.'[31]

The synagogues were not sufficient for all anxious to attend services during the High Festivals, and schools, public halls, theatres all over the East End were brought in to use as auxiliary places of worship, and again as a special attraction, Cantors were imported from Eastern Europe:

This is to inform members, friends, countrymen and the Jewish public generally that we have again this year taken the commodious, beautiful and well ventilated hall – Bonn's Hotel – for the Solemn Days, and that the famous St. Petersburg

Chazan will recite the prayers in it, assisted by a splendid choir.[32]

Sometimes crowds would assemble to hear a *Chazan* and choir even outside synagogue hours. One boot-finisher, acting as a part-time impresario, hired a hall, drilled a choir and let the seats at a profit of £20 a night. 'These apparently poverty stricken Jews', wrote a local paper with awe, 'seem willing to pay as much as three guineas to hear a renowned precentor.'

The second and profane section of Jewry in the East End developed partly through the effects of the assimilationists and partly because of the pressure of economic forces. The latter were perhaps the most insidious. The assimilationists, at least, had an English reverence for tradition and wanted to celebrate Judaism within an English context, to replace the influences of Poland with what they believed to be the more wholesome influence of England. Economic forces, on the other hand, tended to pull them out of Judaism altogether, and could even make them actual antagonists of their ancient faith. Many of them turned towards a vague protesting socialism.

In 1876, before the years of mass immigration, there was founded in 40 Gun Street, Spitalfields (the building still stands), the *Hebrew Socialist Union* with a Lithuanian, Aaron Liebermann, as its secretary and guide. Although he had a traditional Jewish upbringing, he joined the Russian Narodniks, young intellectuals who donned peasant clothes and tried to take socialism to the Russian people. The people were not interested and the movement was suppressed. Liebermann, however, believed that the movement could succeed amongst Jewish workers. He did not, like other Jewish Narodniks, press for complete assimilation and believed that Jews should exist as a distinct entity within a socialist universe. Jews, he believed, were the most exploited of all workers, and the Jewish bourgeoisie and Rabbis had more than a passing share in that exploitation!

We have had to pay for your sins! The race hatred, the religious hatred, with all their terrors have mostly fallen on us. We have to thank you for it that the name Israel has become a curse. The entire Jewish people, suffering and astray, must suffer more than all other peoples because of your greed. It is your fault that we have been exposed to calumny. International speculators, who have dragged our name through the mud, you do not belong to us.[33]

The attacks dismayed the Jewish establishment and there were anguished retorts from Jewish pulpits. The *Jewish Chronicle* dismissed the Hebrew Socialist Union as 'enemies of the Jewish people' and as 'a body which possess no existence whatever except in the imagination of the Union's originator'.[34] This was not far from the truth. The Union, which had nine members at its inception, never had more than forty and foundered within a year, and it is remembered, if at all, for the anger it aroused more than for any positive achievement.[35] Liebermann committed suicide in 1880. Had he lived a decade or two longer his efforts might have proved more effective, for after the mass immigration there was a proliferation of small Jewish socialist groups. They split, reformed and split again almost like the *chevras*. They courted the attention of working men with a torrent of pamphlets urging brotherhood, unity, revolution, a new dawn, a happier world.

In 1884 Morris Wichevsky, a disciple of Liebermann's, founded the *Polisher Yidl*, the first Jewish socialist paper.[36] It folded after fourteen issues but reappeared after a doctrinal split as the *Arbeiter Freint* (The Worker's Friend) which was anarchistic in temper. It urged readers to cast off the yoke of religion and 'to change entirely the present order of tyranny and injustice'. It derided Zionism, which was making rapid headway among the newcomers, and declared that 'no colonisation, no homeland, no sovereignty will help the Jewish nation. Jewish happiness will come with the happiness of all unhappy workers, and Jewish emancipation must come with the emancipation of humanity.'[37] It singled out Sir Samuel Montagu for particular attack as an obstacle to progress, and the acting Chief Rabbi, Dr Hermann Adler, as High Priest of the sweaters.

This latter charge had some foundation, for Adler, who had a genius for misjudging a situation, had preached a sermon when the anti-sweating agitation was at its height, and said that if sweating meant overwork, then he and many of his wealthy congregants were being sweated. He also used the occasion to remind his working-class hearers of the benevolence of their wealthy brethren, and to warn them against socialist agitators.

As a result, on a Saturday in March 1889, some two or three thousand Jewish socialists, according to the *Arbeiter Freint* (three or four hundred according to the *Jewish Chronicle*), took to the streets. Headed by a German band in full blast, they marched upon the Great Synagogue where Hermann Adler was due to preach. They were met by fifty policemen under the Superintendent and Chief Inspector of the City police and forced to retreat to Mile End Waste. There they damned the acting Chief Rabbi in this world and the next in terms suggesting that their belief in unearthly forces had not entirely vanished.

The previous year a number of Jewish socialists had organised a dinner and ball on the eve of Yom Kippur, the Day of Atonement, the most sacred hour of the Jewish year. When God did not strike them dead, as onlookers earnestly prayed He would, it became an annual event which generated – as it was meant to – deep outrage in the Jewish community. It rarely passed without incident and in 1904 it led to an actual riot.

The trouble began in the afternoon when worshippers emerged from the crowded synagogues. What happened next was extensively reported in the local press:

> Thousands of Jews were walking along the streets, when they were met by a body of socialist Jews, who had driven a van containing food along the streets. All the Orthodox Jews were fasting and they at once resented this unseemly display. The Socialists being driven into their club responded by throwing glass bottles out of the windows. Several cases of minor injury occurred and the disorder thus started to spread quickly. Within half an hour the whole area round Princelet Street was in a state of great agitation. Excited groups of Orthodox Jews were parading the street threatening the Socialists with dire penalties for their insults and stones were thrown at the homes of prominent Socialists. Eventually a large force of police arrived on the scene and promptly cleared the streets. . . . It is alleged that the Socialists pelted a Synagogue which stands adjacent to their club, and that they had arranged a concert for the day of fasting – invitations to which they had sent to the principal Rabbis.[38]

Six men and two boys were brought before the Magistrates Court. Two declared themselves to be free-thinkers and declined

9. Matchbox-makers at Bow in the 1870s

10. Parade of coal-heavers on strike, 1889

to be sworn. They admitted that they did not observe the Day of
Atonement but denied they were the aggressors and were discharged. What hurt the Orthodox Jews more than the verdict
itself were the remarks of the magistrates, who thought it
deplorable:

> that a class of persons who for centuries had been distinguished
> as the victims of the fiercest persecutions should when in the
> one free country of the world, turn upon those who disagreed
> with them on religious points, their own co-religionists, and
> stone and persecute them.

At which a correspondent protested:

> In reference to the remarks of the magistrate at the Worship
> Street Police-court, it should be mentioned that the Socialist
> Jews hired a hall opposite the Synagogue, where they held
> revels and feasting. It is needless to say that this exasperated
> the Orthodox Jews, who, to their credit be it said, strictly
> keep their ancient customs. There are no more law-abiding
> people than the Orthodox Jews; but Socialists, whether Jew
> or Gentile – well they are Socialists.[39]

The moving spirit among the Jewish East End socialists was
Rudolph Rocker, a German anarchist of Christian origin, who
had learned Yiddish in order to spread his ideas among the
Jewish masses and, for a time, served as editor of the *Arbeiter
Freint*. He had worked among the Jews in Paris who were
mostly skilled artisans, well fed and well clothed, and he was
struck by the contrast between them and the Jewish East Enders
who 'looked sad, worn and half-starved',[40] conspicuous wretches
of exploitation.

The difficulty with the Jews was that, while they were sometimes open to new and even revolutionary ideas, they were
notoriously difficult to organise – more so even than the Irish.
And like the Irish they were fractious, so that even where they
felt persuaded to join a union they often fell out with its leaders
and joined another, or even tried to form their own. There were
thirteen Jewish trade unions in 1896 and thirty-two in 1902, of
which twenty-six had been formed in the previous six years.
They rose, fused, split, re-fused, split again, re-fused again, and
vanished. Few of them had as many as three hundred members,

*H*

and not all as many as a hundred. Of the fifteen Jewish unions listed in the 1898 *Jewish Year Book*, two vanished by the following year, and one had split and been reduced to the secretary and treasurer.[41] And as with the Jewish Friendly Societies, it was not unknown for the treasurer to make off with the funds.

Yet, given a sufficient degree of provocation, Jews could act in concert and in 1889, when the agitation against sweaters was at its height, ten thousand tailors went on strike. They marched in long processions through the East End, held rallies in Victoria Park. The *Jewish Chronicle*, while agreeing that the workers had a case, was troubled about their tactics. It was, it said:

> questionable policy on the part of the poor foreigners to give an exaggerated idea of their numbers by parading through London, and thus excite further prejudice against their entire body, especially when they place themselves under the leadership of men conspicuously associated with the Socialist movements.

The strike was finally settled through the intervention of Montagu who posted a £100 guarantee demanded by the strike committee as a token of the masters' good faith. Workers' hours were reduced to eight in the morning till eight at night, with an hour for dinner and half an hour for tea, and all meals to be had off the premises. However, many of the small workshops found that they could not both honour this agreement and stay in business, and workers who insisted on their rights were dismissed. The resulting bitterness and unrest in the clothing trades led to further strikes in 1906 and 1912. In the strike of 1912 the East End tailors went beyond their local grievances and came out in support of the West End tailors, an envied, skilled and highly-paid élite. Had the former remained at work orders would have been transferred to them and the West End strike would have been broken. Workers from other trades rallied round them. Bakers provided free bread, cigarette-makers free tobacco. Other unionists adopted a voluntary levy to build up a strike fund. The docks were also on strike and there was a feeling of solidarity in the East End which was both novel and exhilarating, and in the third week of the strike the master-tailors gave in. The dock strike, however, continued and the *Arbeiter Freint* exhorted its readers to give every support to the strikers and their families who were by now in a state of starvation. Jewish shopkeepers offered free food, shoes and clothing, and more than three hundred dockers' children were taken into Jewish homes. It was a brief and improbable honeymoon between the dockside and the Jewish East End.[42]

In 1906 Rocker and his associates established an Anarchist Club in a former Salvation Army depot in Jubilee Street, which was opened by the doyen of anarchists, Prince Kropotkin.[43] It had a meeting hall, library and reading room; it organised courses in history, economics, geography and gave many an East Ender his basic education in radical politics. The difficulty with the Jewish working class, as Rocker and the others discovered, was that they rarely regarded themselves as a class, but as businessmen in temporarily straitened circumstances, and they felt that improvement lay in individual effort and not in mass action. It says something for Rocker's power of advocacy that he brought home the need for unity even to them, nevertheless he and his associates on the *Arbeiter Freint* failed completely to propagate anarchism as a creed.

Yet there were periods before the First World War when readers of the daily press might have thought that the anarchists had the East End in their grip. In January 1911 a couple of self-styled anarchists, who were thought to be connected with a recent murder of policemen in Houndsditch, barricaded themselves in a house in Sidney Street, and when called upon to surrender, opened fire and wounded a police inspector. The Home Secretary, Winston Churchill, arrived to take personal charge of the operation, and troops were called out in support. This was the famous siege of Sidney Street which lasted for less than a day. As preparations were made to storm the house, smoke was seen to be rising from it, and eventually two charred bodies were found inside.

This and similar, if less publicised, episodes led to the belief that the Jewish community harboured in its midst a considerable body of wild and violent men. Nothing could have been further from the truth, as Sir Philip Gibbs, a distinguished journalist, discovered when he visited the Jubilee Street Club:

These alien anarchists were as tame as rabbits. I am convinced that they had not a revolver among them. Yet remembering

the words I heard, I am sure this intellectual anarchy, this
philosophy of revolution, is more dangerous than pistols or
glycerine. For out of that anarchist club in the East End came
ideas.[44]

But they were not the sort of ideas which enjoyed wide currency,
and if the anarchists are remembered at all today it is not for
what they achieved, or even perpetrated, but for the fears they
aroused.

The Jews were more disturbed by the Christian missionaries
than by the so-called anarchists. The Reverend W. H. Davies
who, as Rector of Christ Church, Spitalfields, had more Jews
than Christians in his parish, once put the case for the missionaries to a Jewish gathering. The Anglican Church, he said, with
its parochial system dating back to the seventh century, has
claimed the oversight of all souls within her parishes without
respect to creed or race . . . for whether the clergy of the Church
of England like it or not, the obligation upon them is clear. The
Christian teaching compels them to remember that the middle
wall of partition is broken down, and that there is neither Jew
nor Greek . . . and that the Gospel is to be preached to every
creature.

Although all missionaries were at pains to deny that they
attempted to bribe potential converts, they nearly all offered
inducements of various sorts. Christ Church, Spitalfields, ran
English evening classes which were largely attended by Jews,
and which closed with a religious address. Another common
inducement was the offer of medical aid, which exploited the
Jew's well-known concern for his health. Few Jews, however
poor, resorted to the local workhouse, but they were less hesitant
about making use of the Poor Law hospitals and dispensaries.
In 1901, for example, a peak immigration year, only sixty-two
Jews were admitted to the Whitechapel workhouse but as many as
eight hundred and forty-four[45] applied for medical relief. Medical
missions were able to attract Jews in large numbers, but this did
not mean that many of them were converted to Christianity.
Indeed there were those who considered the whole missionary
effort as something of a joke. They would come for whatever
material benefit might be offered, free excursions, soup, boots or
coal, and if they were required to listen to a passage from the

scriptures in a language they did not understand, it was not too high a price to pay. There was indeed a floating brotherhood prepared to accept anything that was going from whomsoever it came, be they Jew or Gentile, Protestant or Catholic, Established or Dissenter.

The Reverend Davies once protested that, at a special King's dinner organised in his parish, the Jews came, received an allocation of tea, tobacco and chocolate and a special Coronation cup, without joining in the meal (which was non-kosher) or the grace.[46]

The Bishop of Stepney made a similar complaint. There were about five hundred Jews, he said, 'who were in the habit of going round the Mission halls and flocking to the special teas and services which were held from time to time'. But the main attraction was the prospect of medical help.

The first Medical Mission to the Jews was established in Old Saints Parish, Buxton Street, in October 1896 and was consecrated by the Bishop of Stepney. 'Sick persons', he said, 'were more susceptible to spiritual influences and the knowledge put into their mind at such a time might afterwards lead to good results.'[47] A local paper commented that it was 'difficult for the evangelist to reach Jews in the ordinary way', and it looked on the new Mission as a splendid innovation: 'Probably one of the happiest ideas was to associate with gospel propagation medical attendance and advice.'[48]

In 1898 the Church of England went a step further and formally launched 'The Church of England Fund for Work among the Jews of East and North London.' A special committee was formed under the chairmanship of the Bishop of Stepney and several of the local incumbents. It first decided that all parishes with a large Jewish population should regard the mission to the Jews as an integral part of their work. It also urged that 'every care should be taken to obviate the possibility of Jews attaching themselves to the Christian Church for merely mercenary reasons', but at the same time it called for the creation of further medical missions. There were, said the Bishop, about twelve or thirteen missionary groups all working in East London without any coordination.

The Jew, said the Bishop, regarded the missionary not in holy orders as an entrepreneur paid so much per head, and he wanted more clergymen to be actively associated in the work, and to that end he had approached the professors of divinity at Oxford, Cambridge and other universities to facilitate the study of Hebrew and Yiddish, 'and of Jewish modes of thought'. He also attached much importance to house to house visits. Such visiting, he said, should be done by women workers, 'except when the husbands work at home, as the Jewish husbands have oriental ideas about women'.[49]

One of the many groups working in the area was the Stepney Mission in Cambridge Road, headed by Mr D. J. Neugewirtz, a convert. His mission was founded in 1893, and by 1894 he claimed that 'the Mission had carried the good tidings to over five thousand Jewish brethren. Blessed results had followed in many instances' – he did not say how blessed – and that while looking after the spiritual needs of the Jews, 'their temporal needs – in many instances great – had not been neglected'. The Chairman of the gathering, Mr John Marnham, who was a generous supporter of the Mission, confessed that for his part he could not understand why Jews did not like Jesus Christ, 'he was the most perfect Jew and grandest man that ever lived', and he was convinced 'that Israel would never take its proper place among the nations until it had accepted Jesus Christ as the Messiah'. This, in common with almost everything else said at the meeting, was received with loud applause, and the two hundred Jews present must have felt that their tea was well earned.

During the summer months the Rector of one Whitechapel church held outdoor services in his churchyards, and provided neat rows of benches for worshippers. He and his lady harmonium player competed untiringly with the noise of the traffic outside. The audience, mostly Jews, sat and listened stolidly with hats on their heads, sometimes pausing to light a pipe. 'It is sometimes said', the rector declared from the pulpit, 'that Jews are never converted unless they get paid for it. Well you'll not get paid here. Nobody gets anything at all by coming to these services.'[50] But still they came. There were few open spaces in the East End and the sound of a sermon was no deterrent to a man searching for a comfortable seat under an open sky.

The largest, richest, most active and most influential of the missionary groups was the London Society for Promoting

Christianity among the Jews.[51] Its magnificent premises at Palestine Place, Bethnal Green, contained a chapel, a Hebrew missionaries' training centre, a home for any Jewish artisans wishing to undergo conversion, as well as free education and maintenance for any children brought up as Christians. The present inmates, it declared in its 1891 report, 'appear fully to realise the contrast between their former friendless condition and their present life, in which a comfortable home, wholesome food, respectable clothing, instruction in trade, and reward money for attention and industry accumulates until they leave the institution.' Yet, even so, it could claim only twelve converts.

'Imagine the temptation to the poverty-stricken inhabitants of the crowded alleys of the Jewish slum', wrote Beatrice Potter. 'And yet, in spite of comfortable maintenance in the present and brilliant prospects in the future, the number of converts is infinitesimal, a fact that throws an interesting sidelight on the moral tenacity of the Jewish race.'[52]

Some of these converts were perfectly sincere, and being Jewish still, they hardly saw the light before they set up as missionaries in their own account, which added to the number and confusion of the mission halls, and it was these converts who caused the most anger and resentment. When the Bishop of Stepney made an appeal for money and prayers (in that order) to aid the work of one of the missions,[53] it brought forth a rejoinder from Sir Oswald Simon, a Liberal MP and a leading member of the old Jewish community. He summed up perfectly the Jewish attitude to missions and missionaries:

It is reasonable that those who appeal for funds for such a purpose, as well as the readers of *The Times* to whom the appeal is made, should realise the feelings which such a letter arouses in the minds of Jews. We hold that the movement of societies which seek to convert our co-religionists are too often conceived in ignorance and conducted by methods of corruption. . . . To meddle with the settled religious convictions of our neighbours in the hope of supplanting them is a very dangerous exploit. It is a proceeding which in the case of the poor and the weak becomes a stepping stone to temptation and fraud. . . . There is no inherent right in any individual or denomination to interfere with the faith of others . . . there is no lack of spiritual effort among the poor Jews of the East End. It cannot be contended that 'the Church of England Fund for Work Among the Jews of East and North London' will affect their moral improvement because it aims at altering their faith. . . . The three columns of church controversy which, by a strange irony, are preceded by this appeal to convert the Jews, testify that Churchmen are not agreed among themselves as to what they would have Jews do in place of their own venerated faith. There seems almost something immoral in the idea that any society may intrude itself into the homes of private families with the object of altering their faith. It is at any rate a marvellous exhibition of dogmatic arrogance. In the face of widespread poverty and crime amongst the Christian population of London it is deplorable that money so urgently needed and so difficult to collect should be diverted and wasted in the manner proposed. . . . Christian conversion societies for the Jews do not rely upon their open churches. They invade the sanctuary of domestic life. They entice children from parental guidance. They sow discord in the home. Finally, by means which are rarely other than material, and which could not be successfully applied except to those who are in actual physical need, they tempt weak Jews to become doubtful Christians. [54]

There was a deep group feeling among the East End Jews and few of them, even where their beliefs might have carried them that way, could face the loneliness of Christianity. Their Jewishness was bound up with their very being. One could be Orthodox, non-Orthodox, even anti-Orthodox without lapsing from the group, but to go over to Christianity was to go over to the enemy, and to invite hostility and exclusion. Conversion called for either an extraordinary degree of sincerity and courage or of cupidity and fraud. The Jewish class represented by Sir Oswald Simon went over to Christianity in large numbers, but theirs was a class which the missionaries left untouched. In the East End the missionaries, if anything, confirmed the Jew in his Jewishness.

# FOURTEEN

# To Arms

The First World War, once the early disruptions were over, brought full employment to the East End and even pockets of prosperity. The dockers, who a few years before had been charged with holding the nation to ransom, flocked to the colours. Although they were exempted from military service when conscription was introduced, there was such a shortage of labour that troops had to be brought in to handle supplies.[1] The small workshops in the neighbourhood, bolstered by army contracts, were able to offer – and indeed had to offer because of the labour shortage – better wages and working conditions. Women found employment in the new arms industries and for the first time became serious wage-earners in their own right.

The war, in its early phase, was approached by East London in a spirit of cheerful bravado, as something of an adventure, but as the casualty lists lengthened the mood became more sombre and purposeful. With it there came a growing intolerance of those who seemed to be pulling less than their full weight – like the Jews.

There were few Englishmen more earnest in their patriotism than those Jews who had lived here for some generations or who had been born or brought up in England. Their feelings were perhaps best expressed by Basil Henriques, who once said: 'Patriotism is the noblest of sentiments. I just cannot see how a man can feel complete without it. It is one of the most precious things in my life.'[2] He left his East End settlement to join up and had a brilliant war record. His brother was killed at Mons and the oldest son of the minister of the Stepney Green Synagogue died in action on the same front. Or there was the case of the poet Isaac Rosenberg who was born in Bristol and brought up in the East End. He was small, dark, suffered from lung trouble and other ailments. On the advice of his doctor he sailed for South Africa in 1914 but returned in 1915 and enlisted in the army. To the surprise of everyone, including possibly himself, he was accepted and early in 1916 he was sent to France.

'My mind will not relinquish its poetical yearnings', he wrote from the trenches, and his war poems form the most memorable parts of his work. '. . . he endured the inhuman horror of modern war with a great heart', wrote a biographer, 'he would have not liked to be called a hero, but his fortitude was truly heroic.'[3] He was killed in action in April 1918, an event he prophesied in a poem written some weeks before.

It cannot, however, be said that the mass of the new Jewish community felt compelled to rush to arms. Britain, it must be remembered, was allied with Russia against Germany and Austro-Hungary. Both the latter had been comparatively enlightened in their attitude to the Jews, whereas Russia was, in their minds, still the arch-oppressor. Nor had many of them been in Britain long enough to be imbued with a raging sense of patriotism.

But one could not expect the non-Jews of the East End to appreciate that. There was hardly a family among them without a soldier at the front, hardly a family without a casualty. They were being called upon to make every sacrifice, while for the Jews over the road, it seemed, it was business as usual – or, indeed, better than usual.[4] The following, which appeared in a daily paper, was not untypical of the bitterness aroused:

Thirty thousand Russian chaps, fit, and fat, and gay,
Seen 'em swanking in the East End any Saturday;
See 'em prancing up and down, curled and oiled and sleek,
Thirty thousand Yiddishers that lick the word for cheek.

Thirty thousand Russian chaps faring on the best,
Speed the parting Englishman, crowding in his nest;
All with healthy appetites – 'ware the cuckoos brood;
Thirty thousand greedy chops to stuff with British food.
Thirty thousand Russian chaps, fit and fat and young,
(Guileless as old Nick himself) strafe our English tongue;

Bribe and lie to tell the tale – dope to make them sick,
Thirty thousand dodgers they, and up to every trick.[5]

The *East London Observer*, the leading local paper, which had
hitherto, on the whole, been favourably disposed to the Alien,
now turned vehemently against him. It was, it said, time to
ask:

> ... whether as one further result of the war, we shall have to
> alter our methods of offering harbour, refuge and haven for the
> scum and refuse of every low-bred mid-European race. ...
> There is a very strong opinion growing up in East London
> that it is monstrously unjust that we should give the flower of
> the English race to save human liberty for those foreign scal-
> lions who regard themselves, so they say, as 'lodgers in East
> London' without a particle of respect for law, order and good
> behaviour, and lacking the most elemental idea of responsi-
> bility, duty and obligation.[6]

Such attacks were wide of the mark, but they had enough truth
in them to embarrass the established Jewish community and its
mouthpiece, the *Jewish Chronicle*.

In January 1916, when conscription was introduced, tribunals
were set up to hear claims for deferment. They were not without
their moments of comedy. One man sought deferment on the
grounds that he was a Cohen, another on the grounds that he
was needed to conduct morning prayers, a third because he was
saying *kaddish* (memorial prayer) for his father, and a fourth
because he was not permitted to live in a dwelling without a
*mezuzah*. Ministers of Religion were exempt from military service
and one who had turned moneylender reverted to the Ministry
as soon as conscription was brought in. The *Jewish Chronicle*
condemned such efforts and noted scathingly, 'that as soon as
compulsion became law there was in many parts of the country a
rush of young men as recruits, not to the service of the Crown,
but the service of the Synagogue'.[7]

Vladimir Jabotinsky, the Zionist leader, described the Jewish
East End as 'a separate world, shut off, as by a thick wall, from
embattled England'.[8] It seemed wrong to him that about twenty
thousand Russian Jews of military age should escape conscription because they were friendly aliens and not British subjects.

... there are many thousands of youths in the East End who go about in mufti while other youths are in khaki. This fact cannot be explained away especially to the mothers and sisters of the men who are in the trenches. So long as they see healthy young Jews in their thousands at large they will not relax the pressure which led to the present situation. ... They will not be persuaded by any sort of moral objection which may sound right in Jewish ears. ... We cannot blame them, we must understand their psychology ... the situation admits only one honourable end: those who chose England to be their home must defend England.[9]

The *Jewish Chronicle* regarded the situation as unwholesome and unjust and urged the Home Secretary, Herbert Samuel, himself a Jew, to call up all Russian Jews of eligible age for military service, and Samuel made it known that he would do so. The aliens, he said, were 'expected either to offer their services to the British army or to return to Russia to fulfil their military obligations there'.[10] And he added: 'I should have been most blameworthy if I had neglected to bring home to the members of the Jewish community living in this country the fact that where they enjoy rights, they also should share the burdens.'[11]

Jabotinsky now came forward with a new idea, the formation of a Jewish legion to which, he believed, Jews would flock in their thousands. The government was not in favour and to forestall the threat of compulsion Jabotinsky joined with Weizmann and others to exhort Russian Jews of military age to volunteer for service in the British army. These two men were amongst the most persuasive speakers the Jewish world had known, but in this case their powers proved inadequate. The response was derisory. In all four hundred Jews enlisted. The voluntary campaign was abandoned. There was no alternative but compulsion.[12]

The newcomers, left without their usual patrons and protectors, now formed their own Foreign Jews' Protection Committee and found the unlikely help of Lord Sheffield, an eccentric English peer, whose daughter Venetia Stanley was married to Edwin Montagu, Secretary of State for India, and a cousin of Herbert Samuel. Sheffield was concerned above all with England's traditional right of asylum, and agreed 'that we should never threaten to return a man to the country he had repudiated. ...

The right of asylum was fixed in our habits before it found expression in our laws.'[13]

The Foreign Jews Protection Committee wrote to the *Manchester Guardian* repudiating the *Jewish Chronicle* and official Anglo-Jewry's attitude on the Government's plans to deal with Russian Jews, and declared that they in no way represented the views of the great majority of Jews in England. The *Jewish Chronicle* questioned the 'journalistic etiquette' of giving space to such a letter and thought it was a pity that the *Guardian* 'should allow its columns to be the resort of such a method of controversy',[14] but it was otherwise unrepentant. It regretted 'that the element of compulsion had been introduced in the form chosen' – i.e., deportation. 'For this, however, our Russian-born co-religionists have themselves to thank.'[15]

If the Foreign Jews thus found no sympathy in the leading, or indeed, the secondary Anglo-Jewish papers, it found some in the weekly *Nation*, the forerunner of the *New Statesman*, which launched into a vicious personal attack on Herbert Samuel:

> We do not wish to under-rate the difficulties of his scrupulous mind. As other Ministers, when they enter a coalition fear it may be said of them, 'Why the man is a Liberal still', Mr. Samuel seems to fear lest it should be said of him that he is a good Jew. An exaggerated fear. Mr. Samuel mistakes the British character. We give our respect to the Jew who stands boldly for his own race. We have no respect for the Jew who deserts his race. Mr. Samuel need not be afraid that it should be said of him that he is unfit to be Home Secretary because he is partial to the Jews. That is not the verdict. We say of him that he is unfit to be Home Secretary because he is incapable of being just to the Jews.[16]

It was an unfair attack. It was precisely because he was aware of the harm which the anomalous situation was doing to Jewry that he was determined to change it. 'If the mass of the Russian Jews in this country refuse to lift a finger to help when this country is making immeasurable sacrifices in a war in which the cause of Liberty all over the world is bound up,' he wrote, 'the effect on the reputation of the Jewish name everywhere will be disastrous.'[17]

This was not the view of Zangwill who spoke of Samuel as a

Pharaoh, a sort of Russian Jew-baiter who 'panic-stricken by the mob was ready to save English Jewry by the blood of Russian Jews'.[18]

Samuel was by then out of office. Bonar Law took the matter in hand and early in 1917 the Government passed legislation to compel Russian Jews of military age to choose between service in the British army and deportation to Russia.

The Foreign Jews Protection Committee continued its protest and prepared a manifesto which was described by one paper as 'the most shameful, barefaced and selfish appeal which has ever emanated from the alien community'.[19]

The committee harangued, petitioned, prepared handbills, wrote letters to the press, organised large public meetings, and when it was clear that the government would not be dissuaded from its course, insisted that, if the newcomers were to be sent back to Russia, they should be sent with their families. This, wrote *The Times*, was a stalling device: 'They have no real desire to return to the country of their birth, but they seem to think that shipping difficulties will prevent the government from carrying through the wholesale deportations which it asked for.'[20] They were claiming the right of asylum without being prepared to defend their place of asylum.

Yet it was understandable. Patriotism does not go with nineteen centuries of harassment and homelessness. There was nothing in his folk memory or personal experience to instil in the Russian Jew the sort of love of one's birthplace which the Englishman, and indeed the English Jew, took for granted. The thought of Russia itself evoked a shudder. The very instincts which lead to a love of country had been all but cauterised, and it was therefore perhaps natural that the newcomers should have been slow in acquiring any deep love of England. They had not been there long. It was but another, if less bitter, stage in their long night of wandering. They had not, after all, been received with open arms, but with grudging tolerance. Hardly had they settled in any number when an agitation began to keep them out, and even to kick them out. They had been accused of sweating, rack-renting, anarchism, white-slavery, pushing the Englishman out of his job and home, and of bringing crime, squalor and disease to the East End. There were times at the height of the agitation when it was dangerous for a foreign Jew to show his face in the

East End, and if the young men now eligible for army service were too young to remember that, their parents could and did remind them. A Jew's loyalty was first and foremost to his people and to his family. And family pressure, amounting almost to moral blackmail, kept him at home. Charles Landstone, a writer, who served in a labour battalion during World War I, recalls overhearing a woman lament at the time: *Mine zun is kein mentsch nit, er's avecgeloifen tzum krig* – my son's not a man, he's gone to the war. For if the patriotism normal in most human breasts had been stifled in most Russian Jews, it had given way to a fierce group loyalty, first to the Jewish people and beyond that to the ultimate loyalty – the group within the group, the family.

Moreover, Jews who might have been inclined to join the army were not encouraged by the stories which came back about the experiences of some of their compatriots. The bullying NCO, accepted by most privates as a painful and inevitable part of army life, assumed the visage of a pogromist when encountered by a Russian Jew.

Then there was the tragic case of an eighteen-year-old boy, the only son of a Russian Jewish family who, unknown to his parents, joined the army and was tortured by the anxiety and distress he caused them, as could be seen from his frequent letters home:

Dear Mother,
I arrived safe and everything is alright. I was very sorry to leave you, and very sorry to see you cry so much as you did, but never mind, I will be back one day, so be happy at home. Dear Mother, do not forget my nineteenth birthday on Saturday May 1st. Tell Father and Kate to be happy ... from your loving son Aby. Dear Mother, I would like your photo to hold on to me.[21]

A few months later he wrote from the front:

I have been in the trenches four times and come out safe. We are going in again this week. Dear Mother, we go in the trenches six days, and then we get relieved for six days....
You write you was nearly going mad waiting for my letters. You know it takes two days to get to London or more....
Dear Mother, I know it is very hard for you to miss me from

home, but still never mind, be happy and don't cry. I think you know I am sorry I done that, but if I have luck I will come home. . . . I might be home for the Jewish holidays.[22]

But he did not get home for the holidays and early in 1916 his parents received a letter from the War Office informing them that he was 'ill at 38th, Field Ambulance, France, suffering from wounds and shock (mine explosion).'[23]

It was clear from the letters which the boy himself sent from hospital that he had no idea what hit him. He spoke of injuries to his back and his foot, but he was in the main concerned to reassure his mother that he would be all right, and that he was being well looked after and fed. A little later he complained of bed-sores, but there was no reference in his letter to the mine explosion. He was discharged on 20 January after a month in hospital. At the end of February he was in difficulties:

Dear Mother, We were in the trenches and I was ill, so I went out and they took me to the prison, and I am in a bit of trouble now and won't get any money for a long time. I will have to go in front of a Court. I will try my best to get out of it, so don't worry. But, dear Mother, try to send me some money, not very much, but try your best. I will let you know in my next how I get on. Give my best love to Father and Kate.
    From your loving son,
        Aby.[24]

Then followed two months of silence until April when they received a curt note from the War Office:

Sir,
    I am directed to inform you that a report has been received from the War Office to the effect that No. –, 11th Battalion, Middlesex Regiment, GS., was sentenced after trial by court martial to suffer death by being shot for desertion, and the sentence was duly executed on 20th March, 1916.
    I am, Sir, your obedient servant,
        P. G. Hendley,
            2nd Lieut-Colonel I.C. Infantry Records.

In July 1917 the Military Service (Convention with the Allies) Act, which gave friendly aliens a choice between conscription and deportation became law.

In September, the following, signed by the Commissioner of Police, was posted to several thousand Jewish homes:

Take notice that facilities have been provided for you to return to Russia under the above Act, and in order to avail yourself of them you must be at Euston Station, platform 14, at 11.30 p.m. on Saturday, September 29th. . . . Not more than two packages of combined weight of not more than 150 lbs. can be taken, and each package must have a label attached with the words 'Russian Convention' and the name and serial number of the owner clearly written on them.

You are not allowed to take with you letters, English gold or intoxicating liquor.

You are advised to take food for the railway journey.

If you fail to avail yourself of this opportunity to return to Russia the necessary steps to enforce your liability to serve in the British army will be taken as soon as possible.

The journey to Russia was long, hazardous and slow and it is unlikely that anyone so dispatched could have seen active service for in November came the Red Revolution. Russia made an independent peace with the Central Powers and withdrew from the war.

There was also, in the meantime, a more positive development on the home front. The British government, as we have seen, had rejected Jabotinsky's idea of a Jewish Legion, but as a compromise it accepted the idea of a Jewish regiment, or at least a Jewish battalion of a British regiment, the 38th Royal Fusiliers. They came to be nicknamed the Judeans, and, early in 1918, preceded by the band of the Coldstream Guards, they paraded through the streets of the East End.

The paper which in previous years had led the campaign against Jewish 'shirkers', 'funkers' and 'scum' was impressed with the spectacle:

Any impartial observer will admit that the inspection was satisfactory, and that the men bore themselves bravely, and had in a large measure assimilated some of the best traditions of Thomas Atkins Esq. They marched cheerfully, with jets and smile, and showed everything furthest from an unwilling, fearful, Conscript band. . . . It is understood that the new soldiers are shortly off to the Front. . . . We have no doubt that they will fight bravely and make good soldiers now that they are 'in the game', and that they will feel they are fighting for a country which, of all countries, has been just and generous to the Jewish race for centuries.[25]

The agitation died down, but some of the anti-Jewish feeling persisted.

# FIFTEEN

# Blitz

The East Enders who had rushed to the colours at the outbreak of the First World War had returned victorious but disappointed to bleak streets, bleak homes, bleak prospects. Nothing had been improved by their sacrifices. Wages were low, unemployment was high and a sense of brooding frustration pervaded the whole area. The post-war depression had given rise to new ideologies in Italy and Germany, which Sir Oswald Mosley and his British Union of Fascists attempted to emulate.

Its most immediate appeal was to the dejected elements in the British middle class and two years after it was formed in 1932, the BUF claimed to have twenty thousand members. They did not, however, achieve menacing proportions until they turned their attention to the East End. Anti-semitism was not at first part of Mosley's programme, and in later years he was to claim that he never attacked Jews for what they were but for what they did. In his *Notes for Speakers* he added that:

> Speakers will not devote a disproportionate amount of their speech to the Jewish question, the effect of which is to flatter the Jews' sense of self-importance. They should be treated as a problem with which Fascism will deal faithfully, but by no means the only problem which confronts us.[1]

He had plans for the creation of a corporate state and radical economic reforms, but one heard little of them from East End platforms. Here the Jewish issue was central. Mosley's plan was to deport those Jews whose activities were 'inimical to the state' and to deprive others of citizenship. His speakers went beyond that and heaped hysterical abuse on the Jewish community.

The BUF established branches in Shoreditch, Limehouse and Bethnal Green, and they held marches right through the heart of the Jewish area, chanting 'the Yids, the Yids, we've got to get rid of the Yids' – which could have had but one purpose, provocation – and they succeeded.

The Board of Deputies of British Jews established a defence committee to counter the activities of the BUF, and the Association of Jewish ex-Servicemen formed vigilante groups. Both were thought to be too cautious and respectable by young Jewish activists and the gymnasia of the Jewish youth clubs were given over to massively-attended classes in wrestling and boxing. The elderly and the old, cowed by memories of persecution and oppression, rushed to put up their shutters every time they heard the word Jew shouted in the streets; the young were English enough to stand up and fight. As a result, almost every Fascist meeting was the occasion of tussles and fights which were widely reported in the press. This in turn increased the size of the crowds and the degree of commotion. Every Sunday yielded its quota of bleeding noses and broken heads, and every Monday its list of charges for insulting behaviour and causing a breach of the peace. The crowds grew larger still and Mosley gave increasing attention to the Jewish question.

'Up to three years ago', he declared at an Albert Hall rally in 1936, 'anti-Semitism was unknown as a strong force in Britain. Today, in any audience in Britain, the strongest passion that can be aroused is the passion against the corruption of Jewish power.'[2]

This may not have been true of Britain as a whole, but it was true of the East End. The Jews had both by habit and creed largely kept themselves apart from the gentile East End and this inevitably gave rise to a certain amount of hostility and suspicion. Their very qualities, their sobriety, industry, thrift, were such as to incur dislike. The energetic non-Jewish East Ender who made a bit of money generally used it to move into a better part of London, beyond the curious eyes of his neighbours. The Jew on the other hand used his money on clothes and food and travel, all of which gave him the appearance of being better off, and on Sabbath and festivals the parade of Jews in their bowlers and broad-cloth, and their satin-clad perfumed daughters excited comment and envy. The first East End cars, when cars were still objects of curiosity, were mainly Jewish. The Jew seemed to be able to acquire in a matter of years what the Gentiles could not obtain in a lifetime. Everyone knew how they had arrived hungry and penniless at the docks some few decades before, and now they seemed to be living off the fat of the land. The fact that there was also grinding poverty in the Jewish East End was overlooked. It was the opulent who stood out as the symbol of the Jewish capacity to 'make it quick', and the suggestion of the Fascist speakers was that they made it, not by effort or merit, but by cunning and stealth and were, indeed, robbing the Englishman of his birthright.

One of the favourite meeting points of the black-shirted Fascists was Salmon Lane near Stepney Green. A man might get up to speak and within minutes he had a crowd of several hundred round him. Sometimes it would develop into an impromptu demonstration of several thousands, snowballing as it moved, with people pouring out of their houses, women with children, mothers pushing babies in prams, shouting slogans, sometimes hooting and threatening every Jew they passed.

The Communists, who regarded themselves as the party of the working men and the East End as their natural base, never achieved such a following and never had the same grass-roots appeal as the Fascists. However they included in their ranks a number of influential trade union leaders, especially among the dockers, who were fairly well organised and politically conscious. The party also attracted a great many Jews because it was the only one to take the challenge of Fascism seriously. It was also the party to be most directly threatened by the Fascists. Thus, whether as an organisation or through its individual members, the Communist party led the opposition to Mosley in the East End.

In the late summer of 1936 the Fascists announced that they would hold a rally on Sunday, 4 October and march right through the East End including the Jewish areas. It was to be the biggest show of strength the party had made. The Board of Deputies urged the Jewish public to stay at home for Mosley was counting on their opposition to get attention. The advice was ignored and various groups – Jews and non-Jews – came together to stop the march, under the slogan: THEY SHALL NOT PASS. Herbert Morrison, Labour MP for South Hackney and a future Home Secretary, who had earlier drawn attention to threats and attacks on East End Jews, urged the then Home Secretary, Sir John Simon, to ban the march or there would be bloodshed. Sir John felt that he could not interfere. Sir Philip Game, Commissioner of Police, thereupon prepared for battle and drafted six thousand constables, a third of his entire force, into East London, some on foot, many on horse, and others at the ready in buses and cars. A police helicopter hovered overhead, and an elaborate system of radio communications linked different police detachments to head-office.

The streets began to fill from the early hours of the morning and the main thoroughfares of East London became impassable long before Mosley was due to appear. Congestion was particularly heavy where the Whitechapel Road and Commercial Road converged at Gardner's Corner, and people were pushed through plate glass windows by the sheer press of bodies. Fighting between pro- and anti-Mosley factions broke out in several places and police rushing in to restore order were themselves attacked. In Cable Street pavements were ripped up and carts overturned to form a barrier across the street, and bricks and stones were held in readiness for the appearance of the Fascists. In nearby Christian Street broken bottles were scattered across the roadway to impede mounted police. At Wellclose Square police with drawn batons charged the crowd and forced them back into St George's Street. From there they moved into Cable Street and cleared the barricades.[3]

At 2 p.m. a van with barred windows carrying Mosley's advance guard drew up at the rallying point near the Tower of London. At this the crowd, cheering and booing, surged forward. The police hit out in all directions. Tempers flared on both sides, and there was a danger that if the tension continued, the crowd could get out of hand and the police would be overwhelmed. Sir Philip Game telephoned his fears to the Home Secretary who was in his country cottage, and when Mosley drew up in his chauffeur-driven car at 3.30 p.m., he was asked to disperse his followers, which he did, but under protest. 'The government', he declared, 'surrenders to Red violence and Jewish corruption. We never surrender.'[4] Sporadic violence, however, continued for the rest of the day and into the night, and streets were left a shambles, but the day had clearly gone to the anti-Fascists. Mosley and his blackshirts had been stopped.

On the following Sunday a rampaging crowd, wielding sticks, hurling bricks and shouting abuse, attacked every Jew within sight. An eyewitness described the scene:

> Terrorism the like of which has never been witnessed in the East End broke out again last Sunday when a band of hooligans sped down Mile End Road, smashing, looting and pillaging the windows of Jewish shopkeepers. . . . Not one shop bearing an English name was molested. Within five minutes of the attack that section of Mile End Road was a shambles. Broken glass, woodwork, clothing, fruit and vegetables, the contents of the windows were strewn over the pavement. . . . On the main road a man was hurled bodily through a window and a seven year old girl was thrown in after him.[5]

Police were rushed to the spot, but by the time they got there the mob had dispersed. The official explanation was that the police had been drafted to keep the peace at a Communist rally being held in Victoria Park about the same time. It did not convince the East End Jews who felt that the police, and indeed the police magistrates, had more than a sneaking sympathy for their attackers. The BUF denied that they had anything to do with the outbreak, but it bore every mark of their style, and even if they were not directly involved, they certainly provoked it.

'The police', C. Mowat was to write later, 'seemed more concerned to protect the Fascists than to curb their brutality or defend their victims',[6] and every time the Fascists descended into the East End a host of Jews were hauled before the courts. The standard police retort to such charges was that they were impartial between the two sides, which to Jewish eyes meant that they were impartial as between the trouble-makers and their victims, and they felt that they never got fair treatment from the police. However the events of 4 and 11 October had the salutary effect of finally stirring the Home Office to action, and a Public Order Act was hurried through Parliament, which banned political uniforms and gave the police powers to ban processions. The Fascists, deprived of their uniforms and pushed back into mufti, seemed shrunken and drab.

The East End had recoiled at the violence and shame which the Fascists brought to the area. External events, the posturings and aggression of Hitler and Mussolini, the Spanish civil war, further weakened the appeal of Fascism, and Mosley and his followers came to be regarded as enemies not merely by Jews and Communists but much of the nation. They still held the occasional street meeting, and still provoked the occasional fight, but the increasing threat of war was turning the East Enders' minds to graver things. Early in 1938 plans were announced for a £¼ m. air raid scheme to make the East End safe against the bomber. The area, perhaps the most congested quarter of the British Isles, with important dock, harbour and railway installations, was particularly vulnerable. The only real defence was evacuation, and when war was declared on 3 September 1939, East London was suddenly denuded of its children and a great many young mothers. Barrage balloons hung over the river like great flying whales. Anti-aircraft emplacements were built in Victoria Park, and at various points near the docks. Searchlights probed the night sky, and men stumbled through the silent, blacked-out streets.

As autumn turned to winter and all remained quiet on the home-front the fears of massive air raids were allayed. As winter turned into a long, sunny spring, the children began to return. They had found it difficult to adapt themselves to a rural life and missed the sights, sounds, noise and smells of home. By the end of April it was reckoned that about 80 per cent of the evacuees had returned. Their mothers attracted to highly-paid jobs in factories, often left them unattended. The children stayed away from school during the day and ran wild in the streets in the evening. One social worker complained that 'Whitechapel had gone back in education a hundred years'.[7]

Then came the allied disasters on the Western Front but even these did not stem the flow of returning mothers and children. The East End braced itself for more strenuous efforts, and a local paper announced in blaring headlines that Stepney was holding a special scrap iron week. The annual Catholic Whit Sunday Procession organised by St Mary's and St Michael, Commercial Road, was held that year as every year. Hundreds of children from the parochial schools took part and were followed by the Catholic Young Men's Society, the Guild of the Blessed Sacrament, the Guild of St Agnes, the Children of Mary, the Children of the Blessed Sacrament, some in veils and cloaks, some in sashes, some carrying banners, and borne aloft the Statue of the Sacred Heart decorated with lilies and carnations, the procession coursing like a river through the East End, a splash of colour under a sunny sky. The war seemed very distant.[8]

But disaster followed disaster in 1940. France fell under the Nazi advance and the BEF were evacuated from Dunkirk. The warm spring gave way to a hot summer. Then, on Friday 5 September the German Luftwaffe struck. Sixty-eight bombers attacked London causing some casualties and damages in the East End. The next day, two hundred bombers came in broad daylight, one wave behind the other – headed for the docks. Soon the north bank of the Thames was alight. Smoke billowed out across London. Fires burned through the night, leapt and surged and sent a glow into the sky which was not dimmed until the morning. The following night they came yet again, a great armada of three hundred and twenty bombers and six hundred fighters, and the crump of high explosives and the thunder of ack-ack continued through the hours of darkness. Day seemed night and night day as smoke billowed and flames leapt. A seven-storey warehouse in St Katharine's dock stacked with paraffin wax, hemp, copra and timber went up like a giant candle and lit up the shore on both sides of the river.

The bombers returned the following night, and nightly thereafter. Then on 2 November there was remission. No sirens, no bomb, no ack-ack; people were kept awake by the silence. London had been bombed for fifty-seven nights in succession. Twelve thousand people were killed and over sixteen thousand seriously injured, a great many of them in the East End. A large part of the riverside from the Tower to the River Lea had been flattened. Docks, warehouses, bridges, railway sidings, whole streets had vanished. The evacuees who had returned were hurriedly sent back to the country and this time they remained. The most familiar sound of East London, the shrill cries of children at play, was stilled. The town was like Hamelin wrote a war-time visitor:

Going through the highways and by-ways where our budding cricketers and footballers were wont to playfully disport themselves, not to mention the hop-scotch specialists, I missed their shrill and happy voices. The streets seemed strangely quiet.[9]

The respite did not last long and bombing was resumed on 6 November. On 29 November came the great raid on the City which was to be called the second fire of London. Gas mains were set alight, water mains blown up. The Thames was at low tide and little water could be pumped from the river. The fires started by the one wave of bombers, illuminated London for the next and sent up a glow like the midnight sun. Many fires were out of control and burned through the night and for much of the day, crackling here, dancing there, or leaping with a roar into the skies. Sirens sounded nightly and the raids continued into the new year. Whitechapel Station was hit, Charrington's brewery, Crossman's brewery. Incendiaries and high explosives peppered the London Hospital.

'They did what they liked with us', said one woman living near the West India Docks. 'I thanked God my children had been evacuated to Somerset.' She would bed down for the night in the Anderson shelter in the back garden as a matter of course. One night when she emerged after the all-clear, her house was a pile of rubble. Reception centres had been opened in nearby schools, but she went down the street to her sister in Cartom Street, near Poplar Road. As she did so the sirens went again. She quickened her pace and got to her sister as she was going into her shelter. A little later there was a loud explosion, and when they emerged her sister's house too was in ruins.[10]

Not everyone had back-gardens and not everyone felt safe in their Anderson shelters. The nights were warm and thousands of people trekked out to Epping Forest. Others went to the nearest underground station, although the tubes were not regarded as safe against bombing. Not all of them were deep, and many of them lay under a heavy criss-cross of gas and water mains. A direct hit on Balham Station in South London resulted in many deaths by drowning, but still people continued to crowd in every night, bringing bedding and books and sandwiches and flasks, ready for a long siege.

In East London public pressure forced the authorities to open the Tilbury Shelter which was an underground extension of the Liverpool Street goods depot stretching for some distance under the Commercial Road. It was said to be able to accommodate ten thousand people, though on some nights as many as fourteen thousand crammed in.[11] People no longer waited to hear the sirens before rushing for cover. The shelter became an extension to their homes. Tilbury opened at 4.30 p.m. and queues began to form as early as noon. Invalids came in bath-chairs, mothers with babies in prams, young women and old with great bags of sewing and knitting. There was a boom in reading material and almost anything published found a ready market. Prostitutes paraded. Hawkers sold fried fish. Children slept. Evenings were occasionally enlivened by a free fight. East London adapted itself to an underground existence, and one old woman remained underground for seven weeks.[12]

At first there were no sanitary facilities. People urinated and defecated on the line and the air was like a clammy blanket. In the Tilbury Shelter they stacked cardboard cartons to form cubicles and used them as lavatories. Later the Government began to supply latrines, and to fix up bunks, though East Enders preferred the chummy, thigh-rubbing intimacy of the platforms. The health authorities had to cope with a new breed of ailments arising out of the long hours in the shelters. Pressure palsies, bed sores and gravitational oedema became common, but there was no great increase in gastro-intestinal and respiratory infections no great infestation of lice. East London proved to be a cleaner and healthier place than people had expected.[13]

On 11 March 1941 there was the second heavy raid on the docks. The first bombers appeared about eight at night, and the all-clear was not sounded till three in the morning. And so it continued night after night. Sometimes the bombers flew over the area and dropped an occasional bomb, sometimes they made it their prime target. During a heavy attack on 10 May Poplar Hospital received a direct hit and the London Hospital received further damage. Mann's brewery was hit again and their stable demolished. Twenty-five horses were killed, and another six, wild with terror, galloped up Whitechapel Road as bombs and debris crashed about them.

Londoners emerged from the bowels of the earth, washed, ate a quick breakfast, clambered to work over heaps of fallen masonry, through streets made almost impassable by fallen cables and telegraph wires, worked for a few hours, and returned early to queue for a place in the shelter. The next night passed without incident and the next. Although London did not know it, the blitz was over. Hitler was preparing for his attack on Russia.

The East End's worst calamity of the war occurred some two years later in 1943, and it was not the direct result of enemy action. Bethnal Green, because it was so densely populated, had suffered heavily in the bombing. A large part of the area was laid to waste, five hundred and fifty-five people were killed and over four hundred seriously injured.[14] Many of the houses were of a back-to-back type without a yard and without place for an air-raid shelter. Therefore Bethnal Green Underground Station was adapted as a vast shelter with room for ten thousand. The Germans had threatened mass retaliation for an allied bombing raid on Berlin early in the year so that when the warning sounded at 8.17 p.m. on 3 March, people converged on Bethnal Green Station from all directions, some walking, some hurrying and forming a heavy throng near the immediate approaches. Ten minutes later there came a thunderous earth-shaking crash. Bombs did not have such an impact. Land-mines the word went round, the Germans were dropping land-mines. It was in fact a salvo of anti-aircraft rockets discharged from a battery in Victoria Park, some five hundred yards away, but no one knew that. Those walking began to run, those at the approaches to the shelter dived for the entrance and scrambled down the stairs. And then it happened. A woman with a baby in her arms near the bottom step stumbled and fell, those behind fell on top, and those further behind, pressed by a great crash of bodies, fell on top of them. The crowds outside, fearing that they were being kept out, became frantic and pressed harder still. Anxiety gave way to fear and fear to panic. There was shouting, screaming, gesticulations, and muffled cries. The entire stairway was a solid mass of bodies, some dead, some dying, many gasping in agony. Seven or eight infants were pulled free, but not a single adult could be extracted. Ambulances converged from every corner of London. Special operating teams stood by near the mouth of the shelter. The first of the bodies was brought out before nine, the last at 11.40. At the end of the day, one hundred and seventy-three were dead, and sixty-two seriously injured.[15]

There were rumours that local Fascists had induced a state of panic, and William Joyce, formerly one of Mosley's lieutenants, and now broadcasting from Germany, said it was a 'Jewish panic'. Joyce, nicknamed Lord Haw-Haw, had a large audience in the London area, and his charge received wide currency. There were in fact few Jews living in Bethnal Green at the time, and the charge, declared a government inquiry, was not only 'without foundation', it was 'demonstrably false. The Jewish attendance at this shelter was, and is so small as to constitute a hardly calculable percentage.'[16]

The following year 1944, on 10 June, an unidentified flying object fell in Bethnal Green killing six people and seriously injuring others. It was at first thought to be an allied plane which had crashed while trying to make a forced landing. It was soon found to be one of Hitler's first flying bombs, later nicknamed doodle-bugs. They were about the size of small fighters, flew low over the rooftops, with a low, throbbing drone. Then as the engine cut out, there would be a few seconds silence, followed by a whistling noise which grew louder as it drew nearer and finally a terrific crash as the machine exploded. They came over by the hundred, wrote a war historian, and 'this intermittent drizzle of malignant robots was harder to bear than the blitz'.

A white-haired lady, now a resident of an old age home in Poplar, recalled her own experience of a flying bomb.

Things was quiet in the East End in those days, on account of everyone listening out for those doodle-bugs. Every time you heard a noise, you thought ah, is this it, especially any droning noise. I was living with my sister then and we was having a bite, and we both heard it, a low noise. We put down our knife and fork. It gets louder – and stops. We was out of the house and into the shelter before you could say Jack Robinson. And bang. When we come out there's smoke and dust, but no house. My sister and I looked at each other. 'Daft ain't it?' she said. The cat had a lovely time, mice running for cover in all directions. It was a lovely time for cats, the blitz.

On 3 August, a flying bomb hit the London Hospital. It was 1.35 a.m., and Miss Bowell, a night nurse on duty in one of the wards later reported:

Everything was quiet; all the patients asleep. Suddenly I heard the sound of a flying bomb. The engine stopped and then I heard it whistling through the air, and realised that it could hardly avoid hitting us. A moment later there was a terrific explosion, complete darkness, the crash of falling masonry, and the rush of water. My spectacles had been knocked off, a shower of glass and plaster had fallen on my head and shoulders, and my mouth had filled with dust. Complete silence followed, and for a moment I feared that all my patients had been killed.[17]

Damage was extensive but, miraculously, there was only one death.

In September there came a new menace. There was no droning noise, no noise at all. One only knew of it when it landed, and then it was like a minor earthquake. It was the V2 rocket, tall as a two-storey house, and weighing twelve tons. On 10 November, one fell on Petticoat Lane, almost pulling up the street by its roots, and causing over two hundred casualties, many of them fatal. The bombardment continued through the winter and into the spring of 1945. Early in the morning of 27 March, as Londoners were stirring themselves for work, a rocket fell on a block of flats in Vallance Road, razing it to the ground, killing one hundred and twenty-four people and injuring forty-nine. A soldier returning on leave from the front that day found his home destroyed and his family of seven dead.[18] It was the last rocket to fall on London. Two months later the war was over.

When the men returned from the front, the East End they had known had virtually vanished, and not everyone regretted it. At first, small prefabricated houses began to sprout among the tall weeds on the bombed sites. They were intended to be temporary but some of them are still in use. Then one vast housing estate began to rise after another, four, six, eight, ten storeys high, with small balconies and much glass (with steel-walled, steel-doored, vandal-proof lifts), well-spaced with small gardens, and here and there a playground with brightly coloured swings and see-saws. Poplar was rebuilt almost as a new town and became a showplace during the 1951 Festival of Britain. There were new pubs, new shops grouped together in neat parades, and occasionally even a new church, compact, with austere lines and much polished timber. Many churches were burnt-out shells and stood gaping to the skies, but St Dunstan, the mother church of Stepney, its tombstones hugging its ancient walls, stood un scathed amid the ruins.

The reconstruction was rapid and, when the bombed sites were built over, the demolition men moved in and the crash of falling masonry, now echoing benignly, is perhaps the most characteristic sound of East London.

The long lines of two-storey houses, one up one down, with chimneys hidden behind parapets, are vanishing. Here and there a street remains, given a new dignity by its isolation among the high-rise blocks, and suggesting grander days than they in fact enjoyed, but there are still signs the old times.

A widow who lost one husband in the war, and two since, has these recollections:

You should have known Wapping in the old days. It was an island really, docks on three sides of us, and the river on the fourth. There was never much money about, but then you didn't need much. A bob would see you through the day, and if you didn't have a bob you shared with those what had – though if you had a bob you shared with those what hadn't. Surprising the number of people what hadn't a bean and grew fat on it. You saw more fat people then than you do now. And how they worked, the women that is. The men were a lot of lazy narks, always were, still are. Two husbands I've had, and neither knew what it was to do a day's work. Get up any time you like, six in the morning, and you'd find women on their knees scrubbing their doorstep. Some of the Irish was hardly off their knees. In church one minute, on the doorstep the next. They had these processions, the church, right through the streets, with the little girls in white and carrying posies, and fancy uniforms, and Bishops too they had, with all the trimmings, and bands too. Could watch them all day, well we did, standing by the open doorway, or hanging out of the windows. Irish you know, but we all mixed well. And then there was Christmas. You could feel it in the air weeks before it came. Things got quicker and livelier. Windows were full of little fancy lights, and the shops didn't seem to shut at all, not the small corner ones. My two older sisters what never married used to come and stay with us, and oo, we did go wild. No, I never did go to church, not even on Christmas, well people just didn't, not our type of people – unless they was Irish. Not even the Irish go now.

Dockland west of Millwall is silent now. The cranes have
been dismantled, warehouses are being demolished and expensive
cars bounce over the cobbles, with expensive diners headed for
the *Prospect of Whitby*. There are still dockers in plenty and they
form a traffic jam in the early morning as they set out in their
cars on the outward run to East Ham and West Ham and Tilbury,
and again in the afternoon as they turn westwards for home, and
a long evening at ease, shoeless and in sweat-shirt, with beer
can in hand in front of the colour television. A docker, now
retired and living in an old age home, marvels at this new world:

> The money there's about, the money. The nephew, a youngster,
> thinks nothing of spending a fiver on an evening up West –
> spends a quid on parking his bleeding car. A quid! There was
> times I didn't earn that in a week. And they don't work at all
> do they? They're hardly there before they're back, and it's all
> buttons and levers. I used to come home bleeding, my shirt
> stuck to my back, from humping two hundredweight sacks of
> barley. Bleeding. They had to take my shirt off with scissors,
> and I was lucky if at the end of the week I had enough change
> left over for a pint. A pint? These lads have cocktail cabinets.

In Limehouse I was the guest for an evening in the council
flat of a Thames lighterman and his wife. 'I'm not a docker', he
was careful to point out, for laymen are apt to lump all waterside
workers as one, 'we are members of an ancient and honourable
profession.'

One entered through a small hallway made almost impassable
by a tall bookshelf into a small living-room lined with books.
There was no television in sight, but numerous ashtrays, statu-
ettes, paperweights, the bric-a-brac of travel. Lightermen have
enjoyed higher status and greater security of employment than
dockers, but not necessarily higher wages. His wife is a canteen
manageress, and they have no children.

'I suppose you could call me a snob', he said, 'but we don't
have much to do with anyone in this building. They never open
a book – you can't talk to them. They don't speak English, do
they? It's all grunts and "inits?" We're cut off a bit, but we don't
mind. We're both keen readers, and we have friends visiting
from other parts of town.'

His wife is an excellent cook. He knows good wine from bad,

11a. Jewish Immigrants by T. Heath Robinson, 1905

11b. Jewish deserters from the Russian Army in White-chapel, a drawing by Paul Thiriat to illustrate the problem of pauper aliens as the test question in the Mile End Election, *The Sphere*, 14 January, 1905

12b. The Garment Trade, 1972

12a. Kosher butcher in Whitechapel, 1972

and they have frequent dinner parties. At week-ends they drive
out to a cottage in Hertfordshire which they share with a friend.
'If you know how to live, it's a good life', he said.

The East End used to be wild with pets, dogs, cats, budgerigars,
canaries and, nearer the river, huge exotic parrots and cockatoos.
One still finds any number of birds, and small furry animals,
hamsters and gervils, looking out dolefully from between nylon
curtains at the streets below, but it is difficult to keep dogs and
cats in the high-rise flats, and instead East Enders have been
lavishing their care on cars. On sunny evenings and at week-ends
one will find them on their cars and in their cars and under their
cars, washing, waxing, polishing, scraping, painting. On Sundays
in particular so many are in obeisant postures by their vehicles
that a stranger to the planet could take them to be engaged in
an act of worship.

There are numerous caravan owners in the East End and, on
Friday afternoons, they form a long cavalcade, heading eastwards
for Canvey Island and Southend, the cars, low, squat and gleam-
ing, the caravans bobbing behind, in bright pastel shades, high,
with large windows, ungainly.

Evenings are quiet. Roads are busy but pavements are bare,
except for the few minutes when cinemas and pubs discharge
their clientèle. On the housing estates a few children play in the
courtyards and street, but on summer evenings, when windows
are opened, the dominant sound is of gunfire as yet another
Indian bites the dust. Pubs have been pulled inside out and given
subdued lighting, carpets, wrought-iron grilles and plastic
flowers, and sandwiches are served with forceps. But the drinking
places are not as full as they once were and certainly not as
boisterous. 'They spend so much on their cars and their hairdos
and the Costa Brava that they've no money left for drink,' said
a publican. The women, young and old, are elegantly coiffured
with not a hair out of place under a helmet of lacquer, though
here and there one can see an inelegant black eye nursed behind
a pair of dark glasses.

Several East End pubs have introduced topless dancers at
lunchtime, and the crowd come in great variety, builders,
labourers in shortie coats, lorry drivers in string vests, sikhs in
turbans, West Indian porters in railway uniform, medical
students from the London Hospital with stethoscope dangling

from their pockets, truant schoolboys, all with glasses in their hands, and no one drinking. Music blares out on a record, and the dancer moves among them, naked but for a cluster of spangles between her legs, now retreating, now drawing near, her breasts billowing, and sometimes even arching herself over a startled visitor to lower a nipple into his cup – milk stout, East End style.

A new luxury hotel is rising at St Katharine's dock, and in the once solidly working-class Isle of Dogs expensive homes are rising by the river front opposite Greenwich. More luxury homes, and hotels and yacht basins are planned for the riverside, and the area is threatening to become the Chelsea of the East. For over a century one heard complaints that as soon as East Enders made money they left for better places. Now one hears complaints that people with money are driving East Enders from their homes.

Of Hawksmoor's three magnificent East London churches, two were destroyed by enemy action and a third, Christ Church, Spitalfields, has been made unusable by the death-watch beetle and meth drinkers. St George's in the East, with its stately towers and cupolas, was gutted during the war. Within its great shell, a new and smaller church has been built, largely of glass. It is as delicate in conception as a crystal goblet. It is not easy to reach, for it is surrounded by wide, busy roads, with massive lorries thundering by on every side. Once there, it is a restful haven, and the 1973 Easter message of the Vicar, the Reverend A. M. Solomon, could almost be taken as a text for the new East End:

> New every morning is the evidence of life waking up after the winter's sleep. Notice the daffodils who are pressing through into blooms; the tulips are not far behind and we have seen snowdrops and crocuses. In Tower Hamlets there are more open spaces these days and an encouraging increase in flower beds and young trees, especially tubs and receptacles for Nature's flowers on islands and road intersections – let there be more of nature and creative life to soften our concrete and macadam jungles.[19]

East London is a softer and more cheerful place. A look at the area restores one's faith in progress.

If there was one corner of East London less ravaged in the blitz than the others, it was perhaps Whitechapel and Spitalfields. As a result, its present decaying buildings, broken staircases,

shattered windows and refuse piled high in the narrow streets
make it the least wholesome corner of East London. This was
once the heart of the Jewish East End. There are still a few small
Jewish shops, a baker, a grocer, a stationer, small Jewish factories
and workshops and in the daytime a great many Jewish faces.
There are still three or four synagogues catering for small congregations where dozens once flourished. Bloom's restaurant,
resplendent with mirrors and neon lighting, is packed by day
and packed by night. Waiters in spotless jackets rush hither and
thither with laden trays. Cutlery sparkles on starched tablecloths,
and the whole scene is aeons removed from the old-style Jewish
restaurant where the waiter wiped his hands on the tablecloth as
he leant over to take your order, and the altercations in the kitchen
could be heard above the slurping of soup. Only the food and
the hubbub are *heimisch*. Bloom's is in the East End, not of it,
and the clientèle is of the East End by day and of Finchley by
night. Some come from even further afield for the hunger for
Jewish food persists long after the hunger for anything else
Jewish has atrophied. Within every Jewish institution there is a
remembrance of things past and in Bloom's there is a panorama of
Petticoat Lane market stretching along the entire length of a wall.

Petticoat Lane is more busy, bustling and prosperous than
ever, but the old 'Lane' is no more. It is not run by East Enders
for East Enders. The traders descend from the suburbs early in
the morning and depart early in the afternoon, but they have the
old accents and the old style, a mixture of Cockney sauce and
Yiddish *chutspah*. It has become part of tourists' London, part
Carnaby Street, part Speakers' Corner, and livelier and lustier
than both. It has overflowed from Middlesex Street into Wentworth Street and all the side-streets round about, and the crowds
are immobilised by their own numbers. There is a babble of
tongues from many lands and the constant clicking of shutters.
There are – as every East Ender knows – no bargains to be had
at the stalls, but plenty of free entertainment:

Here you are lady, I'm not selling bananas, I'm giving 'em
away. Fifteen pence a pahnd. Who'll give me fifteen pence?
Lovely bananas, look at 'em firm and ripe, think what you
could do with one of 'em, lady eh? And it's edible too. Come
on fifteen pence a pound. Right twelve. Twelve pence a pound.

What do you want blood? Twelve pence a pound. Who'll pay me twelve pence a pound? Lovely ripe bananas, only twelve pence a pahnd. They'd cost you a quid each in a sex shop.

As the morning progresses the crowds thin out. By two the stalls are stripped and the traders have donned their sheepskin coats and are off home in their Volvos and Jaguars. East London returns to itself. Cars whizz eastwards along the great trunk roads to Epping Forest and the Essex coast, or westwards into town.

There is many a sigh for the times that have gone, especially among those who have gone from East London, and even among those who refuse to leave. There is a couple in their eighties in a block of flats in Vallance Road:

No, we didn't even move out in the blitz. We've no children you see, there's only him and me. I was worried when I was here and he wasn't, but when we were both home together what could happen to us? Nothing did. We could have moved after, but you get used to everything, the streets, the smells, the stairs. No, here we've been, here we stop, though I shan't pretend the place hasn't changed. Look at them blacks.

Avrom Stencl, a Yiddish poet, now in his seventy-seventh year, who stubbornly refuses to speak or write in English, feels married to the East End and especially Whitechapel. 'As soon as I stepped off the boat, I felt I was home. It's my Jerusalem. No Jew ever leaves Whitechapel completely, he takes a bit of it with him. I'm now too much part of it to leave. I'm one of the old ruins.':

> Pumpedita, Cordova, Cracow, Amsterdam,
> Vilna, Lublin, Berditchev and Volozhin.
> Your names will always be sacred,
> Places where Jews have been.

> And sacred is Whitechapel,
> It is numbered with our Jewish towns,
> Holy, holy, holy
> Are your bombed stones.

> If we ever have to leave Whitechapel,
> As other Jewish towns were left,
> Its soul will remain a part of us,
> Woven into us, woof and weft.[20]

# SIXTEEN

# Gentle Folk

The Huguenot settlers in the East End were as different from the Irish, as the Irish were from the Jews, and the Pakistanis, the latest wave of newcomers, are different again, but they all encounter a certain consistency of attitude from the native population: they are not wanted. Any established group resents a foreign body and the larger and more foreign the body the greater the sense of resentment.

There are, according to most informed estimates, not more than ten thousand Pakistanis resident in and around the East End, but few local residents believe this to be the actual figure.

'Ten thousand!' said a car-park attendant 'you've got to be joking. There's millions of 'em, *millions*. See for yourself.' And he waved his hand towards Commercial Street. '*Millions*.'

And there indeed were a great many Pakistanis moving to and fro at their characteristically hurried pace, as if conscious of being under scrutiny, many with parcels under their arms, lean little figures in dark suits and white socks, with sunken cheeks and glossy hair. They are particularly numerous in Spitalfields, and the small Jewish shops which used to crowd the narrow streets are under new management. The Samuels and Cohens have given way to the Selims and Kahns, but each little shop displays a bewildering variety of goods, fruit pies and torch batteries, bananas and brilliantine, tea-bags and tights. One gentlemen's outfitters is also a travel agent and some sort of notary public. The Hebrew lettering on the facias has given way to Bengali, though many of the *mezuzoth*, the little scrolls in a metal casing which most Jews have on their doorposts, still persist. Where there were kosher butchers there are now *hallal* butchers. Mosaic law has given way to Moslem law. Business in most shops, at least during working hours, is anything but brisk. Customers linger over and after a purchase and more people seem to drop in to talk than to buy. Voices fall away in the presence of a stranger. Pakistani women in their bright silks give a touch of colour to the scene, but everything about their menfolk blends in with the dark hues of East London. They are about as unobtrusive as one can be without actually vanishing.

'They're model citizens' said a local clergyman 'hard-working, sober, thrifty.' They find the physical environment unpleasant, the moral environment unhealthy, the people sullen and un-friendly. They are here because they found job opportunities not available elsewhere, and because East London, though distant, was not wholly unknown, and because, as in earlier times, the East End offered the least resistance to the newcomers. It never had a sufficient sense of community to form a barrier against the outsider.

The great majority of East End Pakistanis are from Bangladesh, or East Pakistan as it used to be known, an area frequently devastated by famine and flood. Their language is Bengali and they have been familiar figures in the riverside areas as deck-hands on the various lines serving India and the Far East. One found them in the sailors' homes or shopping in the street markets, shadowy, transitory figures, who came and went, and brought back tales of the power, wealth, size and magnificence of London, which seemed to figure in the eastern imagination as a Samarkand of the west – a legendary golden city. The first glimpse of the East End was not entirely in keeping with the legend, but it did offer a promise of stability at a time when India was in turmoil, and an income which in Bengali terms represented a fortune, and after the war as maritime employment contracted, many Pakistanis acquired homes in the East End and brought over relatives, and as one wave of newcomers found jobs, others came out to join them. It was the familiar pattern all over again.

The Pakistanis were needed in a way that no previous immi-grant group had been. The war had depleted the population of the East End, but not the job opportunities in the engineering workshops, chemical concerns, vehicle maintenance plants, and above all, the garment trade. The small Jewish manufacturer remained loyal to the East End, both out of sentiment and habit, the influx of Pakistanis enabled him to remain there.

At first most of the newcomers regarded themselves, and were generally regarded as *guestarbeiter*. Nothing in their circumstances induced them to think of London as their home. They worked hard, lived frugally, and saved to set themselves up in business or to buy a farm in Bengal. Few had their wives with them, and most lived in all-male dormitory houses, with some of the rooms housing one set of tenants by day and another by night. They cooked together, and ate together and, before launderettes became general, washed their clothes together. It was a bleak existence made tolerable by the thought that it was temporary.

Then, as talk grew of restrictions on immigration, and as legislation to this end was tabled before the House of Commons in 1962, many Pakistanis hurriedly brought over their wives and children.[1] Moreover, once their number reached a certain critical size they were able to establish many of the facilities necessary to their way of life, and instead of a few scattered handfuls of individuals, there evolved an organised community, and within a few years East London found itself with yet another foreign colony large enough to impose its character on the neighbourhood. It was a silent invasion. The Pakistanis were there before anyone was fully aware of them.

They arrived at a time of considerable racial tension. Among the few areas of the East End which had survived the blitz almost intact was Cable Street, a long narrow thoroughfare which for most of its course runs parallel between Ratcliff Highway to the south and Commercial Road to the north, and which had been the scene of the famous 'battle' of Cable Street in 1938. It was fairly decrepit already before the war, and the bombs which fell on every side did little to improve it, and as a result it was scheduled for redevelopment. In the meantime, as one plan gave way to another, it sank further into decay, and those families which could afford it made their way into less benighted areas. At the same time, many of the small shops were turned into all-night cafés, which became the haunt of petty-criminals, drug-addicts, pimps, prostitutes and common or garden drunks who roistered in the alley-ways, fought in the streets, or sank quietly into the gutters. The prostitutes and their clients, however, were perhaps the biggest problems, for if Cable Street came to be regarded as a poor man's Soho, few of the cafés aspired to the dignity of a brothel and many of the prostitutes pursued their calling in the small courtyards, the alley-ways and under the railway arches, wherever there was sufficient darkness or shelter to afford a touch of privacy. They had a large clientèle of lorry drivers and, apart from any other nuisance, the road was often made impassable by long lines of articulated lorries.

The prostitutes were in the main wretched little drabs, many of whom had run away from home, or absconded from approved school. Their biggest attraction was their youth, for some were no more than fourteen or fifteen, and they tottered around awkwardly on unaccustomed high heels. The cafés offered them a modicum of companionship and shelter, and more than a modicum of income. Old hags who had retired from the game, were attracted out of retirement by the new opportunities and they thronged Cable Street like walking gargoyles. The old East End seemed to be reasserting itself.

The housing shortage was acute and there were still respectable people in the neighbourhood, and men complained that it was impossible for their wives to go out at night without being molested or importuned.[2] Some of the wives may have been flattered by the experience but for those with young children it was a serious nuisance. Police made occasional raids and in 1956 thirty-five men of different nationalities, twenty-seven of them Maltese, were charged with pimping, but the nuisance continued and local church groups came together in a campaign for the suppression of vice. The fact that most of the individuals involved in running the all-night cafés were from overseas could not be overlooked, and the campaigners did not overlook it. Residents of Toynbee Hall complained of an underlying racialist tone to their literature and pointed out that vice was no monopoly of the immigrant, to which the campaigners retorted with a report from an ex-superintendent of police that '90% of the pimps were West Indian, Cypriots or Maltese', and that the increasing drug problem 'was created here by men from the West Indies, Asians from India, Pakistan and elsewhere'.[3] They urged the deportation of Commonwealth criminals and other undesirables.

A Catholic priest, known popularly as Father Joe, however, went further and demanded restrictions on Commonwealth immigration.[4]

Police stepped up their raids and the number of charges for soliciting in the East End grew from two in 1946 to nine in 1949, to five hundred and eighty-five in 1959.[5] These figures are perhaps more a measure of police activity than the extent of vice, but they helped to spread the feeling among East Enders that immigrants were corrupting their women-folk and polluting the moral atmosphere of Stepney.

It was in this tense situation that the East End gradually became aware of the colony in its midst. It was very rare for a Pakistani to be arrested on a vice or drugs charge. They were as law-abiding a group of people as could be found anywhere, but to the East Enders of this time all immigrants looked alike. By the end of the 1960s much of Cable Street was pulled to the ground, the dim lights of the all-night cafés faded out and it ceased to be a problem area. The expression 'Stepney-Vice', which seemed to have been kept in standing type by some newspapers, vanished from the headlines, but a legacy of ill-feeling remained, and it was one of the factors – though by no means the main one – which was to lead to a series of minor anti-Pakistani pogroms. The first came in the autumn of 1969. Others followed in quick succession. Pakistanis, either singly or in groups, were chased, set upon, attacked with bottles or stones, knocked to the ground, kicked in the face or slashed with knives. The injuries in most cases were more psychological than physical, but they were deep and were accompanied by dazed bewilderment. 'They didn't even steal anything', said one middle-aged victim. 'They didn't even take my watch.' There were thirty-two attacks in December alone.[6] They were widely reported in the press. Camera crews descended on every wind to interview attackers and attacked, with the inevitable result that the attacks increased both in number and scale and 'Paki-bashing', as it came to be called, rose to the level of a local sport.

An elderly Pakistani, who had been living in London for years, tried to view it all philosophically. There have always been troubles, he said, they came in waves and he recalled being set upon by a gang called the 'Billy Boys'. The new attackers were mostly skinheads, so called because of their closely-cropped heads. Their particular weapon was their boots, 'bovver-boots' as they called them, heavy, steel-capped, and, when sharply applied, lethal. They were teenage thugs of limited intelligence and very limited education, who found a certain camaraderie in their common appearance, their common search for mischief and in the notoriety which it brought. They were particularly active over bank holiday week-ends and were often involved in pitched battles with the police at seaside resorts. Their attacks on the Pakistanis were more workaday affairs, but early in 1970 there was a sizeable riot involving several dozen skinheads who surged down Brick Lane, shouting obscenities, throwing stones, shattering windows, and assaulting almost anyone in sight. The incident, albeit on a smaller scale, was repeated the following evening. A few days later a middle-aged Pakistani working as a kitchen porter in a West End restaurant, was followed home from the underground station by two youngsters and stabbed in the back. He crawled, writhing and screaming, up two flights of stairs, apparently unheard by his neighbours, and died as he reached his front door.[7]

A docker who said, with some pride, that his two sons were skinheads, argued that the Pakistanis deserved all they got. 'You get used to living in the East End with all sorts', he said, 'but the Pakistanis were creeps. No one liked them.'[8]

Some of the charges made against them echoed the charges made against the Jews, and were equally without foundation, but in one respect they were not wholly erroneous. The Pakistanis, like the Jews, helped to make an already critical housing shortage more acute. Five or six Pakistanis prepared to share a room could always outbid a man with a young family, but it was also said that they were jumping the queue for Council housing.

A Russian Jew who came to England at the age of seven and who was not properly housed before he was nearly seventy said:

I always said the English was crazy, now I know it. See this block. Take a walk on the landing about eight at night. It's black with *schwartzes*, Indians, Mohammedans, full of them. Yet you can see young families with small children walking about the streets without a roof over their heads. And English families, I mean, not drunken, Irish yoks, but respectable English people. Aren't they crazy?

What usually happens is that when Pakistanis club together to buy a property they generally do so in about the only areas to which their funds will stretch, and that is the near-derelict back street slums, usually forsaken by their white inhabitants, and as these become subject to demolition, they have to be rehoused. But the number is not large and most Pakistanis still live in conditions which few English people would find tolerable. It is not unusual to hear the other criticism that their homes are a breeding place for vermin and disease, that they did not inherit slums, but created them through insanitary habits and overcrowding.

One hears frequent sexual jokes about Pakistanis which suggests an undercurrent of sexual jealousy, but again all immigrants, and especially West Indians, are the subject of such humour. West Indians, however, have frequently been charged with drug offences or living on the earnings of prostitutes, yet they have come to enjoy an acceptance in the East End bordering almost on popularity, though perhaps the very animosities aroused by the Pakistanis may have helped to make them acceptable. 'Up the Blacks, down the Paks', read the scrawl on one East End wall.[9] The term 'Black' in the mouth of an East Ender is almost free of disdain. The West Indian speaks the same language, his dress is not too outlandish, he attends local church (rather more frequently than his English neighbours who, if not particularly Christian themselves, tend to admire Christianity in others), his wife may belong to the local Women's Institute, his sons to the Boy Scouts, and, if he may not always eat the same food, he drinks the same drink as other working men, and shares their passion for cars. The West Indian is also a sportsman, good at football, excellent at cricket and like most working men he likes a flutter at the dogs or horses. He is clubbable, almost matey. 'He's not the same colour', said a printer, 'and he pongs a bit, but he's almost one of us.' The Pakistanis were none of these things. 'They couldn't be more foreign, could they?' said the printer, and there is, as a Jewish writer once observed, an inherent dislike of the unlike. The West Indian, moreover, if attacked usually stood his ground and could return more than he got, whereas the first instinct of the Pakistanis – and a fairly sensible one where one is outnumbered – was to run. Their timidity is proverbial and was regarded almost as an incitement in itself. 'They cringe', said a youngster. 'If they would stand up to people we'd respect them.'

What made it rather difficult for them to 'stand up to people' was the feeling that the entire world about them was hostile; they could not even look to the police for protection. On the contrary, as attack followed attack without anyone being apprehended, many Pakistanis began to feel that the police were not merely turning a blind eye on the incidents, but that they were in league with the attackers. After the Brick Lane riot in April 1970, a large body of Pakistanis with banners and placards, marched on Arbour Square police station demanding police protection. One of the banners read: AN END TO POLICE BRUTALITY.

'That was the limit of our hopes', said a young Pakistani who acts as a spokesman for his community. 'We don't really expect the police to protect us. We only wish they weren't against us.'

He described how he once saw a Pakistani knifed in the foyer of a local cinema. He rushed for help and found two policemen round the corner. They listened, they nodded and remained where they were. 'They just didn't want to know.'

There is an echo here of the complaints against the police by Jewish immigrants, and they were perhaps equally justified, or unjustified, though, as with the Jewish immigrants, one does sometimes find an excessive officiousness on the part of the police. There was, for example, the case of the elderly Pakistani who, walking home during the height of the Paki-bashing terror, saw a crowd of youngsters approaching and picked up an empty milk bottle to defend himself. He was promptly arrested for carrying an 'offensive weapon', to wit, the milk bottle, and fined £5.[10] Such incidents made it difficult to believe police protestations of impartiality. On the other hand, there was the inevitable language difficulty. Twelve policemen volunteered to undergo a course in Bengali. One does not know how far they succeeded, but suspicions have not been allayed and a Pakistani, seeing a policeman approach, will be inclined – traffic permitting – to cross to the other side of the road.

In May 1970, after the march on the Arbour Square police station had proved wholly ineffective, the Pakistanis held a rally in Hyde Park, followed by a march to 10 Downing Street, where they handed a letter to the prime minister drawing attention to their fear and resentment: 'People say Pakistanis are attacked because they are known to be gentle and peaceful people, because they are there and will not fight back. But they are now coming to regret their reputation for gentleness. If nothing further is done to protect them, the time will come when they will fight back.'[11]

The idea of self-defence groups had been active in the minds of younger Pakistanis for some time. In February 1970 there was a meeting in Toynbee Hall of representatives of all the coloured communities in East London addressed by a Black Power leader who called for united action against their assailants, for, if Pakistanis were the prime victims, he said, Indians and West Indians too had been attacked.[12] Nothing practical emerged, and nothing practical was to have been expected, for, although one might not have thought so from the press reports, skinheads were not the only Paki-bashers in the district. They included youngsters in mufti, and even some West Indians who, no doubt, must have felt all the more integrated for having found a common victim.

The Pakistanis, who felt themselves increasingly beleaguered, lobbied Peter Shore, Labour MP for Stepney, who in turn saw the police and was assured that everything possible was being done to protect the immigrants and bring their attackers to justice,[13] but this was not borne out by the experience of the Pakistanis, and they began to be infused with what one might call a *Sinn Fein* mentality. There was no prospect of united action with other immigrants. They could not depend on the police, and against the advice of Shore and the Bishop of Stepney and some of their own elders,[14] they formed a Vigilante Association.

The Bishop, who had the deepest sympathy with the immigrants, was afraid that the Association might perpetuate what he regarded as a passing phenomenon. Others feared race riots, pitched battles in the East End reminiscent of the battles between Fascists and Jews before World War II, but the attacks petered out. This was due neither to the existence of the Vigilante Association, nor even to increased vigilance by the police. The news media tired of the subject, and the less frequently one read of the attacks or saw them on television, the less frequently they occurred. It did not mean that they ceased entirely. Pakistanis walking home of an evening still tend to go in convoy and look over their shoulders even now, and they will quicken their pace if they hear footsteps. One still hears of the occasional attack, but one does not have to be a Pakistani to have one's head broken in East London, though perhaps it helps.

The number of Pakistanis in East London has now been virtually static for almost a decade, for though the birth-rate is high, the marriage rate is low. There is nothing which so sustains an immigrant community in its ways as a constant flow of newcomers from the old country, but the flow has virtually ceased and given the smallness of the community one would expect it gradually to fade away. But there are barriers, many of them self-imposed.

There is, first of all, the simple devotion to faith, a silent fanaticism which is inculcated into the child from his first conscious moments. Thus, like the Jewish immigrant, the Pakistani child will rush from his school every evening to attend religious classes. These are held in two main centres and remind one of the old style Yiddish *cheder*, except that they are even more crammed and chaotic. One class meets in the East London mosque which is a converted shop in Commercial Road, another in the back room of a council flat in Cannon Street Road. The flat could, one feels, accommodate a small man and a large wife comfortably, but the children begin to pour in, five, ten, twenty. A divan by the wall is rapidly filled and latecomers crowd on the floor, thirty, forty, and still they come, each stooping to remove his shoes as he enters. Small, dark-eyed girls huddle against older brothers. An English woman, a Moslem convert, is there with a big stick to keep order, but the children, for all their large number and cramped conditions, are very orderly indeed.

There is a smell of cooking from the kitchen, somebody is running a bath, and there is much coming and going in the corridors. Latecomers, pulling hats from their pockets, continue to pour in and somehow they still find room. The air is heavy and the walls moisten. The children are aged from about six to fourteen. Some of the boys begin to chatter and laugh. The woman waves her stick, and that is silence. The *Mufti* enters. They all rise and he waves them down. He is a robust man in an astrakhan hat, black face, and a red beard. He enunciates his words very carefully and reveals a set of teeth, large, and almost startling in their magnificence, as if he could bite iron spikes in half.

The class awaits his word, and he begins, in Arabic, and they follow in chorus, line by line. There is not a textbook between them, it is all by word of mouth, handed down from father to son. Like the Jewish immigrant children they grapple with three languages, one in school, one at home, and a third for their religion.

Like the Jewish immigrants they treat their dietary laws with great meticulousness. They have their own ritual slaughters, their own *hallal* butchers, as the Jews had their own kosher butchers and, said a young Pakistani, they never eat out. 'Not even a sandwich, for even an egg sandwich could have lard in the bread.'

They are abstemious by nature, training and religious injunction. They must not, and do not, touch alcohol, and like the Jewish newcomers they are a godsend to the soft drinks industry. A large pub in a part of Commercial Road largely inhabited by Pakistanis has gone out of business, and some local grocers are also feeling the pinch. A Jewish grocer, now retired, voiced a familiar complaint: 'Nothing I sold they ate, nothing I had they wanted, nothing they wanted I had. Thank God I retired when I did.'

Most of the Pakistanis are from rural areas, ill-educated and untrained. Few have knowledge of English and one finds them in a great variety of unskilled occupations, but most of them are in the garment trade, which is easy to learn and for which one needs little capital to set up as proprietor, and one, moreover, which the English working class has always found unattractive. Jewish immigrants went into it because they had no alternative, and got out of it as quickly as they could. It offers the first rung on the ladder for the small capitalist. But conditions are extremely competitive and a man can stay in business only by cutting corners, by working longer hours, paying lower wages, circumventing the provisions of the Factory Acts, so that there have always been areas of the trade where conditions have not risen far above the sweatshop and, with the Pakistani immigration, they have in some places slumped back to it.

In one workshop I found eight men, sitting shoulder to shoulder, bent over sewing machines, in an atmosphere heavy

with dust, sweat and decaying cloth. There was the low voice
of a cricket commentator burring in the background, but it
could not be heard above the clatter of the machines and the
chatter of the machinists. They looked like brothers, and they
were in fact all brothers and cousins. The room was overcrowded and under-ventilated by any standards, and it was not
unlike other workshops one could find in the neighbourhood.

As one walks through the back streets, lights burn and
machines rattle late into the night, but if this is indeed sweating,
it must be added that the victims are cheerful in their plight. If
they work long hours rather than short and accept stifling
conditions rather than comfortable ones, it is because the small,
cramped workshop, with its smaller overheads, is in a position
to pay, and does pay higher wages.

Though as unskilled as the Jewish immigrants, the Pakistanis
have more options open to them. There was high unemployment
during the years of Jewish immigration; there is a shortage of
labour now, and it is this shortage, indeed, which has acted as a
vacuum and pulled them into the East End. Without it, few
could have found jobs at all, for, unlike the Jews, they had no
substantial body of co-religionists ready to employ them.

The Jews, moreover, were dependent on Jewish employers
because they were, in the main, strict Sabbatarians. The Pakistanis suffer from no such handicap. Friday is their Sabbath and,
ideally, they should be off work, but the laws surrounding it
are not so rigorous that they must risk their livelihood to be at
rest. If they have to go to work – and they do – then they may.
Their handicap is the month of Ramadan, which, being based
on the lunar calendar, can shift from month to month. They
have to fast during the daylight hours which, if Ramadan falls in,
say, January, is no great trial, but if it falls in June, it can be
debilitating. But they observe it loyally and accept its rigour
cheerfully and, fast or no fast, put in a full day's work.

'They look as if you could knock them down with a feather',
said an employer, 'but they're wiry little chaps, with more
stamina than you give them credit for.'

Where Pakistanis lay themselves open to exploitation is that
they are not always aware of their rights. Some of the newcomers
have not been able to believe their luck in getting here at all
and tend to look over their shoulders in case they are put on the

next plane back. They are helped with labour permits and other papers by their employers and are sometimes left to believe that they are dependent on them for their continued stay. They are nervous of changing jobs, for that can mean a meeting with officialdom and officials, they fear, are invariably against them.

One substantial employer, a mattress maker, tried to tie his workforce down to their jobs by offering 'free accommodation', which was in effect hardly more than a bed in an old public house converted into barracks. A bed is as much as most Pakistanis want when they first get here, and it was only the active intervention of the trade unions and local trades councils which made them realise they were being exploited.

Pakistanis, like most newcomers, are difficult to unionise. There is the language difficulty. They tend to be chary of white trade union officials – as they are chary of all white men – and especially of white officials. They are, moreover, nervous of displeasing their employers, and they are more interested in overall earnings than a basic wage. An employer who offers ample scope for overtime will get away with lower wages than the man who can only offer a forty-hour week. A seventy-hour week is not uncommon, and even an eighty-hour week is not unheard of, but Pakistanis do not regard that as exploitation. It's exactly what they came for. They look doleful and ill-at-ease when not working.

Some of them work at one job during the day and then rush off to another, usually as kitchen hand or porter in the evening. Earnings of £50 or £60 are not uncommon, but there is little evidence of what one might call conspicuous or, indeed, inconspicuous consumption. They are a frugal community. They save the lumps of sugar from their tea-break, said an employer. All immigrants are keen savers, but Pakistanis top the league, possibly because they have the heaviest weight of dependents. For every Pakistani wage earner in Stepney there could be a dozen relatives in Bengal waiting to be fed.

They will suffer long hours and harsh conditions cheerfully, partly because they suffered even harsher conditions at home and because, like the Jew, they hope that given hard work, a bit of luck and a consortium of relatives they might become master themselves. And if not as a workshop proprietor then as a shopkeeper, for trade exercises a strong fascination. A small

K

trader may hope to become a large trader, but few East End Pakistanis that one encounters set their sights on the professions.

Language is, of course, a great barrier. If the children are quick to learn English, the adults are slow, and there is no system of adult English classes compared to those maintained by the Russo-Jewish Committee during the days of mass Jewish immigration. Of the many and varied Commonwealth immigrants in East London, the Cypriots are perhaps the most favoured and the Pakistanis the least. Yet, they are generally reckoned to be the least troublesome.

'They'll never come to you with a complaint', said an employer, 'on the other hand, you never know if you've been rubbing them up the wrong way until they come to you in a solid body – never in ones or twos, always as a whole family – and ask for their cards.'

They do not, as a rule, compete with Englishmen for employment, but one old lady, who used to take some work in for a clothing manufacturer to eke out her pension, said she had had to give up because of the low pay. 'These people (the Pakistanis) don't let their women go out to work. They're at home all day and are happy to do anything they can get. I used to make a decent few bob before they started coming. They've got their children at it too, you know, and keep them off school. It shouldn't be allowed.' The latter point might be difficult to substantiate, for the school attendance of the Pakistani children is good. 'They're ideal pupils', said a school teacher, 'if you like them hard-working and subdued', which he, one suspected, did not. 'Give them a page of homework, and they'll do a book. They're not as bright as the Jewish kids you used to get, but they're not as insolent. They don't open their mouth, at least for the first year or two, but then after a time a bit of sparkle comes into their eyes, and they get a bit cheeky, and you feel you're making progress.'

The little girls tend to be ragged because of their distinctive attire and long plaits, and all the Pakistanis tend to huddle together in the playground for protection: 'very timid little chaps, they don't fight, they shrink back – and they're slow to make friends, but that changes once they pick up the language, and, on the whole, they make better progress than the English kids. I wouldn't say they're brighter, but they try harder. They're

also better looked after. You'd be surprised at the number of
East End kids who come to school without a crumb in their
belly – you can see it by the way they guzzle down the school
milk and dive on the revolting school meals. Not the Pakistanis,
though, they're well looked after, if anything they're a bit molly-
coddled. In winter some of them arrive with about a dozen layers
of clothing.'

They leave school early and one finds few Pakistanis in the
fifth and sixth forms of the secondary schools. On the other hand,
a visit to the Whitechapel Library on almost any evening of the
week evokes memories of the peak years of Jewish immigration.
The faces are a little duskier, the hair a little blacker, the figures
a little slighter, but the intensity of concentration is the same,
and the air is almost humming with effort. However, most of
them are not members of the local Pakistani community, but
Pakistani students studying at one or the other of several poly-
technics and technical colleges in the neighbourhood. They are,
moreover, mainly from West Pakistan and have little to do with,
and look down upon the Bengalis who have made their homes in
East London, and this has nothing to do with the recent dis-
ruption over Bangladesh. A Pakistani medical student, who tried
to put the relationship in an English context, explained that the
Bengalis were the Irish of Pakistan, which would seem to indicate
a gross misunderstanding of the character of both Irish and
Bengalis.

The community, in spite of the influx of wives and children
in the early 1960s, is still predominantly a male one and females
are outnumbered by about twelve to one. Some Pakistanis have
been too appalled by permissive London to expose their families
to it, though not all have been above enjoying its pleasures and
the rate of venereal disease in the immigrant community is not
low.[15] Many of the Pakistanis live in austere, all-male communes,
and English bystanders have sometimes commented darkly on
their way of life. 'They're not natural', said a docker. 'A lot of
queers if you ask me, look at the way they hold hands.'[16]

They meet together of an evening in one of the many small
gloomy cafés on and off the Commercial Road. There is animated
chatter as one approaches, which stops dead the moment one
enters, and is not resumed till the moment one leaves, and one
feels almost pierced by the scrutiny of dark eyes. One is received

with every courtesy when escorted by a Pakistani, but to enter such a place alone is to invite immediate suspicion and cause more than a tremor of apprehension.

Pakistanis seem to be keen cinema goers and there are two cinemas in the Commercial Road and a third in Brick Lane showing Bengali films. The fare is decent, wholesome, unsubtle and, to judge by the rapt attention it receives, entertaining, and it reminds one vaguely of the Hollywood films of the 1940s with Maria Montez and Yvonne de Carlo. Many houris and much muslin, and strangers on horseback from distant lands and mysterious comings and goings. The villains are very villainous, and the heroes are truly heroic, and the maidens are beautiful and chaste. There is much heartache and many a chase, but evil is confounded, virtue is rewarded and everything comes right in the end – and the lights come on, dimly and uncertainly, upon three hundred dusky male faces still taking in what they had seen.

There is nothing so bleak as the English Sunday as experienced by the Pakistanis. It is not their Sabbath. They do not drink. Few of them have cars to polish. In the mornings many of them go shopping, or push their way through Petticoat Lane in search of a bargain they never find. In the afternoon one finds them in desultory bands, walking up the Mile End Road, and down again. Those who have been here a little longer have discovered Epping Forest and the Essex coast, and those with cars visit relatives in the Home Counties and the Midlands.

The great pleasure to be yearned and saved for was the occasional trip home by charter flight, but there is a nervousness about leaving the country at all, as if afraid that some one might change the law once their backs were turned. There is, moreover, a dread of Heathrow as the most inhospitable place on earth. Immigration officials are especially feared, as if a mere glance from them could nullify one's papers and permits. 'They look at you', said a Pakistani, 'not only as if you've no right to be in England – but as if you've no right to be on earth.'

Nor can it be said that they are completely at ease even in the East End. They have the anxious pace of men who fear they might miss the last bus. They have not the volubility of men at ease. They look unutterably subdued.

A distinguished journalist, Rawle Knox, has suggested that

they have been subdued by their geography. They stem from an
area of Bengal lashed almost yearly by typhoons which kill
thousands and reduce their towns and villages to a muddy
wilderness. The survivors shrug their shoulders, sigh, rebuild
their homes, and wait for the next time. 'They never give up',
writes Knox, 'and they never expect to win', and they approach
life in London with the same fatal resignation.[17]

The Pakistanis, though hard-working, are not ambitious.
They may indeed rise from the ranks of machinist to that of
proprietor or shopkeeper, but even so they merely become
working men who happen to have more money. They may
spend more, they will certainly save more, but their change of
income will not affect their way of life. They remain solidly
working-class and their class loyalty (though such a concept
might perhaps seem meaningless to a Moslem) in turn sustains
their religious loyalty. Moslems may not share the Catholic
belief in holy poverty, but poverty, or at least lack of riches, has
helped to keep the people holy, and certainly the tenacity with
which they adhere to their faith, in spite of every temptation and
inconvenience, is remarkable and in some ways touching. Yet
the Jews who settled here some eighty years ago were no less
poor or tenacious, yet they are largely integrated into English
life, as were the Irish before them, and the Huguenots before
them.

The Huguenots and Irish were, of course, Christians in a
Christian land – the latter even speaking the same language –
and it would have needed a miracle to keep them apart as distinct
groups. With the Jew the situation was more complex, but he
was part of Western history, and once exposed to Western culture,
he took to it with a hunger which made up for all the centuries
of exclusion, and, as we have seen, he was helped in his transition
by co-religionists who had migrated before him and had acquired
a high place in English life. They had assimilated themselves by
their exertions and were assimilating the newcomers by their
example. Jews, moreover, are supremely ambitious and, if it was
necessary to drop this usage or that to get on in life, they found
reasons for doing so, and having dropped the first few, the rest
came easy. And even then, it should be added, they have never
become wholly integrated.

The Pakistani is different in almost every respect. He is entirely of the East with no hunger for a Western education beyond the minimum necessary to do his job, and every instinct beyond the necessity to earn a living draws him home. He is fresh from there. Much that he earns goes back there. When he marries he takes a wife from there. When he dies – for there is no Moslem cemetery in London – he will be buried there. Now that is something the Jew never knew. He spoke of Russia as *der Heim*, but it was a place of torment. There was Zion, of course, but that was a vague concept enshrined in prayer.

The Pakistanis are thus more consciously in exile than the Jews ever were. They are not accepted readily, nor do they seek to be readily accepted. Their language, their manners, their religion, their diet, their clothes, keep them apart. Pakistani children may join readily in games at school, but once at home they will play among themselves. The men may meet Englishmen at work but will move exclusively among themselves after work. And the women, at home all day, do not even have this limited contact. 'The lack of meaningful links with the wider community', a social observer has written, 'is an indication that Pakistani leaders do not know, or do not want to know, how they can help Pakistanis integrate.'[18] But they do not regard it as part of their function to help Pakistanis integrate, except in the limited sense of helping them to learn English and find their way about the country. In the past, when a stranger sought to make his home in England, it was axiomatic that he wished to become English. Today, neither the newcomers nor their hosts feel that Englishness is necessarily the ideal form of cultural expression, and that one is, if anything, a better Englishman for remaining a good Moslem. Certainly Pakistanis have suffered none of the importunities from Christian missionaries which the Jewish newcomers experienced or, as one of them put it: 'In Bengal yes, in London no'.

Pakistanis are less inclined to gamble and take risks than the Jew and, if determined, their determination is softened by resignation. They leave more – some might say too much – to Allah. And perhaps not only to Allah. 'They're like sheep', said a voluntary social worker who has moved widely among immigrants, 'they don't ask for anything, but they expect somehow to be looked after and they just look mournful when they're not.'[19]

Each wave of Jewish immigrants was helped by the waves before, and even the Irish received an occasional hand from the old Anglo-Catholic families and eager assistance from English converts, but Pakistani immigrants receive no such help from co-religionists. If there are old Pakistani families in London, they are not at the service of the new. The East End Pakistanis are, with few exceptions, working-class, and if they get any outside assistance at all, it is from their English neighbours. The Bishop of Stepney, Father Trevor Huddlestone, has been particularly helpful and has placed the crypt of St George's in the East at their disposal for social gatherings and religious classes.

Father Huddlestone, a lean, ascetic-looking man with grey hair, bright smiling eyes, and massive, determined jaw, who could have been a Gary Cooper-type hero in an old time Western, takes an ecumenical view of his functions and feels that there is an interdependence among the faithful, not merely in the obvious sense – that they are all challenged by the same materialism – but in that the faithful of one group help to sustain faith in others, that, in short, good Moslems and good Jews make it less difficult for the wider community to remain good Christians. He feels that any group which takes a pride in its own culture and traditions and has a close sense of its own identity, is bound to enrich the life of the nation as a whole. East London, in his view, is a richer, better, more colourful place for its immigrants, and this is one of the reasons why he has made his home in the heart of it, in a drab terrace house, where the heavy lorries thunder eastwards along the Commercial Road.

Islam is less restrictive for its followers than Judaism. Judaism abhors mixed marriages, but the prevailing attitude amongst many Jews is for it. Islam permits it, but the prevailing attitude amongst Pakistanis is against it. 'Can a white woman be a good wife?' asked a Moslem paper recently, and the consensus amongst readers was that white women were 'domineering, slovenly and apt to be unfaithful'.[20] The last point is perhaps the crucial one. Many Pakistanis regard the typical white woman as a whore. 'They fuck about', said one in a phrase he had probably picked up from his workmates without fully understanding its import.

White people, moreover, have not the same sense of family as Pakistanis, nor is their life built round their children in the same way. They may be more indulgent and spend more money on them, but they are less caring and affectionate. The Pakistani is not, and does not think of himself, as an individual with a life of his own. The family is all. For the family he will starve, for the family he will slave. It is only the pressure of his family's needs that has brought him here and keeps him here in the first place. For the sake of his family he will leave his family to spend a lifetime in gloomy exile.

Whatever attitudes some young Pakistanis may have towards whites, their marriages are generally arranged by their parents,[21] and parents certainly can be relied upon to set their face against miscegenation. There is also the barrier of colour, which did not affect earlier newcomers. And there is finally the crucial point we have mentioned before, that Englishmen are no longer confident in the superiority of their way of life so, that they feel others should conform to it. And the growing tendency to sameness is breeding a greater tolerance for distinctiveness.

The present Pakistanis are, of course, first-generation immigrants. It may be that the next generation will be more receptive to change and more ambitious for themselves and their children, and the third will disperse to the suburbs and vanish, but given the present tendencies it seems unlikely, and one would say that the Pakistanis are here to stay as a distinct group, an exotic thread in the bright fabric of East End life.

# Notes

ONE Pagan Place

1. *Times*, 7/4/1879
2. *John Bull*, 12/7/1879
3. *Daily Telegraph*, 25/6/1872
4. G. R. Sims, *How the Poor Live*, p. 9 (London, 1889)
5. *East London Observer*, 3/5/1879

6. *ibid.*, 1/1/1859
7. *ibid.*, 29/1/1859
8. *ibid.*, 26/3/1859
9. *ibid.*, 26/4/1862
10. *John Bull*, 12/7/1879

TWO The Garden Suburb

1. Stow, John, *Survey of London*, 1598, 6th edition, Vol. II, p. 32 (London, 1755)
2. H. L. Smith, *History of East London*, p. 22 (London, 1939)
3. Stow, *op. cit.*, p. 47
4. Smith, *op. cit.*, p. 47
5. P. Ziegler, *The Black Death*, p. 159 (London, 1969)
6. Stow, *op. cit.*, p. 94
7. Smith, *op. cit.*, p. 211
8. J. A. Birch, *Limehouse Through Five Centuries*, p. 17 (London, 1930)
9. Stow, *op. cit.*, p. 33
10. *ibid.*, p. 44

11. *ibid.*, p. 34
12. *ibid.*, p. 40
13. *ibid.*, p. 42
14. D. Defoe, *Journal of the Plague Year*, pp. 16–17 (Routledge ed., 1884)
15. *ibid.*, p. 82
16. D. Lysons, *The Environs of London*, vol. III, p. 449 (London, 1792)
17. Defoe, *op. cit.*, p. 28
18. W. Harrison, *A History of London and Westminster*, p. 278 (London, 1776)
19. Defoe, *op. cit.*, p. 137
20. *ibid.*, p. 125
21. Harrison, *op. cit.*, p. 279

### THREE On the Waterfront

1. T. de Quincey, *Select Essays,* p. 92 (London, 1888)
2. *ibid.,* p. 93
3. *Times,* 9/12/1811
4. *ibid.,* 16/12/1811
5. *ibid.,* 21/12/1811
6. *ibid.,* 21/12/1811
7. *ibid.,* 23/12/1811
8. *ibid.,* 2/1/1812
9. *ibid.,* 27/12/1811
10. *ibid.,* 2/1/1812
11. P. Colquhoun, *Treatise on the Police of the Metropolis,* p. 214 (London, 1806)
12. *ibid.,* p. 220
13. *ibid.,* p. 215
14. *ibid.,* p. 228
15. *ibid.,* p. 226
16. *ibid.,* p. 228
17. *Times,* 28/8/1802
18. M. Rose, *The East End of London,* p. 125 (London, 1951)
19. *East London Observer,* 9/1/1864
20. W. Hale, *Observations on the Distress of the Poor Peculiar to Spitalfields* (London, 1806)
21. Quoted in *East London Observer,* 6/1/1912
22. J. L. & B. Hammond, *The Age of the Chartists,* p. 148 (London, 1930)
23. *Report of 1834 Committee on Drunkenness,* p. 197
24. An American, *London in 1838,* pp. 94–5 (New York, 1839)
25. C. Dickens, *Sketches by Boz,* p. 158 (London, 1892)
26. A. McEwen, *East London Papers,* Vol. III, No. 2, p. 67
27. *East London Observer,* 10/10/1857
28. W. Besant, *East London,* p. 81 (London, 1901)

### FOUR Profitable Strangers

1. *Publications of the Huguenot Society,* Vol. 8, p. 8 (1893)
2. *ibid.,* p. 10
3. *ibid.,* p. 21
4. *Catalogue of State Foreign Papers,* Edward VI, p. 119, 1547–53
5. S. Smiles, *Huguenots in England and Ireland,* p. 76 (London, 1895)
6. F. Warner, *The Silk Industry of the U.K.,* p. 40 (London, 1921)
7. A. J. Grant, *The Huguenots,* p. 190 (London, 1934)
8. Smiles, *op. cit.,* p. 269
9. *Huguenot Society,* Vol. 10, p. 302 (1914)
10. Warner, *op. cit.,* p. 42
11. W. Harrison, *A History of London and Westminster,* p. 546
12. *L.C.C. Survey of London,* Vol. 27, p. 5 (London, 1957)
13. *Huguenot Society,* Vol. 8, p. 206

14. *ibid.*, p. 286
15. Warner, *op. cit.*, p. 57
16. W. H. Manchee, *Memoirs of Spitalfields*, p. 13 (London, 1914)
17. *Survey of London*, p. 4
18. *Huguenot Society*, Vol. 8, p. 332 (1893)
19. *ibid.*, p. 314
20. *ibid.*, p. 332
21. Smiles, *op. cit.*, p. 287
22. *East London Observer*, 14/3/1868
23. *ibid.*, 14/3/1868
24. *East London Observer*, 24/2/1906
25. Manchee, *op. cit.*, p. 39
26. *Huguenot Society*, Vol. 10, p. 341 (1914)
27. *ibid.*, Vol. 8, p. 291 (1893)
28. *Select Committee on Public Libraries*, 1849. Minute 2730
29. C. Marmoy, *The Huguenots and their Descendants in East London* (Address to East London History Group, 10/6/1970)
30. Manchee, *op. cit.*, p. 22
31. Marmoy, *op. cit.*
32. *Huguenot Society*, Vol. 10, p. 319 (1914)
33. Manchee, *op. cit.*, p. 22
34. Marmoy, *op. cit.*
35. *ibid.*
36. *ibid.*
37. *ibid.*

FIVE Troublesome Strangers

1. A. Redford, *Labour Migration in England*, p. 132 (London, 1964)
2. J. A. Jackson, *East End Papers*, Vol. 6, No. 2, p. 106
3. *ibid.*, p. 106
4. *Annual Register*, 25/5/1768
5. *ibid.*, 26/7/1786
6. J. Denvir, *The Irish in Britain*, p. 78 (London, 1892)
7. *East London Observer*, 6/4/1912
8. J. A. Jackson, *East End Papers*, Vol. 6, No. 2, p. 106
9. *Select Committee on Emigration*, p. 9 (1829)
10. Redford, *op. cit.*, p. 142
11. J. Swift, *Tracts Concerning the Present State of Ireland*, Vol. 81 (1792)
12. Committee on Emigration, p. 7
13. H. A. Irvine, *Journal of Transport History*, November 1960, p. 233
14. *ibid.*, p. 233
15. Committee on Emigration, p. 259
16. Denvir, *op. cit.*, pp. 157–8
17. *ibid.*, p. 83
18. Edwardes & Williams, *The Great Famine*, p. 329 (London, 1956)
19. *Limerick Chronicle*, 18/1/1848
20. Edwardes & Williams, *op. cit.*, p. 328
21. Redford, *op. cit.*, p. 158
22. *Chambers' Journal*, 17/10/1848
23. *Select Committee on Poor Law*, 1847. Par. 5239
24. Redford, *op. cit.*, p. 159

25. Hammond & Hammond, *op. cit.*, p. 104
26. *Report on the Practice of Internments in Towns,* 1843, pp. 45–6
27. J. A. Jackson, *op. cit.*, p. 112
28. *ibid.*, p. 113
29. *Rambler,* 1852, Vol. 1, pp. 109–10
30. *ibid.*, p. 111
31. H. Mayhew, *London Labour and the Poor,* Vol. 1, p. 461 (London, 1851)
32. *Dublin Review,* December 1856, p. 487

33. Mayhew, *op. cit.*, p. 466
34. *ibid.*, p. 458
35. *Westminster Journal,* 1/1/1835, p. 83
36. Mayhew, *op. cit.*, Vol. 1, p. 448
37. *Nation,* 17/1/1846
38. *Tablet,* 24/1/1846
39. Denvir, *op. cit.*, p. 253
40. J. Clay, *The Prison Chaplain,* p. 569 (London, 1861)
41. *Nation,* 17/1/1846
42. W. L. Arenstein, 'Victorian Prejudice Re-examined', *Victorian Studies,* June 1969

## SIX The Double Burden

1. W. L. Arenstein, *op. cit.*
2. E. R. Norman, *Anti-Catholicism in Victorian England,* p. 15 (London, 1968)
3. H. Mayhew, *op. cit.*, Vol. 1, p. 88 (London, 1851)
4. S. Garratt, *The Irish in London,* p. 210 (London, 1852)
5. *ibid.*, p. 215
6. *ibid.*, p. 221
7. *Spectator,* 21/6/1879
8. *Catholic Standard,* 4/5/1850
9. S. Gilley, *Evangelical and Roman Catholic Missions to the Irish in London,* p. 56. Cambridge, Ph.D. thesis No. 7420, 1970. Unpublished
10. Garrett, *op. cit.*, p. 196
11. Gilley, *op. cit.*, p. 91
12. *ibid.*, p. 108
13. *East London Observer,*

9/11/1861
14. *Tablet,* 14/1/1865
15. L. Charlton, *Recollections of a Northumbrian Lady,* p. 244 (London, 1949)
16. W. Salmon, *St. Anne's Parish, Underwood Road,* p. 6 (London, 1950)
17. *Tablet,* 26/6/1847
18. Gilley, *op. cit.*, p. 260
19. S. Gilley, *Recusant History,* July 1969, p. 125
20. *ibid.*, p. 125
21. *Tablet,* 6/1/1844
22. *Recusant History,* July 1969, p. 261
23. Garrett, *op. cit.*, p. 200
24. Mayhew, *op. cit.*, p. 115
25. Salmon, *op. cit.*, p. 6
26. *Recusant History,* July 1969, p. 127
27. *Tablet,* 24/4/1858
28. *ibid.,* 24/4/1843

29. *ibid.*, 17/3/1855
30. Gilley, *op. cit.*, p. 230
31. *ibid.*, p. 231
32. *Tablet*, 17/3/1855
33. Minutes Book, Spitalfields Catholic Schools, 3/12/1851
34. Dingle & Harrison, 'Manning as Temperance Reformer': *Historic Journal*, Vol. XII, p. 487
35. *ibid.*, p. 501
36. *Report of Committees*, 1868, Vol. XLV, Q. 2444
37. Dingle & Harrison, *op. cit.*, p. 496
38. E. S. Purcell, *Life of Manning*, Vol. II, p. 598 (London, 1895)
39. *ibid.*, p. 595
40. *ibid.*, p. 595
41. *Blackwoods*, July 1901, pp. 125–6
42. *ibid.*, p. 126
43. J. A. Jackson, The Irish in East London: *East London Papers*, Vol. 6, No. 2, p. 111

44. *Blackwoods*, p. 133
45. W. G. Todd, *Dublin Review*, December 1856, p. 472
46. J. Denvir, *op. cit.*, p. 462
47. Dingle & Harrison, *op. cit.*, p. 498
48. *East London Observer*, 18/1/1868
49. C. Booth, *Life and Labour of the People of London*, Third Series, Vol. 1, p. 47 (London, 1902)
50. *Blackwoods*, p. 133
51. J. A. Jackson, *op. cit.*, p. 118
52. *ibid.*, p. 116
53. B. Tillet, *A Brief History of the Dockers' Union*, p. 3 (London, 1919)
54. J. A. Jackson, *op. cit.* p. 116
55. Gilley, *op. cit.*, p. 372
56. Mayhew, *op. cit.*, p. 107
57. *ibid.*, p. 108
58. C. C. Martindale, *Father Bernard Vaughan*, pp. 127–8 (London, 1923)
59. Gilley, *op. cit.*

SEVEN Christmas Day in the Workhouse

1. S. & B. Webb, *English Poor Law, The Last Hundred Years*, Vol. 1, pp. 10–11 (London, 1929)
2. *ibid.*, p. 8
3. J. Townsend, *A Dissertation on the Poor Law*, p. 34 (London, 1785)
4. *East London Observer*, 1/1/1870
5. *ibid.*, 2/1/1858
6. *ibid.*, 2/1/1858

7. *ibid.*, 2/7/1862
8. *Times*, 28/12/1857
9. *East London Observer*, 2/8/1862
10. *ibid.*, 20/4/1861
11. *ibid.*, 22/8/1863
12. *Standard*, 12/5/1862
13. *Morning Post*, 12/5/1862
14. *East London Observer*, 22/11/1862
15. *ibid.*, 27/12/1862
16. *Bethnal Green Times*, 14/2/1863

17. *London City Mission Magazine,* July 1839, p. 100
18. *East London Observer,* 4/12/1865
19. *ibid.,* 3/9/1864
20. *ibid.,* 16/8/1862
21. *ibid.,* 6/8/1862
22. *ibid.,* 16/8/1862
23. *ibid.,* 10/10/1863
24. *ibid.,* 10/10/1863
25. A. E. Clark-Kennedy, *The London Hospital,* p. 41 (London, 1963)
26. *ibid.,* p. 42
27. *ibid.,* p. 44
28. *ibid.,* p. 46
29. *ibid.,* p. 47
30. *Daily Telegraph,* 19/12/1867
31. *East London Observer,* 8/1/1870

EIGHT Home of Good Causes

1. R. Collier, *The General Next to God,* p. 51 (London, 1964)
2. H. Barnett, *Canon S. A. Barnett,* Vol. 1, p. 30 (London, 1918)
3. Dingle & Harrison, *op. cit.,* p. 509
4. Chaim Bermant, *The Cousinhood,* p. 169 (London, 1971)
5. Barnett, *op. cit.,* p. 38
6. *ibid.,* p. 53
7. *ibid.,* p. 76
8. E. K. Abel, *Canon Barnett.* Unpublished Ph.D. Thesis, London University, p. 19
9. Barnett, *op. cit.,* p. 70
10. *ibid.,* p. 118
11. *ibid.,* p. 142
12. *ibid.,* p. 268
13. *ibid.,* p. 139
14. Abel, *op cit.,* p. 25
15. *ibid.,* p. 26
16. *ibid.,* p. 27
17. Barnett, *op. cit.,* p. 154
18. *ibid.,* p. 196
19. *ibid.,* p. 307
20. *Handbook of Settlements of Great Britain*
21. *East London Observer,* 21/6/1913
22. Barnett, *op. cit.,* p. 297
23. C. Burdett Paterson, *Angela Burdett-Coutts,* p. 2 (London, 1953)
24. *ibid.,* p. 65
25. *ibid.,* p. 208
26. *ibid.,* p. 201
27. *Truman the Brewers,* p. 25 (London, 1966)
28. G. Thorne, *The Great Acceptance,* p. 11 (London, 1913)
29. *ibid.,* p. 21
30. *ibid.,* p. 25
31. *ibid.,* p. 53
32. *ibid.,* p. 201
33. *ibid.,* p. 90
34. *ibid.,* p. 161
35. *ibid.,* p. 159
36. *ibid.,* p. 163
37. *ibid.,* p. 112
38. *ibid.,* pp. 129–32
39. Collier, *op. cit.,* p. 77
40. E. Bishop, *Blood and Fire,* p. 6 (London)
41. Collier, *op. cit.,* p. 21
42. *ibid.,* p. 68
43. A. E. Clark-Kennedy, *op. cit.,* p. 50

44. Barnardo & Merchant, *Memoirs of Dr Barnardo*, p. 79 (London, 1907)
45. *ibid.*, p. 84
46. *ibid.*, p. 96
47. *ibid.*, p. 144
48. *ibid.*, p. 145
49. *ibid.*, pp. 210–12
50. *ibid.*, p. 227
51. *ibid.*, p. 243
52. Barnardo & Merchant, *op. cit.*, p. 137
53. *Times*, 21/9/1905
54. Barnardo & Merchant, *op. cit.*
55. H. Walker, *East London*, p. 60 (London, 1896)
56. *ibid.*, p. 61

### NINE Jacob the Ripper

1. *Jewish Chronicle*, 14/9/1888
2. *East London Observer*, 15/9/1888
3. *Standard*, 2/10/1888
4. *Times*, 2/10/1888
5. *Times*, 2/10/1888
6. *Times*, 3/10/1888
7. *East London Observer*, 15/9/1888
8. D. McCormick, *The Identity of Jack the Ripper*, p. 33 (London, 1970)
9. R. Odell, *Jack the Ripper in Fact and Fiction*, p. 153 (London, 1965)
10. McCormick, *op. cit.*, p. 62
11. *ibid.*, p. 116
12. *Times*, 2/10/1888
13. McCormick, *op. cit.*, p. 98
14. *Pall Mall Gazette*, 8/10/1888
15. *ibid.*, 12/10/1888
16. McCormick, *op. cit.*, p. 114
17. *Pall Mall Gazette*, 12/10/1888
18. R. Anderson, *The Lighter Side of My Official Life*, p. 137 (London, 1910)
19. McCormick, *op. cit.*, p. 74
20. D. Farson, *Jack the Ripper* (London, 1972)

### TEN Perfect Strangers

1. *Whitaker's Almanac*, 1892
2. B. Gainer, *The Alien Invasion*, p. 11 (London, 1972)
3. *ibid.*, p. 7
4. S. H. Jeyes, *Fortnightly Review*, July 1891
5. *East London Observer*, 18/1/1902
6. *East London Observer*, 1/3/1913
7. P. Colquhoun, *Treatise on the Police of the Metropolis*, p. 120
(London, 1806)
8. *ibid.*, pp. 189–90
9. *ibid.*, p. 320
10. E. H. L. Emmanuels, *A Century and a Half of Jewish History*, p. 11 (London, 1910)
11. Colquhoun, *op. cit.*, p. 321
12. *Times*, 15/2/1832
13. *ibid.*, 18/2/1832
14. *Chambers' Journal*, 2/12/1848
15. Mayhew, *op. cit.*, Vol. II, p. 129

16. *ibid.*, p. 130
17. *ibid.*, p. 133
18. *ibid.*, p. 136
19. *ibid.*, p. 138
20. *ibid.*, p. 138
21. *ibid.*, p. 138
22. *ibid.*, p. 140
23. *ibid.*, p. 141
24. *ibid.*, p. 142
25. S. S. Levin, *Jewish Historical Society*, Vol. XIX, p. 16
26. *Jewish Chronicle*, 8/7/1898
27. G. Lansbury, *Looking Forwards and Backwards*, p. 15 (London, 1935)
28. V. D. Lipman, *A Century of Social Service*, p. 5 (London, 1959)
29. I. Zangwill, *Children of the Ghetto* (one-vol. edition, London, 1893)
30. *ibid.*, p. 83
31. *ibid.*, p. 179
32. *ibid.*, p. 225
33. *East London Observer*, 28/5/1881

ELEVEN  The Deluge

1. C. Booth, *op. cit.*, Vol. II, p. 103
2. W. H. Wilkins, *The Alien Invasion*, p. 50 (London, 1892)
3. L. P. Gartner, *The Jewish Immigrant in England*, p. 24 (London, 1960)
4. *ibid.*, p. 52
5. A. White, *The Modern Jew*, p. XII (London, 1899)
6. Cmd. Paper, 1741, 1903. Q. 330
7. *East London Observer*, 18/1/1902
8. *ibid.*, 1/3/1902
9. *Eastern Post*, 9/11/1901
10. *East London Observer*, 25/1/1902
11. *ibid.*, 15/2/1902
12. *Daily News*, 5/9/1904
13. *Pall Mall Gazette*, 17/2/1902
14. *Eastern Post*, 19/10/1901
15. *Lancet*, 3/5/1884
16. Lipman, *op. cit.*, p. 126
17. *East London Observer*, 18/12/1900
18. *Lancet*, 3/5/1884
19. Cmd. Paper, 1741. Q. 4290
20. *ibid.*, Q. 4222
21. *ibid.*, Q. 3963
22. *ibid.*, Q. 4295
23. *Parliamentary Papers*, Vol. LXXXIX, p. 256, 1887
24. Booth, *op. cit.*, Vol. IV, p. 49
25. *ibid.*, p. 60
26. Gartner, *op. cit.*, p. 116
27. Cmd. Paper, 1741. Q. 11685
28. *Fortnightly*, Vol. LXXVII, p. 1103, 1905
29. W. Fishman, *History Today*, January, 1966
30. *Transactions of Jewish Historical Society*, Vol. XXI, p. 210
31. *ibid.*, p. 210
32. Cmd. Paper 1741. Q. 9932
33. G. Lansbury, *op. cit.*, p. 218
34. *East London Observer*, 17/3/1906

35. Cmd. Paper, 1741. Q. 11657
36. *Jewish Association for the Protection of Women and Girls,* Annual Report 1905
37. Gainer, *op. cit.,* p. 5
38. Cmd. Paper, 1741. *d.* 9897
39. *ibid.,* Q. 9636
40. *ibid.,* Q. 17681
41. Gainer, *op. cit.,* p. 183
42. *Pall Mall Gazette,* 17/2/1902

43. Lipman, *op. cit.,* p. 128
44. Gainer, *op. cit.,* p. 44
45. *ibid.,* p. 43
46. Cmd. Paper, 1741, p. 5
47. *East London Observer,* 4/6/1904
48. Gainer, *op. cit.,* p. 163
49. *ibid.,* p. 199
50. *ibid.,* p. 163
51. *ibid.,* p. 199

TWELVE Men at Work and Play

1. *East London Observer,* 13/6/1896
2. *ibid.,* 13/6/1898
3. *The Link,* 14/7/1888
4. *ibid.,* 14/7/1888
5. *ibid.,* 21/7/1888
6. Booth, Vol. IV, p. 241
7. Thompson & Yeo, *The Unknown Mayhew,* p. 109 (London, 1971)
8. Hammond & Hammond, *op. cit.,* p. 25
9. *East London Observer,* 13/6/1896
10. *Truman the Brewers,* p. 47 (London, 1966)
11. *Eastern Post,* 7/9/1901
12. *East London Observer,* 1/1/1859
13. *ibid.,* 26/2/1859
14. *Nineteenth Century,* October 1887, p. 488
15. *ibid.,* p. 486
16. *ibid.,* p. 489
17. *ibid.,* p. 495
18. *ibid.,* p. 496
19. F. Williams, *Ernest Bevin,* p. 32 (London, 1952)

20. B. Tillet, *op. cit.,* p. 24
21. *ibid.,* p. 30
22. D. Wilson, *Dockers,* p. 48 (London, 1972)
23. *Nineteenth Century,* October 1887, p. 490
24. E. M. Page, *East London Papers,* Vol. IX, No. 1, p. 27
25. W. W. Jacobs, *A Master of Craft,* p. 1 (London, 1900)
26. Morrison, *Child of the Jago,* Introduction
27. *ibid.,* p. 48
28. *ibid.,* p. 49
29. *ibid.,* p. 103
30. T. H. Smith, *East London Papers,* Vol. II, No. 1, p. 40
31. *ibid.,* p. 41
32. *East London Observer,* 15/8/1908
33. *ibid.,* 26/9/1857
34. *ibid.,* 9/6/1860
35. *ibid.,* 13/6/1868
36. *ibid.,* 2/3/1889
37. *The Rambler,* 1852, Vol. 1, p. 357
38. Walker, *op. cit.,* p. 96

39. G. Goodwin, *Queen Mary College*, p. 20 (London, 1939)
40. *ibid.*, p. 44
41. *ibid.*, p. 54
42. *East End News*, 29/7/1938
43. *ibid.*, 7/10/1949
44. *ibid.*, 11/12/1953
45. *St. Anne's Spitalfields, Minutes Book*, 18/4/1849
46. *East London Observer*, 29/8/1868
47. *ibid.*, 29/8/1868
48. *ibid.*, 15/12/1868
49. *ibid.*, 23/1/1858
50. *Daily Telegraph*, 20/11/1862
51. *East London Observer*, 2/3/1861
52. G. Gaunt, *East London Papers*, Vol. XIV, No. 2,

pp. 101–103
53. J. Melling, *East London Papers*, Vol. XIII, No. 1, p. 43
54. *East London Observer*, 21/8/1859
55. *ibid.*, 23/1/1897
56. *ibid.*, 27/1/1906
57. *ibid.*, 16/5/1908
58. *ibid.*, 16/5/1908
59. *ibid.*, 16/5/1908
60. *ibid.*, 27/1/1906
61. *Quiver*
62. *Daily Chronicle*, 12/5/1908
63. Quoted in *East London Observer*, 8/8/1896
64. *East London Observer*, 16/7/1904
65. *ibid.*, 2/1/1904

THIRTEEN The Two Communities

1. *East London Observer*, 30/9/1905
2. *ibid.*, 7/10/1905
3. Booth, *op. cit.*, Vol. III, p. 169
4. *ibid.*, p. 170
5. *Jewish Chronicle*, 23/1/1880
6. *ibid.*, 5/12/1884
7. Quoted in *East London Observer*, 18/1/1908
8. *ibid.*, 11/8/1906
9. *Jewish Chronicle*, 19/4/1912
10. Cmd. Paper, 1741. Q. 16771
11. Jew's Shelter Annual Report, 1886
12. Russel and Lewis, *The Jew in London*, p. 60 (London, 1900)
13. J. L. Bensusan, *Windsor Magazine*,

14. Gartner, *op. cit.*, p. 223
15. *Windsor Magazine*
16. Cmd. Paper, 1741. Q. 10281
17. *ibid.*, Q. 18329
18. *Daily Chronicle*, 12/8/1908
19. Russel & Lewis, *op. cit.*, p. 24
20. *East London Observer*, 11/7/1902
21. *ibid.*, 7/1/1882
22. A. White, *op. cit.*, p. 201
23. Victoria Club Papers
24. Victoria Club Log Book
25. Oxford & St George's *Anniversary Review*, p. 17
26. *City and East London Observer*, 29/3/1929
27. *Jewish Chronicle*, 6/9/1901
28. Cmd. Paper, 1742. Q. 18280

29. *Daily Chronicle*, 12/8/1908
30. *Jewish Chronicle*, 13/3/1891
31. *Eastern Post*, 7/9/1901
32. *ibid.*, 7/9/1901
33. W. Fishman, *European Judaism*, p. 31, December 1972
34. *Jewish Chronicles*, 11/8/1876
35. W. Fishman, *Jewish Immigrant Libertarians in London* (Unpublished)
36. *ibid.*,
37. Gartner, *op. cit.*, p. 114
38. *East London Observer*, 24/9/1904
39. *ibid.*, 24/9/1904
40. W. Fishman, *This Is Whitechapel*, p. 32
41. Russel & Lewis, *op. cit.*, p. 83
42. W. Fishman, *European Judaism*, p. 19
43. *ibid.*, p. 15
44. *ibid.*, p. 23
45. Cmd. Paper, 1742. Q. 9150
46. *ibid.*, Q. 9759
47. *East London Observer*, 24/10/1896
48. *ibid.*, 24/10/1896
49. *ibid.*, 7/10/1899
50. *Daily News*, 10/9/1899
51. *East London Observer*, 24/10/1896
52. Booth, *op. cit.*, Vol. III, p. 178
53. *Times*, 4/3/1899
54. *ibid.*, 7/3/1899

FOURTEEN To Arms

1. Wilson, *op. cit.*, p. 72
2. C. Bermant, *op. cit.*, p. 384
3. G. Bottomley (ed.), *Poems by Isaac Rosenberg*, p. 11 (London, 1922)
4. *Colour*, October 1919
5. *Globe*, 26/5/1917
6. *East London Observer*, 29/6/1916
7. *Jewish Chronicle*, 21/7/1916
8. L. Stein, *The Balfour Declaration*, p. 488 (London, 1961)
9. *Jewish Chronicle*, 30/6/1916
10. Stein, *op. cit.*, p. 489
11. *East London Observer*, 5/8/1916
12. Stein, *op. cit.*, p. 489
13. *East London Observer*, 13/3/1917
14. *Jewish Chronicle*, 18/8/1916
15. *ibid.*, 17/7/1916
16. *Nation*, 7/8/1916
17. Stein, *op. cit.*, p. 489
18. *East London Observer*, 20/1/1917
19. *ibid.*, 5/8/1917
20. *Times*, 25/1/1917
21. S. Pankhurst, *Home Front*, p. 308 (London, 1932)
22. *ibid.*, p. 309
23. *ibid.*, p. 309
24. *ibid.*, p. 310
25. *East London Observer*, 9/2/1918

### FIFTEEN Blitz

1. C. Cross, *The Fascists in Britain*, p. 153 (London, 1961)
2. *ibid.*, p. 158
3. *East London Observer*, 10/10/1936
4. Cross, *op. cit.*, p. 161
5. *East London Observer*, 17/10/1936
6. C. Mowat, *Britain Between the Wars*, p. 474 (London, 1955)
7. *Times*, 22/4/1940
8. *East London Observer*, 8/6/1940
9. *ibid.*, 21/7/1944
10. *Evening News*, 7/9/1965
11. C. Fitzgibbon, *London's Burning*, p. 89 (London, 1970)
12. F. R. Lewey, *Cockney Campaign*, p. 44 (London)
13. A. E. Clark-Kennedy, *op. cit.*, Vol. II, p. 255
14. G. Vale, *Bethnal Green's Ordeal*, p. 141 (London)
15. Cmd. Paper, 6583. p. 7
16. *ibid.*, p. 12
17. Clark-Kennedy, *op. cit.*, Vol. II, p. 274
18. *ibid.*, p. 279
19. *The Highway*, April 1973
20. A. Stencl, *This is Whitechapel*, p. 3

### SIXTEEN Gentle Folk

1. *Observer Magazine*, 5/12/1971
2. E. Young, *Vice Increase in Stepney* (London)
3. *East London Advertiser*, 24/11/1961
4. *ibid.*, 24/11/1961
5. Young, *op. cit.*
6. *East London Advertiser*, 27/2/1970
7. *ibid.*, 10/4/1970
8. *Spectator*, 9/5/1970
9. *New Society*, 12/10/1970
10. *East London Advertiser*, 1/5/1970
11. *ibid.*, 29/5/1970
12. *ibid.*, 27/2/1970
13. *ibid.*, 17/4/1970
14. *Times*, 14/4/1970
15. K. Leach, *Race Relations News Letter* (Supplement), 1964, p. 10
16. *Spectator*, 9/5/1970
17. *ibid.*, 9/5/1970
18. *New Society*, 12/10/1970
19. *Spectator*, 9/5/1970
20. *Sunday Times*, 13/7/1969
21. *Times*, 24/2/1971

# Select Bibliography

Abel, E. K., *Canon Barnett*. Unpublished Ph.D. Thesis, London Univ.

An American, *London in 1838* (New York, 1839)

Anderson, R., *The Lighter Side of My Official Life* (London, 1910)

Barnardo & Merchant, *Memoirs of Dr. Barnardo* (London, 1907)

Barnett, H., *Canon S. A. Barnett*, Vol. I (London, 1918)

Bermant, C., *Troubled Eden* (London, 1967)

———, *The Cousinhood* (London, 1971)

Besant, W., *All Sorts and Conditions of Men* (London, 1882)

———, *East London* (London, 1901)

Birch, J. A., *Limehouse Through Five Centuries* (London, 1930)

Bishop, E., *Blood and Fire* (London, 1964)

Booth, C., *Life and Labour of the People of London*, Third Series, Vol. I (London, 1902)

Bottomley, G. (ed.), *Poems by Isaac Rosenberg* (London, 1922)

Burdett Paterson, C., *Angela Burdett-Coutts* (London, 1953)

Charlton, L., *Recollections of a Northumbrian Lady* (London, 1949)

Clark-Kennedy, A. E., *The London Hospital*, 2 Vols (London, 1963)

Clay, J., *The Prison Chaplain* (London, 1861)

Collier, R., *The General Next to God* (London, 1964)

Colquhoun, P., *Treatises on the Police of the Metropolis* (London, 1806)

Cotter, J. R., *The Sacred Harp of Ireland* (London, 1852)

Cross, C., *The Fascists in Britain* (London, 1961)

Defoe, D., *Journal of the Plague Year* (Routledge Edition, London, 1884)

Denvir, K., *The Irish in Britain* (London, 1892)

Dickens, C., *Sketches by Boz* (London, 1892)

Edwardes, —. & Williams, —., *The Great Famine* (London, 1956)

Emmanuel, E. H. L., *A Century and a Half of Jewish History* (London, 1910)

Farson, D., *Jack the Ripper* (London, 1972)

Fitzgibbon, C., *London's Burning* (London, 1970)

Gainer, B., *The Alien Invasion* (London, 1972)

Garratt, S., *The Irish in London* (London, 1852)

Gartner, L. P., *The Jewish Immigrant in England* (London, 1960)

Gilley, S., *Evangelical and Roman Catholic Missions to the Irish in London.* Unpublished Ph.D. Thesis No. 7420, 1970, Cambridge

Goodwin, G., *Queen Mary's College* (London, 1939)

Grant, A. J., *The Huguenots* (London, 1934)

Hale, W., *Observations on the Distress of the Poor Peculiar to Spitalfields* (London, 1806)

——, *Appeal to the Public in Defence of the Spitalfields Act* (London, 1822)

Hammond, J. L. and Hammond, B., *The Age of the Chartists* (London, 1930)

*Handbook of Settlements of Great Britain*

Harrison, W., *A History of London and Westminster* (London, 1776)

Jacobs, W. W., *A Master of Craft* (London, 1900)

Lansbury, G., *Looking Forwards and Backwards* (London, 1935)

Lewey, F. R., *Cockney Campaign* (London)

Lipman, V. D., *A Century of Social Service* (London, 1959)

Lysons, D., *The Environs of London*, Vol. III (London, 1792)

Maguire, J. F., *Father Mathew* (London, 1865)

Manchee, W. H., *Memoirs of Spitalfields* (London, 1914)

Martindale, C. C., *Father Bernard Vaughan* (London, 1923)

Mayhew, H., *London Labour and the Poor*, 2 Vols (London, 1851)

McCormick, D., *The Identity of Jack the Ripper* (London, 1970)

Mills, J., *The British Jews* (London, 1853)

Morrison, A., *Tales of Mean Streets* (London, 1894)

——, *A Child of the Jago* (Panther edition, 1969)

Mowat, C., *Britain Between the Wars* (London, 1955)

Norman, E. R., *Anti-Catholicism in Victorian England* (London, 1968)

Odell, R., *Jack the Ripper in Fact and Fiction* (London, 1965)

Purcell, E. S., *Life of Manning*, 2 Vols (London, 1895)

Pankhurst, S., *Home Front* (London, 1932)

de Quincey, T., *Select Essays* (London, 1888)

*Quiver*

Redford, A., *Labour Migration in England* (London, 1964)

Rose, M., *The East End of London* (London, 1951)

Russel, —. & Lewis, —., *The Jew in London* (London, 1900)

Salmon, W., *St. Anne's Parish, Underwood Road* (London, 1950)

Stallard, J. H., *London Pauperism Among Jews and Christians* (1967)

Sims, G. R., *How the Poor Live* (London, 1889)

Smiles, S., *Huguenots in England and Ireland* (London, 1895)

Smith, H. L., *History of East London* (London, 1939)

Stencl, A., *This is Whitechapel* (London, 1973)

Stein, L., *The Balfour Declaration* (London, 1961)

Stow, John, *Survey of London*, 1598, 6th ed. (London, 1755)

Swift J., *Tracts Concerning the Present State of Ireland* (1792)

*Survey of London*

Thompson, —. & Yeo, —., *The Unknown Mayhew* (London, 1971)

Thorne, G., *The Great Acceptance* (London, 1913)

Tillet, B., *A Brief History of the Dockers Union* (London, 1919)

Townsend, J., *A Dissertation on the Poor Law* (London, 1785)

*Truman the Brewers* (London, 1966)

Vale, G., *Bethnal Green's Ordeal* (London)

Walker, H., *East London* (London, 1896)

Warner, F., *The Silk Industry of the U.K.* (London, 1921)

Webb, S. & B., *English Poor Law, The Last Hundred Years*, 2 Vols (London, 1929)

*Whitaker's Almanac* (London, 1892)

White, A., *The Modern Jew* (London, 1899)

Wilkins, W. H., *The Alien Invasion* (London, 1892)

Williams, F., *Ernest Bevin* (London, 1952)

Wilson, D., *Dockers* (London, 1972)

Young, E., *Vice Increase in Stepney* (London)

Zangwill, I., *Children of the Ghetto* (1 Vol. ed., London, 1893)

Ziegler, P., *The Black Death* (London, 1969)

# Index